"*Those who believe that Pope John Paul II is not in touch with the world's most important questions and events will find this book a revelation. Those who believe that being in touch with the world's Creator is the best way to be in touch with the world itself will find this book a confirmation. All of us will find it a comfort and perhaps another occasion for thanking God for Karol Wojtyla's life and ministry.*"

—Francis Cardinal George, OMI
Archbishop of Chicago

"*Out of the number of substantial biographies of the Holy Father, this one stands out for its clear focus on his life and motivation. It avoids speculation and theories about him. Instead, the reader learns from the Pope's own personal writings and recorded statements what he actually is feeling and the reasons behind what he does. The author provides an insider's view of the life and vision of this very great man of our time.*"

—Benedict J. Groeschel, CFR
Director, Office for Spiritual Development
Archdiocese of New York

Man of the Millennium
John Paul II

By
Luigi Accattoli

Translated by
Jordan Aumann, O.P.

Pauline
BOOKS & MEDIA
BOSTON

This is a translation of the Italian book entitled *Karol Wojtyła: L'uomo di fine millennio*, by Luigi Accattoli, published by *Edizioni San Paolo*, Piazza Soncino, 5, 20092 Cinisello Balsamo (Milano), Italia, 1998.

Distribuzione: Diffusione San Paolo s.r.l.,
Corso Regina Margherita, 2,
10153 Torino, Italia.

Photo credits:

Cover photos—Arturo Mari/*L'Osservatore Romano* Photo Service: front; *L'Osservatore Romano* Photo Service: back; Estella M. Gogan: (spine)

Photo section I—Arturo Mari/*L'Osservatore Romano* Photo Service: pp. 7, 8, 9, 10 (bottom), 13 (top); Baramtini/© Periodici San Paolo, Milan, Italy: p. 5; Del Canale/© Periodici San Paolo, Milan, Italy: pp. 1 (bottom right), 2, 3, 4 (top left, bottom); Edizioni San Paolo: pp. 11, 13; FSP Photo, p. 6 (bottom); Giancarlo Giuliani/© Periodici San Paolo, Milan, Italy: pp. 6 (top), 12, 15, 16; *L'Osservatore Romano* Photo Service: pp. 10, 14 (top); Sipa Laski/© Periodici San Paolo, Milan, Italy: p. 1 (top, bottom left); © Periodici San Paolo, Milan, Italy: p. 4 (top right).

Photo section II—Arturo Mari/*L'Osservatore Romano* Photo Service: pp. 1 (bottom), 2 (top right), 3, 4, 5 (bottom), 6 (middle left), 7, 8 (right), 9 (top & bottom), 10 (top; bottom right), 11 (middle), 12; Felici/Pontificia Fotografia, Rome, Italy, pp. 2 (middle, bottom right), 5 (top), 6 (top left; middle right), 8 (left), 9 (middle), 10 (middle) 11 (bottom); FSP Photo, p. 6 (top right); Giancarlo Giuliani/© Periodici San Paolo, Milan, Italy: pp. 1 (top), 2 (bottom left), 5 (middle), 10 (bottom left), 13; *L'Osservatore Romano* Photo Service: pp. 14-16; Sekino/© Tropical Center Color, p. 2 (top left).

Printed and published in the U.S.A. by Pauline Books & Media, 50 Saint Paul's Avenue, Boston, MA 02130-3491.

Pauline Books & Media is the publishing house of the Daughters of St. Paul, an international congregation of women religious serving the Church with the communications media.

1 2 3 4 5 6 7 8 9 10   09 08 07 06 05 04 03 02 01 00

The author, *Luigi Accattoli,* has been Vatican correspondent for the Italian newspaper *Corriere della Sera* for sixteen years. He is also the author of *When a Pope Asks Forgiveness: The Mea Culpas of John Paul II,* published by Pauline Books & Media.

∽

The translator, *Jordan Aumann, O.P.,* is an American Dominican based in Washington, D.C. He has authored and translated several books, including *Spiritual Theology.*

Contents

Preface

John Paul II's pontificate has been one of profound significance for the Church and for the world. He has moved forward in relaunching Christian preaching throughout the world and in seeking unity among the churches. John Paul has acknowledged Gospel deviations that have marked Christian churches both in the past and in recent times. He is the first Slav pope in the history of the Catholic Church, and the only pope in modern times to be threatened with assassination. John Paul will be remembered as the pontiff who triumphed over communism.

With the pontificate of John Paul, the papal image has changed and has been brought closer to the people of our day. The Pope takes vacations, skis in the mountains of Italy, swims in a pool at Castel Gandolfo, seeks medical treatment in a public hospital. He continues to travel around the world despite the tremor of his left hand and the uncertainty of his gait. Indeed, John Paul's pontificate has been an authentic *aggiornamento* (renewal), an adaptation to the Church and spirit of the Second Vatican Council.

Mikhail Gorbachev once remarked: "Without this pope, it would be impossible to understand what happened in Europe at the end of the 1980s." To John Paul's great credit, he encouraged the people of his Polish homeland to find a peaceful way of exiting from the communist system, and when they did, it was also to the Pope's credit that his countrymen did not harbor a spirit of revenge.

Elected pope in October 1978, John Paul immediately announced his desire to return to Poland for a visit. When he finally arrived in June of the following year, it was the first time since the signing of the Warsaw Pact that the entire population was allowed to gather publicly for an event. They came out in droves to acknowledge a spiritual leader and to applaud a message that was a direct challenge to an atheistic and repressive regime.

That visit planted a seed from which the organization known as *Solidarnońć* (Solidarity) grew. From Rome the Pope defended Solidarity when others accused it of being a clandestine movement. He strongly defended all the liberation movements which sprang up in communist countries throughout the 1980s, following Poland's example. When he visited Prague in April 1990, after the crumbling of the Berlin Wall and the collapse of the iron curtain, the Pope stated that "a new Tower of Babel has been torn down" and that the latter part of the twentieth century had made significant progress in providing greater freedom for all people.

In the course of his numerous travels, John Paul has energetically defended human rights, even against the dictatorships of the Third World, but he has also spoken out against capitalism, insisting that the defeat of communism does not justify the unrestricted control of capital by individuals or nations.

Perhaps John Paul's greatest gift to the Church and to the world has been his proposal for the "examination of conscience at the end of this millennium," in preparation for the Great Jubilee. He admits there are "dark pages" in the Church's history with the same courage with which he has vindicated the rights of the Church. To the consternation of a number of individuals within the Church, he has asked forgiveness for the scandals which still burn in peoples' memories, such as the violence used during the Inquisition and, in this century, the cooperation of Christians with dictatorships, and the anti-Semitic prejudice that prevented them from taking a stand against the Nazi slaughter of the Jews.

In the ecumenical field, his most daring initiative has been to open discussion on the role of the pope. John Paul has invited Protestants and Orthodox Christians to indicate what form of the "primacy of Rome" they believe would be most suitable today. He discussed this question in the 1995 encyclical *Ut Unum Sint* (On Commitment to Ecumenism), but so far he has had little success in moving closer to an agreement.

Though a great desire of his, the Pope has not yet been able to visit a single country where the majority of Christians are Orthodox; and relations with both the Anglican Church and Protestants are, in general, colder than when he first became pope. But John Paul II has extended his hand and continues to do so with the hope that during the year 2000, a general gathering of all Christians and a meeting with Jews and Muslims on Mount Sinai can take place.

John Paul has formulated a "theology of the body" which may one day have a great impact on the understanding of the human person. He preaches incessantly in defense of life, for the advancement of peace, and for aid to the poor. Catholics are proud of his courageous denunciation of every kind of injustice, but some fail to take to heart his strict teaching on sexual morality and married life. He does not soften, to any degree, the traditional moral precepts that bind believers. Nevertheless, the radical thrust of the Gospel message, which he considers necessary in order to respond to the "deep-seated distrust" of our age, is not an obstacle to his popularity. On the contrary, it seems to attract young people who flock to the gatherings to which John Paul invites them.

John Paul is much more a missionary pope than one of government and administration. To date, there is not a single major reform that bears his signature; the Curia remains as he found it. Yet, no pope of the twentieth century has had a stronger impact outside the Catholic Church.

While the Pope asks forgiveness from women, who have been poorly treated by the Church in the past, he has not changed their role in the apostolic structure of the Church. He calls the bishops to Rome regularly in order to keep alive the *communio* between the local churches and the Vatican, but he has not modified the structure of the Synod of Bishops, something he had once judged necessary.

In regard to the relations between local churches and the pontificate of John Paul, conflicts do exist. At times these conflicts are provoked by his missionary zeal, but more often they arise from the juridical restraints on requests for decentralization or substantial changes in matters touching the local churches. John Paul II has had confrontations with some of the most important episcopates in the Church: with the bishops of Brazil regarding the theology of liberation; with the bishops of the United States in the area of greater freedom of action for the laity; with the bishops of Italy concerning political involvement; and with the bishops of Germany regarding the secularity of the State. Some tensions remain.

The first twenty years of John Paul's pontificate—the longest of the twentieth century and one of the longest in the history of the Church —can be divided into three stages. Each of these stages is marked by a particular maxim of the Pope that has been especially helpful in communicating his message to people.

He pronounced the first of these maxims on October 22, 1978, at the celebration that inaugurated the beginning of his papal service: *"Open wide the doors to Christ!"* The first phase of his pontificate was marked by a missionary outreach to every continent; by creative use of the media; by the first encounters with the "powerful" of the world; by the struggle with Communism and the Soviet regime; and by the dramatic attempt on his life.

The second maxim is found in John Paul's encyclical *Dominum et Vivificantem* (The Holy Spirit in the Life of the Church and the World): *"We need to look further and go further afield"* (n. 53). This marked the stage of extending the mission *ad gentes* (to the people), far beyond traditional limits. John Paul called the Jews "our elder brothers"; he went to meet Islamic people; he convoked interreligious assemblies; he made a clean break with the rigid traditionalism of Marcel Lefebvre; he asserted the incompatibility of an "integralist temptation" with authentic evangelical inspiration.

This period also culminated in the sudden collapse of his ecumenical hope for a reunion between the Orthodox and the Roman Catholic Churches to occur before the dawning of the third millennium.

After this disappointment, Pope John Paul II entered a phase of physical suffering. This marked the stage of the third theme of his pontificate: *"In the name of the Church, I ask forgiveness."* The Pope first spoke these words during a visit to the Czech Republic in May 1995, but he repeats them again and again. He has scheduled a penitential ceremony for the year 2000. There the Pope will ask pardon for all the errors, infidelities, and irregularities for which members of the Church have been responsible during the millennium that has drawn to a close.

This book will probe each stage of the past twenty years of the pontificate of Pope John Paul II, composing a biographical narrative that will revolve around three significant periods:

❖ 1978–1979: beginning of the pontificate; the charter encyclical, *Redemptor Hominis* (The Redeemer of Man); pastoral visits to Mexico, Poland, and the United States.

❖ 1985–1986: meeting with Muslim youth at Casablanca; journey to India; visit to the Jewish Synagogue in Rome; ecumenical day of prayer at Assisi.

❖ 1994–1995: proposal for an examination of conscience at the end of the millennium; Extraordinary Consistory to discuss the Great Jubilee; Apostolic Letter *Tertio Millennio Adveniente* (On Preparation for the Jubilee of the Year 2000); the encyclical *Ut Unum Sint*.

The beginning of the Great Jubilee, toward which John Paul's pontificate has tended from its beginning, will likely mark a new creative phase and will console the Pope with some sign of ecumenical harmony. Here he stands, on the brink of the third Christian millennium, with his gaze firmly fixed on the future.

Luigi Accattoli

Author's Note

For information and suggestions, thanks are due to Emilio Vinci-Guerra; Fr. Georges Cottier, O.P.; Fr. Michal Jagosz; Fr. Adam Boniecki; Senator Giulio Andreotti; Bishop Pierfranco Pastore; Bishop Clemente Riva; Joaquín Navarro-Valls; and Benjamin and Matilda Accattoli.

CHAPTER ONE

Lolek Wojtyła

*S*ince a pope is a public figure, whatever he says or does attracts the attention of the world. This book will look at the specifically human background of John Paul, considering what part his past has played in determining his way of acting as pope. Therefore, we will not limit ourselves to the accomplishments of his pontificate. We will also scrutinize the signs destiny has engraved on John Paul's human countenance. We will explore his spontaneous expressions of emotion, trying somehow to discern the extent to which his memory of places and events in Poland has left an imprint on his soul.

Shortly after his election to the papacy, John Paul sent a message to the people of Poland:

> Dear fellow-countrymen:
>
> It is not easy to renounce the return to my country, "to those fields rich in varied flowers, silvered with wheat and gilded with rye," as Mickiewicz writes; to these mountains and valleys, lakes and rivers; to the people loved so much; to our royal city (Oct. 23, 1978).

Earliest Years

Wadowice, with its 15,000 inhabitants and surrounded by fields of rye, is the city where Karol Wojtyła was born on May 18, 1920. The city is located in southern Poland, on the River Skawa at the foot of the Beschidi Mountains, some 40 kilometers west of Kraków and 30 kilometers from Auschwitz. When Karol was born, Poland had only recently regained its independence after 123 years of domination by a foreign power, and it was struggling to regain territory on its eastern border.

The Wojtyła family lived in a small rented house on Rynek (today called Koszielna) Street, near the parish church. When Karol arrived, his father, after whom he was named, was 41 years old; his mother, Emilia Kaczorowska, was 36; and their first-born son Edmund was 14.

The infant was baptized on June 20, one month after his birth, and given two names; along with Karol he received the name Józef, after the national hero, Marshal Józef Piłsudski, who was waging war against Soviet Russia. The family immediately began calling the boy by the affectionate nickname, "Lolek." On June 7, 1979, when Pope John Paul visited the church where he had been baptized, he said: "As I look back, the wheels of my life carry me into the midst of this place and people, into this parish, into the midst of my family, and finally, to this baptismal font in this church in Wadowice."

The elder Karol Wojtyła was born in Lipnik and was the son of a tailor. After finishing secondary school, he also first worked as a tailor, but in 1900 he was called to service in the army where he became a noncommissioned officer. When the Austro-Hungarian Empire dissolved, he transferred to the Polish army and served there until 1928. He was a reserved man, well suited for a life of military discipline. Pope John Paul once stated in a conversation with biographer André Frossard: "He was so hard on himself that he had no need to be hard on his son; his example alone was sufficient to inculcate discipline and a sense of duty."[1]

Emilia Kaczorowska was born in Biata, the fifth of eight children. Thin and frail, she died on April 13, 1929, at the age of 45. Her death certificate attributes the cause of death to an infection of the heart and kidneys. Ten years after his mother's death, in the springtime of 1939, Lolek wrote a poem in her honor, perhaps not the first he ever wrote, but at least the first one that has been preserved.

> *Around your white tombstone*
> *The white flowers of life are blooming.*
> *Oh, how many years have already passed*
> *without you; how many years?*[2]

Very likely it was Lolek's mother who reminded him several times of the exact hour of his birth. And, as is typical of the Poles regarding anniversaries or family history, he retained the precise details. Much later, while visiting the parish of St. Athanasius in Rome, he said: "I was born between the seventeenth and eighteenth of May; and fifty-eight years later, at practically the same hour, I was elected Pope!"

Another detail Karol learned from his father was his birth during the First World War. Recently, on January 3, 1998, he visited the city of

Macerata in central Italy, after an earthquake. He commented: "Some day [these children] will hear their parents say: 'You were born at the time of the earthquake,' and they will not understand. I was born in a time of war but I understood nothing; I have always had great admiration for those who were victorious in that war."

John Paul tells us that it is important to know what our mothers and fathers were doing when we came into the world. The great passion that gripped the Polish people in the 1920s was the rebirth of their nation. At the end of the First World War, shortly after gaining independence, Poland was engaged in war against Russia. The conflict terminated with the signing of the Polish-Soviet Peace Treaty at Riga, Latvia, on March 18, 1921. This event marked the reunion of the Poles who had been subject to Austria with their countrymen who had been under the jurisdiction of Russia. To understand what that meant to a man who was a soldier and a Polish patriot, one must remember that Wadowice had participated energetically in the national insurrection against Russian rule in 1863, and that Karol's father had fought on the Russian front in the early phase of World War I.

The fact that John Paul was born during the First World War helps us understand the passion with which Karol Wojtyła, as Pope, would recall certain events. For example, in his letter to the Polish episcopate on August 26, 1989, he remembered the fiftieth anniversary of the outbreak of the Second World War—the Molotov-Ribbentrop Pact that led to the fourth division of Poland when he was 19 years old. It also helps us to imagine the tone of the letter he wrote in March, 1981, to Leonid Brezhnev, head of the Russian Kremlin, to deter him from an armed intervention in Poland (see Chapter 16). Although that particular letter never became public, we do know it was written a month before Ali Agca's attempt on the Pope's life.

Karol's older brother Edmund obtained a degree in medicine. He died tragically in 1932, at the age of 26, after contracting scarlet fever while serving his internship at the hospital in Bielsko. Karol had been very close to his brother, and he suffered greatly from the loss.

Between Edmund and Karol there had been another child named Olga, but she had died only a few days after birth. So, Lolek remained alone with his father, who was a very attentive parent, friend, and confidant. After Karol was elected pope, old neighbors told journalists how they remembered the Wojtyłas, father and son walking hand in hand to the restaurant near their home for a meal, or simply out strolling.

John Paul has said very little about the deaths of his mother and brother. But his words to Frossard regarding his father's grief help us to imagine something of his own sense of loss: "...Quite soon I became a motherless only child. My father was admirable and almost all the memories of my childhood and adolescence are connected with him. The violence of the blows that had struck him had opened up immense spiritual depths in him; his grief found its outlet in prayer."[3]

It was the elder Wojtyła who taught his son piety and devotion, as John Paul acknowledged in a written testimonial marking the fiftieth anniversary of his priestly ordination: "Sometimes I would wake up during the night and find my father on his knees, just as I would always see him kneeling in the parish church."[4]

John Paul told Frossard that his father had been the first inspiration for the encyclical *Dominum et Vivificantem*:

> When I was 10 or 12 years old I was a choirboy, but I wasn't very dedicated, I must confess. My mother wasn't with us anymore...but my father, when he noticed my lack of diligence, said to me one day: "You are not being a very good choirboy. You don't pray to the Holy Spirit enough. You ought to pray to him." And he taught me a prayer to say.... That was a major spiritual lesson, longer lasting and more powerful than anything I got from my reading or from the courses I took later on. What conviction his voice held as he told me that! I can still hear his voice saying those words, even today. The end product from that lesson from my childhood is my encyclical on the Holy Spirit.[5]

After the death of his wife Emilia, Karol took his two sons on a pilgrimage to the shrine *Kalwaria Zebrzydowska*, not far from Wadowice. The young Karol would return many times; in fact, he did so before leaving for the conclave that elected him Pope. After his election, he again returned on June 7, 1979, commenting: "I don't know how I can thank divine Providence that I am once again visiting this place, *Kalwaria Zebrzydowska*, the sanctuary of the Mother of God. I have visited this sanctuary many times, beginning from my childhood and adolescence. I visited it especially as Archbishop of Kraków and as Cardinal. I came here with the priests and celebrated Mass before the Mother of God."

Several thousand Jews lived in Wadowice during Karol's early years. In fact, the owner of the apartment house the Wojtyłas rented was a Jew named Chaim Balamuth, and on the ground floor of the building he had a glassware store. Many of his associates and some of Lolek's best friends were Jewish; for example, Regina (called Ginka) Beer, the daughter of the director of the bank of Wadowice, and Jerzy Kluger, whose father was a lawyer and president of the local Jewish community. Years later, John Paul would write: "I remember, above all, the Wadowice elementary school, where at least a fourth of the pupils in my class were Jewish. I should mention my friendship...with one of them, Jerzy Kluger—a friendship that has lasted from my school days to the present."[6]

Karol Wojtyła's relationship with the Jews was one of mutual understanding and friendship. Years later, Jerzy Kluger would say: "Life was not easy for us Jews before the war. Offenses were not lacking, nor wounds to our sensibility. But from Lolek, never; there was never any rudeness from him."[7]

From the time of St. Peter to the present, no pope has ever shown such constant good relations with the Jews. "I can vividly remember the Jews who gathered every Saturday at the Synagogue behind our school. Both religious groups, Catholics and Jews, were united, I presume, by the awareness that they prayed to the same God."[8]

That peaceful coexistence did not last, but it planted a seed in Karol which one day would bear fruit. The Second World War, with its concentration camps and methodical extermination of the Jewish people, dramatically turned everything upside down. "First and foremost the sons and daughters of the Jewish nation were condemned for no other reason than that they were Jews. Even if only indirectly, whoever lived in Poland at that time came in contact with this reality. Therefore, this was also a personal experience of mine, an experience I carry with me even today."[9] Some day humanity will be grateful for such an honest admission, which contradicts countless excuses such as: "We didn't know; we could never have imagined such a thing was happening."

Two Passions: Literature and Theater

In the autumn of 1926, six-year-old Lolek started elementary school, and in 1930 he was admitted to the middle school, *Marcin Wadowita.* Looking back on that time, Jerzy Kluger relates: "Lolek was a special person. He was in first place: at school, in the theater, and in everything. If he had gone to General Motors, he would have become its president."[10]

Lolek studied assiduously under the watchful eye of his father. The young boy was especially interested in literature and in the Polish language. He read the works of Henry Sienkiewicz (*Quo Vadis?*, *The Deluge, With Fire and Sword*), Adam Mickiewicz (a romantic poet and herald of Polish independence), and the poet and dramatist Juliusz Słowacki. He also read the Greek and Latin classics and modern philosophical works in German (a language which he had learned at home)—among them,

Immanuel Kant's *Critique of Pure Reason* and Karl Marx's *Das Kapital.* Lolek also played sports, and he especially liked skiing, swimming, soccer, and hockey. He enjoyed holidays and took an active part in feast day celebrations.

Almost every morning before classes Lolek assisted at the Mass celebrated by his pastor, Father Edward Zacher, who later, at the age of 84 in 1979, would receive a visit from the Pope at Wadowice. Karol also visited the Carmelite Fathers' monastery, which was situated behind the market square in Wadowice. There he met Father Joseph Prus who became an invaluable counselor. Lolek was fascinated by Carmelite spirituality; as a priest he would frequently ask and be denied the permission of Adam Stefan Sapieha, Archbishop of Kraków, to enter the Carmelite Order.

On May 4, 1938, Lolek graduated with the following grades: *excellent* in conduct, religion, the Polish language and literature, Latin, Greek, German, mathematics, philosophy, and physical education; *good* in history, physics, and chemistry. During that same month he received the Sacrament of Confirmation. "My religion teacher, Father Edward Zacher, chose me to give the address of welcome.... I know that after my speech the Archbishop asked the religion teacher what university course I would be taking.... Father Zacher replied: 'He will study the Polish language and letters.' The Archbishop apparently replied: 'A pity it is not theology.'"[11]

During his years at secondary school, Lolek developed another interest: the theater. His first performance, at the age of 14, consisted of a collection of songs and patriotic verses which he recited in the school auditorium and in the city park. His interpretation of the poem "Promethidi" by Cyprian Norwid won second place in a competition. Lolek was a versatile actor. On one occasion he had to take two roles in the same comedy (perhaps because a colleague failed to show up); he played them both quite naturally because he knew the script in its entirety from first page to last.

Sometimes Lolek gave formal recitations together with his classmates, especially with Ginka Beer and Halina Krolikiewicz. Ginka's family would eventually flee Wadowice to escape the Holocaust; Halina later became a well-known professional actress in the Polish theater.

His companions were aware that Lolek had a special liking for Ginka. His first love, however, was the theater. "Perhaps some of [my friends] thought that if a young man with such evident religious inclinations did not enter the seminary, it had to be a sign that there were other loves or interests involved. Certainly I knew many girls from school and, involved as I was in the school drama club, I had many opportunities to get together with other young people. But this was not the issue. At that time I was completely absorbed by a passion for literature, especially dramatic literature, and for the theater."[12]

The summer of his eighteenth year marked a change in his life. He spent the month of June at a preparatory camp for military service at Zubrzyca Gorna, organized by the youth section of the Department of Labor. Then, before the end of the summer, he moved to Kraków with his father in order to take courses at the Jagiellonian University, where he enrolled in the department of Polish philology in the faculty of philosophy. "As for my studies," he says, "I would like to point out that my choice of the Polish language and letters was determined by a clear inclination toward literature. Right from the beginning of the first year, however, I found myself attracted to the study of the language itself. We studied the descriptive grammar of modern Polish as well as the historical evolution of the language, with a special emphasis on its ancient Slav roots. This opened up completely new horizons for me; it introduced me to the mystery of language itself."[13]

The young Karol and his father now lived in a small apartment on Tyniecka Street in the Debniki quarter, which is separated from the historical section of the city by the Vistula River. The house was owned by two of Lolek's unmarried aunts, sisters of his mother.

On October 15, 1938, one of the city's hotels posted an announcement of a literary evening to be held at the Catholic House of Kraków. The featured presentations included works by Jerzy Bober, Jerzy Kalamacki, Tadeusz Kwiatkowski, and Karol Wojtyła. Lolek was already writing poetry and composing scripts for the theater.

*A*dulthood is a time for making decisions and pursuing one's destiny. One of the mysterious abilities of youth is to quietly make a decision, at a certain moment, that will affect the rest of one's life. John Paul calls his decision to choose a celibate life instead of marriage "a gift and a mystery" in the memorial he composed to mark the fiftieth anniversary of his priestly ordination. Regarding his decision, he explains: "A day came when I knew for certain that my life would not be fulfilled in the human love, the beauty of which I have always felt deeply."[14]

In 1939, war broke out and carried everyone toward their destiny.

NOTES

1. A. Frossard, *"Be Not Afraid!"* (New York: St. Martin's Press, 1984), p. 14.

2. K. Wojtyła, *Giobbi ed altri inediti* (Rome: Libreria Editrice Vaticana, 1982), p. 83.

3. A. Frossard, *"Be Not Afraid!"* (New York: St. Martin's Press, 1984), p. 14.

4. John Paul II, *Gift and Mystery* (New York: Doubleday, 1996), p. 20.

5. A. Frossard, *Portrait of John Paul II* (San Francisco: Ignatius Press, 1990), p. 74.

6. John Paul II with Vittorio Messori, *Crossing the Threshold of Hope* (New York: Alfred A. Knopf, 1994), p. 96.

7. J. Chelini, *Jean Paul II* (Paris: Editions Jean Goujon, 1980), p. 37.

8. John Paul II with Vittorio Messori, *Crossing the Threshold of Hope* (New York: Alfred A. Knopf, 1994), p. 96.

9. Ibid., p. 97.

10. G. Svidercoschi, *Lettera a un amico ebreo* (Milan: Mondadori, 1993), p. 92.

11. John Paul II, *Gift and Mystery* (New York: Doubleday, 1996), p. 5.

12. Ibid., p. 7.

13. Ibid.

14. A. Frossard, *"Be Not Afraid!"* (New York: St. Martin's Press, 1984), p. 15.

❀   CHAPTER TWO   ❀

Laborer, Actor, Priest

*W*hen the first bombs fell on Kraków, Karol was in the cathedral: "I will never forget the day of September 1, 1939: it was the First Friday of the month. I had gone to Wawel for confession [and Mass]; the cathedral was completely empty. That was perhaps the last time that I was able to enter the church freely."[1] As soon as Mass was over, Karol rushed home to his father, who was in poor health. They gathered their things together and, with about ten other refugees, fled eastward on foot. The trek was difficult, in spite of a ride a truck driver offered them, and Karol's father was exhausted. But they discovered that war was also being fought in the east. The Ribbentrop-Molotov Pact had made it possible for Stalin's Red Army to invade eastern Poland. The refugees were forced to return to Kraków.

Two-thirds of Poland, including Kraków, was in German hands while the remaining third, in the direction of Lithuania and Belorussia, was already in the hands of the Russians. In World War I that land had been taken from Marshal Piłsudski, so much admired by Karol's father.

The university in Kraków reopened, but classes lasted only until November 6, the day the Nazis arrested the professors and sent them to the concentration camp at Sachsenhausen. Very few of them ever returned.

Forced labor was imposed on all Poles between the ages of 18 and 60, unless they were already engaged in regular work. Lolek was 20 years old, so he was liable to be drafted. "In order to avoid deportation to do forced labor in Germany, I began in the autumn of 1940 to work as a laborer in a stone quarry attached to the Solvay chemical plant. This was at Zakrzówek, about half an hour from my home, and every day I would walk there."[2] The Nazis considered Solvay a strategic plant because its production supplied materials needed for the war. Consequently, the young laborer and his companions had permission to move about freely.

"The managers of the quarry, who were Poles, tried to spare us students from the heaviest work. In my case, they made me the assistant to the rock-blaster; his name was Franciszek Łabus. I remember him because he would occasionally say things like: 'Karol, you should be a priest. You have a good voice and will sing well; then you'll be all set.'"[3] The Poles also gave him time to study and to pray: "It did not bother them that I brought books to work. They would say: 'We'll keep watch; you go ahead and read.'"[4]

In February 1940 Karol met a person who would leave a definite mark on his formation. Jan Tyranowski was a 40-year-old tailor of quite ordinary appearance but extraordinary spiritual depth. Tyranowski had formed a clandestine prayer group which he called "The Living Rosary." "Tyranowski, whose own spiritual formation was based on the writings of St. John of the Cross and St. Teresa of Avila, helped me to read their works, something uncommon for a person my age."[5] Later, as Cardinal and as Pope, John Paul would remember that special teacher, calling him "an apostle of the love of God" and describing with emotion his example of dedication to God alone.

Lolek worked in the stone quarry until the springtime of 1942, when he was transferred to the Solvay factory. "Having worked with my hands, I knew quite well the meaning of physical labor. Every day I had been with people who did heavy work. I came to know their living situations, their families, their interests, their human worth, and their dignity."[6]

On one occasion Lolek saw a fellow-worker killed in an accident. It disturbed him greatly, and later he recalled the incident in a poem entitled "The Stone Quarry." He wrote the poem in 1956 in memory of the workers who died in the uprising at Poznan.

> They took his body, and walked in a silent line.
> Toil still lingered about him, a sense of wrong.
> They wore gray blouses, boots ankle deep in mud.
> In this they showed the end....
> White stone now within him, eating into his being,
> taking over enough of him to turn him into a stone.[7]

Suddenly Alone

Lolek's father died on February 18, 1941, but Lolek had sensed for some time that the end was near. He had already turned for help to a family friend, Julius Kidrinski, who was also devoted to the theater. The two young men took turns sitting beside Karol's father, and Mrs. Kidrinski, Julius' mother, usually prepared meals for the Wojtyłas. When Lolek returned from work on February 18 and found his father dead, he called for Julius. The two kept an all-night vigil. Looking back on that night years later, in a private conversation John Paul said: "I never felt so alone." Perhaps it was also on that night that he began to think seriously about how to give some meaning to his solitude.

He did not make an immediate decision. For a whole year Karol continued as before, working in the factory and involving himself with the theater. In fact, now that he had no family, Karol lived with the family of Mieczysław Kotlarczyk, a professor of Polish literature who was totally dedicated to the theater and had previously started a university theater at Wadowice. In time Kotlarczyk became host, friend, and teacher to Karol, and together they founded the "Theater of the Living Word." "Sharing the same house, we were able not only to continue our conversations about the theater, but also to attempt some actual performances. These took the form, precisely, of a 'theater of the word.' It was all quite simple. The scenery and decorations were kept to a minimum; our efforts were concentrated essentially on the delivery of the poetic text."[8] The great names of Polish literature performed by the Theater included Slowacki, Kasprowicz, Wyspianski, Norwid, Mickiewicz, all of whom proclaimed the glories of the fatherland and its identification with Christianity.

Because of the simplicity of the "Theater of the Living Word," which could be staged in private homes, its founders considered it a form of peaceful resistance and a defense of Polish culture against their Nazi invaders. Karol opposed violence and did not want to be part of any opposition that would lead to an armed struggle, although he was willing to collaborate in raising funds for resistance efforts.

The actors and audience of the "Theater of the Living Word" met secretly in private homes or in basements, with at least twenty persons taking part in each gathering. They posed a challenge to the Gestapo who patrolled Kraków street by street every night. In the theater's productions Karol always had a key role as actor, scriptwriter, scene designer, or interlocutor. None of the regular members had any doubt that Karol's future lay in the theater. He possessed everything needed for an acting career: voice, gestures, emotion, memory.

One evening, however, in the autumn of 1942, Karol told his friend Kotlarczyk not to count on him any more; he had informed Adam Stefan Sapieha, Archbishop of Kraków, of his intention to become a priest. Karol's last theatrical performance was in March 1943, in the play

Samuel Zborowski. The vocation that had surfaced during the night of his father's wake had now come to full maturity.

"The story of my priestly vocation? It is known above all to God. At its deepest level, every vocation to the priesthood is *a great mystery*; it is a gift which infinitely transcends the individual."[9] These are the words with which John Paul begins his autobiographical document, *Dono e Mistero* (Gift and Mystery), written to mark the fiftieth anniversary of his priestly ordination. He did not become aware of his vocation in a sudden flash; it developed slowly and perhaps was apparent to others before he himself recognized it. Concerning his last years in Wadowice, the Pope writes: "In that period of my life *my vocation to the priesthood had not yet matured,* even though many people around me thought that I should enter the seminary."[10] Two traumatic events lie at the core of his decision to become a priest: the war and the death of his father.

> In the face of the spread of evil and the atrocities of the war, the meaning of the priesthood and its mission in the world became much clearer to me. The outbreak of the war took me away from my studies and from the university. In that period I also lost my father, the last remaining member of my immediate family. All this brought with it, objectively, *a progressive detachment* from my earlier plans; in a way it was like being uprooted from the soil in which, up till that moment, my humanity had grown. But the process was not merely negative. At the same time a light was beginning to shine ever more brightly in the back of my mind: *the Lord wants me to become a priest.* One day I saw this with great clarity....[11]

Karol had also deepened his life of prayer, nourished by membership in "The Living Rosary" and by his reading of the great Spanish mystics. To these classics he added the reading of *True Devotion to the Blessed Virgin Mary* by St. Louis de Montfort, the book from which, more than thirty years later, he would take the motto of his pontificate: *Totus Tuus* (I am all yours).

Another important influence was Karol's devotion to Brother Albert, known in the world as Adam Chmielowski, an artist and Polish hero from the 1800s who had abandoned everything to dedicate himself to the poor. "For me he was particularly important, because I found in him a real *spiritual support and example* in leaving behind the world of art, literature and the theater, and *in making the radical choice of a vocation to the priesthood.*"[12] In 1949 Father Karol Wojtyła would dedicate to Brother Albert his drama, *Our God's Brother*.

From Clandestine Actor to Underground Seminarian

In 1942 Karol secretly began to take classes from the theology faculty at the university in Kraków as a seminarian for the archdiocese of Kraków. The seminary was instituted by Archbishop Sapieha, but hidden from the Nazis who permitted only those registered as seminarians before 1939 to study theology openly. Karol passed his examinations with grades of *excellent* and *very good*. During this time he continued to live in the neighborhood of Debniki in Kraków and to work at the Solvay factory.

Each morning Karol left his house for the archbishop's residence to serve Mass in Sapieha's private chapel. He was always accompanied by another clandestine seminarian named Jerzy Zachuta. "One day [Zachuta] did not appear. After Mass I stopped by his house in Ludwinów (near Debniki) and learned that he had been taken away by the Gestapo during the night. Immediately afterward, his name appeared on the list of Poles who were to be shot."[13]

On the night of February 29, 1944, while walking home from the factory, a German army truck hit Karol. The driver did not stop, and Karol lay unconscious with a fractured skull. A woman found him by the side of the road and he was taken to the city hospital. Karol did not regain consciousness for several days and spent the next two weeks in the hospital, reflecting on the mysterious designs of Providence.

Some time later he narrowly escaped arrest during a search by Nazi soldiers. To avoid further risks, Sapieha decided in August to move the six or seven clandestine seminarians into his own residence. There they remained hidden for several months while continuing their studies. A friendly hand erased Karol Wojtyła's name from the list of workers at the Solvay plant and, as a result, the Nazis no longer checked for him among the workers. On September 9 Karol received the tonsure.

Kraków was liberated on January 18, 1945, when the Red Army drove out the Nazi forces. At the end of the war, Karol was elected vice-president of *Bratnia Pomoc*, an organization to aid university students in difficulty. At the same time he completed all his courses in theology. On November 1, 1946, Karol was ordained to the priesthood in Sapieha's private chapel.

> I can still remember myself in that chapel during the singing of the *Veni, Creator Spiritus* and the Litany of the Saints, lying prostrate on the floor with arms outstretched in the form of a cross, awaiting the moment of the imposition of hands.... There is something very impressive about the prostration of the ordinands, symbolizing as it does their

total submission before the majesty of God and their complete openness to the action of the Holy Spirit who will descend upon them and
consecrate them.[14]

The following day, the Feast of All Souls, Karol celebrated his first
Mass in the crypt of the cathedral at the altar of St. Leonard. He offered
the Mass for his mother and father, basing his priesthood firmly on the
keystone of his parents' faith.

Priesthood marked the end of one decisive chapter in Karol Wojtyła's
life and the beginning of another. He had passed through the war years
essentially unharmed, but greatly changed spiritually.

I was spared much of the immense and horrible drama of the Second
World War. I could have been arrested any day—at home, in the stone
quarry, in the plant—and taken away to a concentration camp. Sometimes I would ask myself: so many young people of my own age are
losing their lives. *Why not me?* Today I know that it was not mere
chance.... What I have said about the concentration camps represents
only a part, albeit dramatic, of this "apocalypse" of our century. I have
brought it up in order to emphasize that *my priesthood, even at its beginning, was in some way marked by the great sacrifice of countless
men and women of my generation.* Providence spared me the most difficult experiences; and so my sense of indebtedness is all the greater,
both to people whom I knew and to many more whom I did not know;
all of them, regardless of nationality or language, by their sacrifice on
the great altar of history, helped to make my priestly vocation a reality.[15]

Soon after his ordination, Father Karol Wojtyła departed for Rome.

NOTES

1. John Paul II, *Gift and Mystery* (New York: Doubleday, 1996), p. 26.

2. Ibid., p. 8–9.

3. Ibid., p. 10.

4. Ibid., p. 22.

5. Ibid., p. 24.

6. Ibid., pp. 21–22.

7. K. Wojtyła, *Collected Poems* (New York: Random House, 1982), p. 87.

8. John Paul II, *Gift and Mystery* (New York: Doubleday, 1996), p. 11.

9. Ibid., p. 3.

10. Ibid., p. 5.

11. Ibid., pp. 34–35.

12. Ibid., p. 33.

13. Ibid., pp. 42–43.

14. Ibid., pp. 43–44.

15. Ibid., pp. 36, 38–39.

CHAPTER THREE

Studies in Rome, Teaching Position at Lublin

*K*arol left for Rome at the age of 26 on November 15, 1946. He briefly describes that lengthy autumn journey: "For the first time I was leaving the borders of my homeland. From the window of the moving train I looked at cities known previously only from my geography books. For the first time I saw Prague, Nuremberg, Strasbourg, and Paris...."[1]

He enrolled at the Angelicum (the Pontifical University of St. Thomas Aquinas), staffed by the Dominicans, and after residing for a brief period with the Pallottines, he moved to the Belgian College. The rector at the time was Maximilian De Fürstenberg, who later became a cardinal. "How can I fail to remember that during the conclave of 1978 Cardinal De Fürstenberg came up to me at a certain moment and uttered the significant words: *'Dominus adest et vocat te'* [God is here, and calling you]? It was like a subtle and mysterious completion of the role he had played, as rector of the Belgian College, in my priestly formation."[2]

Among Karol's professors at the Angelicum were the internationally known theologian Reginald Garrigou-Lagrange and the future cardinals Luigi Ciappi and Paul Philippe. Among his fellow students was Jorge Mejía of Argentina, later named by the Pope as a collaborator in the Curia and entrusted with arranging the papal visit to the Synagogue of Rome.

John Paul has happy memories of the Angelicum and the Dominicans, and he has visited the University numerous times as Pope. On one such occasion he told the students: "You are all my colleagues, but in my day there were no Sisters, who today make up the majority in this *aula magna*. I must congratulate you, dear students at the Pope's *alma mater!*" (Nov. 24, 1994)

John Paul has a great love for Italy. In one of the chapters of *Gift and Mystery,* titled "Learning Rome," he describes his arrival

> I remember the first Sunday after our arrival, when I went with Stanislaw Starowieyski to St. Peter's Basilica and attended the Pope's solemn veneration of a newly proclaimed Blessed. From afar I saw Pope Pius XII being carried on the *sedia gestatoria*.... I would set off every day from the Belgian College...to attend lectures at the *Angelicum*. I would always make a stop at the Jesuit Church of St. Andrea al Quirinale, where the relics of St. Stanislaus Kotska are enshrined.... I remember that among the visitors to his tomb there were many seminarians from the *Germanicum*, easily recognizable by their characteristic red cassocks. At the heart of Christendom, and in the light of the saints, people from different nations would come together, as if to foreshadow, beyond the tragic war which had left such a deep mark on us, a world no longer divided.[3]

During Christmas and Easter vacations, Karol was accustomed to visit other Italian cities, beginning with Assisi. During the long summer vacations he visited France, Holland, and Belgium.

> There I came to appreciate the broader European context.... These experiences, in my first and second years of priesthood, proved enormously important to me.... From different and complementary angles, I was coming to an ever greater appreciation of *Western Europe*, the Europe of the postwar period, a Europe of splendid Gothic cathedrals and yet a Europe threatened by increasing secularization. I understood the challenge that this posed to the Church, and the need to confront this impending danger through new forms of pastoral activity open to a broader participation by the laity.[4]

Karol spent two years in Rome. In June 1948, he successfully defended his thesis, *The Doctrine of Faith According to St. John of the Cross*.[5] Although he received a *summa cum laude*, Karol Wojtyła could not receive his doctoral degree until he submitted the required number of copies of his thesis to the University. Karol could not pay for the printing, however, so when he returned to Poland, he delivered his thesis before the theology faculty of Jagiellonian University. He received the degree of doctor of theology in December 1948.

Initial Ministry in Poland

Once back home, Karol asked Archbishop Sapieha's permission to enter the Carmelite Order, but the answer was a definitive "no." The Archbishop reminded Karol of the shortage of priests following the war,

The Pope's parents, with his older brother Edmund, in 1908.

The future pope with his mother, Emilia Kaczorowska.

Karol Józef Wojtyła was born on May 18, 1920, and was called Lolek by his mother.

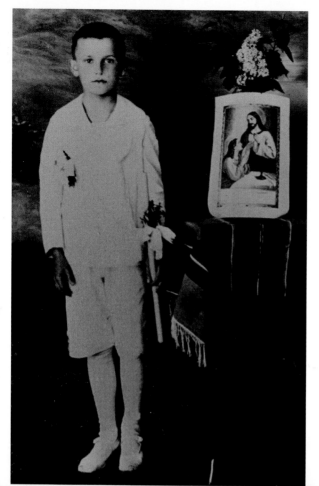

On his first Communion day, in 1929.

With a group of fellow students in elementary school, 1930. Karol is in the top row, far right.

Around 1939. During his university days he worked in a quarry while also pursuing his love for the theater.

Karol Wojtyła often enjoyed mountain sports.

The Archbishop of Krakow in a lighter moment.

Karol Wojtyła as Archbishop of Krakow (1967–1978). During this time he was a key figure in the Church's opposition to the communist regime.

The future pope during Vatican Council II sessions.

Pope John Paul II shortly after his election on October 16, 1978.

Pope John Paul II has made a practice of hearing confessions on Good Friday at St. Peter's.

At a general audience in St. Peter's Square.

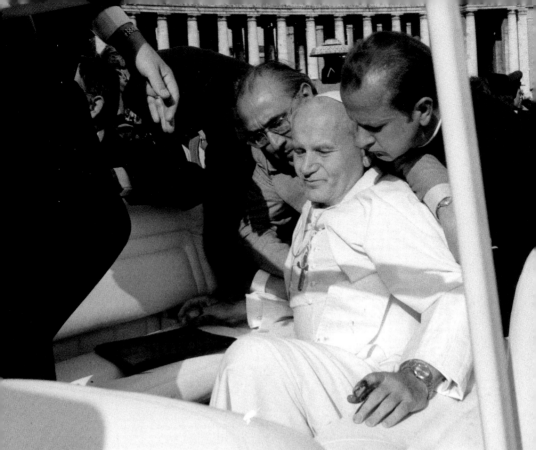

Assassination attempt, May 13, 1981.

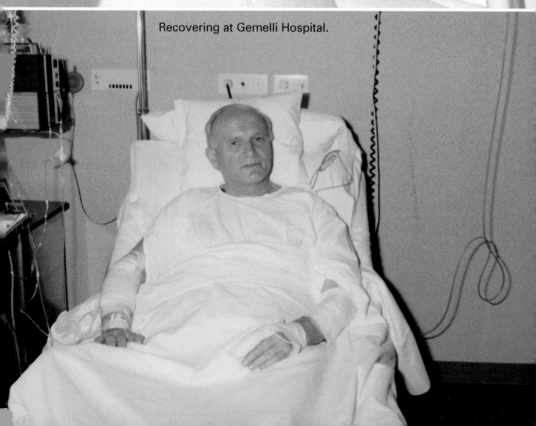

Recovering at Gemelli Hospital.

Pope John Paul II's meeting with his would-be assassin, Ali Agca.

Entering Auschwitz.

A moment in the daily life of John Paul II.

Pope John Paul II on the icy
peaks of Adamello, where he
celebrated Mass for the
people of the Alpine (1988).

Despite his busy schedule, the Pope makes time for prayer and reflection.

A pensive moment in his private study.

The Pope spends many hours
in his study preparing documents
and planning his trips.

John Paul II stands at the door of the House of Slaves on the Senegalese island of Gorée.

and besides, Sapieha insisted, Wojtyła was "needed much more in the diocese." Then he added what now seems a premonition, "and in the future for the entire Church."[6]

Father Wojtyła's first assignment was to serve as associate pastor in the village of Niegowic, some 50 kilometers from Kraków and east of Wadowice. "Immediately I inquired how to get to Niegowic and made plans to be there on the day appointed.... It was harvest time. I walked through the fields of grain with the crops partly already reaped, and partly still waving in the wind. When I finally reached the territory of Niegowic parish, I knelt down and kissed the ground. It was a gesture I had learned from [the life of] St. John Vianney."[7]

The fields of grain constantly return to John Paul's memory and are frequently mentioned in his poetry. One of his poems uses the image of grain fused with light, reminiscent of the fields of Provence, so dearly loved and often depicted by the artist Vincent Van Gogh.

When I think—my Country—I still hear
the swishing scythe, it strikes the wall of wheat,
merging into one profile with the arched sky; the light stoops.[8]

Young Father Wojtyła stayed less than a year in Niegowic—a village which did not yet have electricity—but it was enough time for him to get to know the young people there. In March 1949, he was called back to Kraków and assigned to St. Florian's Church in the university quarter. There he was in his element. He organized courses of formation for couples and families. He also took part in the so-called "distance university," which consisted of university level courses that did not fall under the control of Communist authorities because they were conducted secretly in churches or religious houses.

Father Wojtyła also founded a group for young boys called *Srodowisko* (Environment). The group's purpose was to bring boys in contact with nature, something Wojtyła. considered a special means for coming in contact with God. Years later he would say to a gathering of more than 5,000 young people:

Sun and stars, water and air, plants and animals are all gifts with which God has made comfortable and beautiful the dwelling which his love has prepared for man on earth. Anyone who has understood this cannot fail to look with reverent acknowledgement at the creatures of the earth and treat them with the proper care that a dutiful glance at the divine Giver reveals to us (Viterbo, Italy, May 27, 1984).

Even more than his fond image of grain, the memories of the young people he had known in the early years of his priesthood would never leave him. They would help him to dialogue with young people of every nation.

> You are determined to establish a just, free, and prosperous society.... In my youth I experienced the same convictions. God willed that they should be tempered in the fire of a war whose atrocities did not spare my family. I have seen these convictions trampled on in many ways. I have feared for them, seeing them exposed to the tempest. One day I determined to confront them with Jesus Christ.... If a young person such as I, called upon to live my youth at a crucial time in history, was able to say something to young people like you, I think I would say: Don't let yourselves be manipulated! Strive always to be fully aware of what you desire and what you do! (Belo Horizonte, Brazil, July 1, 1980)

Father Wojtyła spent his vacations with young people in the mountains or in semi-clandestine summer schools which were forbidden by the Communist authorities. In order not to arouse suspicion, he removed his cassock and wore civilian clothes. Photographs show him seated on the grass socializing with young people or playing with the children of married couples. "In my own life I have identified these priorities in the lay apostolate and particularly in the pastoral care of the family—an area in which lay people themselves have helped me so much—in youth ministry and in serious dialogue with the world of learning and culture."[9]

Professor of Theology

Stalin's death in 1953 affected many lives in Poland. Cardinal Wyszynski, the Primate of Poland, was arrested because the Communist regime never forgave him for his opposition to Poland's new Constitution, which increased the power of the Communist government and restricted the rights of the Church. He was imprisoned, together with numerous priests, and released three years later. The government also shut down the magazine *Tygodnik Powszechny,* to which Wojtyła had been contributing under a pseudonym, because the magazine's editors refused to publish a eulogy in honor of Stalin. The theology department at Jagiellonian University in Kraków, where Wojtyła had only recently become professor of social ethics, was also closed. He was promptly offered the chair of theology at the Catholic University of Lublin, a position he would occupy until his election as pope.

The courses Wojtyła taught were crowded with students. His fundamental thesis was that "the subject of morality is the living individual; the existing person is the supreme form of reality, and this reality must be respected in its concrete form."[9] This was a traditional Thomistic principle, renewed and revived by Jacques Maritain and embellished by the personalism of Emmanuel Mounier, two authors whom Wojtyła had read with great interest during his stay in France the summer of 1947.

This Thomism was one revived and renewed by the method and language of the phenomenology of Max Scheler (1874–1928), the German philosopher whose theories Wojtyła used to promote freedom of research and teaching at the university in Kraków. Similarly, these theories later became the point of reference for his greatest philosophical work, *Osoba i Czyn* (1969), published in English under the title, *The Acting Person.* In the book's preface Wojtyła wrote:

> I have indeed tried to face the major issues themselves concerning life, nature, and the existence of the human being—with its limitations as well as with its privileges—directly as they present themselves to man in his struggle to survive while maintaining the dignity of the human being: man, who sets himself goals and strives to accomplish them, and who is torn apart between his all too limited condition and his highest aspirations to set himself free.[10]

The philosophical work of Karol Wojtyła, produced over a period of twenty-five years—from 1952 until shortly before his election to the papacy—is described by the experts as a unique "treatise on man"[11] and a research culminating in a "philosophy of man."[12] He affirms a humanism that is solidly anchored in reality and experience.

Playwright and Poet

Besides his philosophical output, and more readily accessible to the ordinary reader, are Wojtyła's literary works: the poems and dramas published in *Tygodnik Powszechny* under the penname Andrzej Jawien or, in *Znak*, under the pseudonym Stanisław Andrzej Gruda. Perhaps he chose a penname out of modesty or, as the Marist priest Adam Boniecki has stated, in order to keep his literary activity separate from his priestly ministry. Actually, Wojtyła considered writing a secondary occupation: "If I had not become Pope, no one would have paid any attention to my poetic writings."

Wojtyła's earliest poems and stage plays date back to his days in secondary school. The first play, *David,* is no longer extant, but Wojtyła mentions it in a letter to his friend and teacher Kotlarczyk: "I have written a play, or rather a dramatic poem called *David.* The hero is clothed in biblical dress and at the same time in crimson. I have placed in him many things, many sentiments that fill my soul. I am curious to know what you think."[13] The following year, he composed two scripts within a few months of one another: *Job* and *Jeremiah*. In a letter to Kotlarczyk, he commented that *Job* was "a theatrical piece, Greek in style, Christian in spirit, eternal in substance, like everyone. A drama about suffering. It is for anyone who likes it. It is in part the result of my reading of the Old Testament. I have read the psalms of David, the Book of Job, the Book of Wisdom, and now I am reading the Prophets."[14]

As a meditation on suffering and pain in a religious context, and also from a patriotic perspective, *Job* contains the seeds that would germinate 40 years before bearing fruit in his 1984 apostolic letter, *Salvifici Doloris* (On the Christian Meaning of Human Suffering). This letter contains his more recent comments on the sufferings of Job: "And if the Lord consents to test Job with suffering, he does it *to demonstrate the latter's righteousness.* The suffering has the nature of a test."[15]

Jeremiah also has a religious and patriotic theme. The drama is set in the period between the sixteenth and seventeenth centuries when Poland was at war against the Turks. The two most significant events of this period were the victory of the Turks in 1620 and the definitive victory of the Poles in the battle at Khotim (Russia) in 1621.

> *Here is the Bulwark—our Glory.*
> *As a holy bulwark you placed us, O Lord—*
> *and never did we resist your order,*
> *but with your roses stuck in our armor,*
> *leaning on our swords, we watched the border.*[16]

After these three biblical dramas, composed between 1939 and 1940, ten years would pass before Wojtyła's next theatrical composition: *Our God's Brother*. The main character in this drama is Adam Chmielowski, a Polish painter and patriot of the 1800s who abandoned pen and sword to become Brother Albert, hailed as the St. Francis of Poland. As Pope, Wojtyła would beatify him in 1983 and canonize him six years later. Echoes of the play, *Our God's Brother,* can be found in John Paul's encyclical *Dives in Misericordia* (On the Mercy of God).

Wojtyła describes his next drama, *The Jeweler's Shop,* which he wrote in 1960, as "a meditation on the Sacrament of Matrimony, which from time to time is transformed into a drama." It is composed of three parts and recounts events in the lives of three couples.

> In the first act, Teresa and Andrew become engaged and then get married. The second act portrays the marriage of Stephen and Anna, which is in an advanced stage of crisis. Deeply hurt by Stephen's indifference, Anna tries to make contact with other men and tries to sell her wedding

ring, but the jeweler refuses, saying: "This ring doesn't weigh enough...
only the two rings together are of sufficient weight." In the third act,
Monica and Christopher, the children of the two couples, fall in love
and get married, but their union is not an easy one.[17]

An important role is played by a "mysterious stranger" named Adam
who, as witness, spokesman, counselor and judge, portrays the figure of a
confessor. "Adam represents those who have never married and have no
family but have a profound understanding of human love and marriage."[18]

The final play Karol Wojtyła wrote (in 1964) is called *Radiation of
Fatherhood.*[19] He describes the play as a "mystery," suggesting that it is
more of a philosophic-religious reflection than a drama in the strict sense
of the word. Actually, *Radiation of Fatherhood* is an analysis of various
themes of human existence—solitude, parenthood, infancy—which were
only hinted at in *The Jeweler's Shop.*[20]

Confronting Communism

To be a priest and an educator in Communist Poland, especially under Stalin, meant one had to confront the regime on a daily basis. It was a
battle that Karol Wojtyła waged—first as priest and later as bishop and
cardinal. He fought this battle on three distinct fronts: his ministry to
young people, the struggle to obtain permission for the construction of
new churches, and the annual procession for the Feast of Corpus Christi
which became a platform for denouncing every violation of human freedom. Wojtyła fought his battle against the Communist regime, but the
then Archbishop of Kraków did not use clamorous denunciations or explicit political interventions.

Karol Wojtyła had little or no interest in politics. His friend Jerzy
Turowicz, editor of the weekly *Tygodnik Powszechny*, said, "He is neither on the right nor the left, and he is not even a nationalist."[21] Nevertheless, Wojtyła's scant political interest did not prevent him from supporting
the initiatives of the Catholic laity. In fact he made an important contri-
bution to the politico-cultural organization called *Znak* (Sign), which had
a small representation in the parliament in Warsaw and published a
magazine to which Karol Wojtyła often contributed. He also collaborated
with *Odrodzenie*, a clandestine group directly dependent on Cardinal
Wyszynski.

Naturally, Karol Wojtyła understood Marxism very well and was totally against it. His opposition to Marxism is comparable only to that of
Nazism. He writes in *Gift and Mystery:*

[The Church in Poland] had to endure a dramatic struggle for survival against two totalitarian systems: the regime inspired by the Nazi ideology during the Second World War and then, in the long postwar period, a Communist dictatorship and its militant atheism.... The two totalitarian systems which tragically marked our century...I came to know, so to speak, from within. And so it is easy to understand my deep concern for the dignity of every human person and the need to respect human rights, beginning with the right to life.[21]

As a bishop in 1962 Karol Wojtyła experienced his first real brush with the Communist regime. The Communist authorities in Kraków planned to take over the seminary in order to turn it into a teacher's college. Wojtyła protested directly to the regional secretary. Then he did something unprecedented for a Polish bishop: he entered Communist Party headquarters to discuss the matter. The result was a compromise; the third floor of the building would be used for the school of pedagogy, and the rest of the building would remain a seminary.[22]

The battle Wojtyła fought for the parish church at Nowa Huta has become legendary. Communist authorities consistently refused to grant permission for the construction of the new church. So, on a rainy Christmas night, Wojtyła celebrated midnight Mass on the open field of the site chosen for the church. He called it "a new cave of Bethlehem." The authorities finally granted permission and construction began on May 18, 1969. Pope Paul VI sent a stone from the Basilica of St. Peter's in Rome to be the first stone in the new edifice. In his homily at the consecration of the new church in 1977, Wojtyła said: "This city is not a city of persons who do not belong to anyone, persons to whom anyone can do as he pleases; persons who can be manipulated according to the law of supply and demand. This city is a city of the children of God."[23]

In 1966 the Catholic Church celebrated its millennium in Poland, but authorities refused to approve the Polish bishops' invitation to Pope Paul VI to visit. The refusal did not prevent the Church celebrations from taking place. On September 3 the icon of the Black Madonna was scheduled to solemnly enter the Diocese of Wadowice, but the procession was blocked by a group of demonstrators. The Archbishop's automobile, which carried the icon, came to a stop. Karol Wojtyła got out of the car and was vehemently shouted down, in spite of his attempts at dialogue. There was nothing else to do; the icon had to return to Czestochowa. But the faithful did not give up. The procession moved forward, parish by parish, with an empty picture frame and a lighted candle symbolizing the flame of solidarity. Such is the spirit of resistance among the Poles.[24]

On October 28, 1967, the Archbishop organized a ceremony for the reception of the Black Madonna in Kraków. This "visitation of the Blessed Virgin Mary" ended on December 12 of the following year; Wojtyła himself was present at 120 ceremonies in various parishes and presided over fifty-three solemn liturgies.

One of his biographers, Jean Chelini, described one of Wojtyła's last public charges against the Communist regime. It occurred in June 1978, during the national pilgrimage of Polish miners at Piekary Slaskie in Upper Silesia:

About 100,000 [pilgrims] were shouting: "Long live the Cardinal; long live our bishops!" Karol Wojtyła advanced to the center of the crowd at the side of Cardinal Baum, Archbishop of Washington, D.C., who was visiting him. He was smiling broadly and he acknowledged the acclamation of the crowd with a wave of his hand. Dressed in his crimson robes, Wojtyła was a picture of strength and serenity. In his homily he spoke to the miners in very simple language but with great energy. He vehemently attacked the atheistic ceremonies the government wanted to sponsor. He defended the Sunday rest for the miners, who were forced to work on that day. "A family without Sunday is a family without a father, and a wife without a husband." He also demanded that the government authorize the opening of new factories and the reconstruction of churches that were destroyed during the war. "This refusal is contrary to the rights of man and the interests of the workers; it is an injustice. It is necessary to change this situation."

Speaking of the press in his country, Cardinal Wojtyła emphasized the disproportion between the numerous Marxist publications and the one and only publication of Catholic inspiration. "We have only one officially Catholic publication; that is intolerable." He then continued: "To say that the faith pertains to idealism is stupid. It has been said that faith is the opium of the people; I say that it is a right of the workers. What is man, if not the son of God?"[25]

John Paul II would adopt this tone whenever he returned to Poland as Pope. He adopts it every time and place in the world when questions arise concerning the rights of people and of the Church. He always expresses his opinions by returning to his Polish experience. He did this when, after twenty years of his pontificate, he told journalists what he planned to say in Cuba: "I know well what I shall say about human rights. Human rights are the foundation of every civilization. I brought this conviction out of Poland, from my confrontation with the Soviet system and communistic totalitarianism. Nothing other than this can be expected from me!" (Jan. 21, 1998, on the flight from Rome to Havana)

NOTES

1. John Paul II, *Gift and Mystery* (New York: Doubleday, 1996), p. 50.
2. Ibid., p. 59.
3. Ibid., pp. 51, 53.
4. Ibid., pp. 55–56.
5. Published in English by Ignatius Press, San Francisco, in 1981.
6. C. Bernstein, M. Politi, *Sua Santitá* (Milan: Rizzoli, 1996), p. 79.
7. W. Gramatoeski, Z. Wilinska, *Karol Wojtyła negli scritti* (Rome: Libreria Editrice Vaticana, 1980), pp. 61–62.
8. K. Wojtyła, *Collected Poems* (New York: Random House, 1979), p. 151.
9. J. Chelini, *Jean-Paul II* (Paris: Editions Jean Goujon, 1980), p. 52.
10. K. Wojtyła, *The Acting Person* (Boston: D. Reidel, 1979), p. vii.
11. T. Styczen, "Metoda antropologii filozoficznej w Osobie i czynie karadynala Wojtyła" in *Analecta Kraków*, 1973/1974, vol. 5/6, pp. 107–115.
12. K. Wojtyła, *Perché l'uomo* (Milan: Mondadori, 1995), p. 8.
13. M. Malinski, *Le radici di Papa Wojtyła* (Rome: Borla Editore, 1979), p. 112.
14. K. Wojtyła, *Opere letterarie, Poesie e drammi* (Rome: Libreria Editrice Vaticana, 1993), p. 179.
15. John Paul II, *Salvifici Doloris* (Boston: Pauline Books & Media, 1984), n. 11.
16. K. Wojtyła, *Collected Plays and Writings on the Theater* (Berkeley: University of California Press, 1987).
17. K. Wojtyła, *Opere letterarie, Poesie e drammi* (Rome: Libreria Editrice Vaticana, 1993), p. 442.
18. Ibid., p. 443.
19. K. Wojtyła, *Fratello del nostro Dio e Raggi di paternitá* (Rome: Libreria Editrice Vaticana, 1982).
20. K. Wojtyła, *Opere letterarie, Poesie e drammi* (Rome: Libreria Editrice Vaticana, 1993), p. 503.
21. John Paul II, *Gift and Mystery* (New York: Doubleday, 1996), pp. 66–67.
22. J. Offredo, *Jean-Paul II* (Paris: Editions Carrière-Michel Lafon, 1986), p. 77.
23. K. Wojtyła, *Opere letterarie, Poesie e drammi* (Rome: Libreria Editrice Vaticana, 1993), p. 104.
24. Cf. J. Offredo, *Jean-Paul II* (Paris: Editions Carrière-Michel Lafon, 1986), p. 88.
25. J. Chelini, *Jean-Paul II* (Paris: Editions Jean Goujon, 1980), pp. 60–61.

❀ CHAPTER FOUR ❀

Bishop, Cardinal, World Traveler

*K*arol Wojtyła was one of the last bishops named by Pope Pius XII, three months before the end of that Pope's pontificate. Twenty years later, Wojtyła would radically change the papal image by bringing it closer to the language and life of ordinary people.

On July 4, 1958, Pius XII named Karol Wojtyła auxiliary bishop of Kraków; Wojtyła was 38 years old. When Church officials looked for Father Wojtyła to give him the news, they found him out camping with a group of young people. He hurried back to town, accepted the responsibility immediately, and asked permission to return to his group.

A year later, when a discussion arose about topics to be covered in the upcoming Second Vatican Council, Bishop Wojtyła suggested "an opportunity for priests to have a closer relationship with all areas of life in the world, including sports and the theater."[1] Evidently he was thinking of his own personal experience (see Chapter 19).

Bishop Wojtyła's response to the preparatory commission for the Council, dated December 30, 1959, fills eight pages of the *Acts of Vatican Council II*. His comments show he had a keen perception of what was necessary for renewal in the Church. In ecumenism, less emphasis should be placed on what divides Christians and greater concentration placed on our common heritage. A stronger indication of the vocation and responsibility of the laity in the Church was needed, as well as a reform of the breviary and revitalization of the liturgy to respond to an ever-increasing materialism and to promote a system of ethics based on Christian personalism.

Bishop Wojtyła left for Rome to attend the Council on October 5, 1962. He had not been outside Poland since the completion of his studies in 1948. His participation in the assembly of the Fathers of the Council evoked in him strong emotions, which he described in the poem "Church."

We have words to lean on, spoken long ago
still spoken in trembling for fear we should change them in any way.
But is this all?

For there are invisible hands that hold us
so that it takes great effort to carry the boat,
whose story, despite the shallows, follows its course.
Is it enough to dip deep in the spring,
not to seek the invisible hands?[2]

Bishop Wojtyła immediately became the spokesman for the Polish bishops. He intervened eight times during the Council, submitted thirteen written texts and three more in conjunction with other Council Fathers. He was one of thirteen members of a commission for the study of questions dealing with population, the family, and birth, under the presidency of Cardinal Alfredo Ottaviani. He was also a member of the subcommittee charged with drafting the text of the document *Gaudium et Spes* (Pastoral Constitution on the Church in the Modern World). Worthy of note are his interventions on ecclesiology, religious freedom, and atheism. In two interventions (Oct. 21, 1963 and Oct. 8, 1964) he insisted strongly that in the schema on the Church, the chapter titled "The People of God" should precede the chapter on the hierarchy.[3]

On September 22, 1965, in an intervention on religious liberty and atheism, Wojtyła stated: "It is necessary to declare that the divine right of religious liberty, since it is a natural right (that is, based on the natural law and hence on divine law), cannot suffer any limitation except what flows from the natural law itself."

In an intervention on September 28, he allied himself with the Fathers who criticized parts of the document for being overly optimistic: "In the schema, the vision of the world as it ought to be overshadows that of the world as it is; therefore, it lacks a sense of Christian realism." Regarding atheism, he said: "It would be well to distinguish between atheism that is based on personal conviction and that which is imposed from outside by various kinds of pressure, both physical and moral, especially when it becomes impossible to profess the faith in public life or official life, and the profession of atheism is demanded, so that the instruction of young people is permeated with this even against the will of the parents."

Bishop Wojtyła's interventions during the Council were prompted by his determination to point out to the bishops of the West the difficult situation of Catholic communities in Communist countries.[4] The tensions within the delegation of Polish bishops, and the tendency of Cardinal Wyszynski to remain in the shadows, most likely acted as a brake on a fuller discussion of any strongly controversial topics. Although Bishop Wojtyła was somewhat limited in the degree of his participation, his receptivity to the work of the Council was complete and creative. Years later, he told André Frossard in an interview: "I must admit on this point that it was the Second Vatican Council that helped me, so to speak, to synthesize my personal faith; in the first place Chapter 7 of the Constitution *Lumen Gentium*, the one titled 'The eschatological character of the pilgrim Church and its relation with the Church in heaven.'"[5]

As to what extent the Second Vatican Council has influenced the pontificate of Pope John Paul II, we have this statement from Cardinal Casaroli, former Secretary of State:

> We can say that he is the first pope who was formed by the Council, who has lived his priestly maturity and his years of service as a bishop in the spirit of the Council, taking from it perduring attitudes of thought and action.[6]

An author who has painstakingly reviewed Bishop Wojtyła's participation in the Council gives us this description: "In 1962, at the beginning of the Council, the auxiliary bishop of Kraków was in the lowest ranks of the worldwide episcopate. In the hall of the Council, the bishops were ranked according to seniority. The young generation of bishops sat in the lower section of the Basilica, and it was from that section that the applause that greeted favorable proposals first emanated before spreading to the assembly as a whole. Wojtyła was a member of that group of young bishops and was in fact in the vanguard."[7]

John Paul recalls his days at the Second Vatican Council: "At the beginning of my participation in the Council, I was a young bishop. I remember that at first my seat was right next to the entrance of St. Peter's Basilica. From the third session on—after I was appointed Archbishop of Kraków—I was moved closer to the altar."[8]

At the end of the Council, Archbishop Wojtyła returned to Kraków with the realization that he had participated in an event without precedent. He described it as "a great gift to the Church, to all those who took part in it, to the entire human family, and to each of us individually."[9] Now the problem and challenge was to carry out the teachings of the Council in the life of the local church. Wojtyła did so very directly. First he wrote a book titled *Sources of Renewal: The Implementation of Vatican II.*[10] Published in 1972, the book begins with the statement: "A bishop who took part in Vatican Council II feels greatly indebted to it." That same year, Wojtyła called the entire archdiocesan community together, both clergy and laity, to form an archdiocesan synod. He officially closed the synod on his first return visit to Poland as Pope in June 1979.

The Synod of Kraków was Wojtyła's crowning work as archbishop. It shows how seriously he took the teaching of Vatican Council II as his pastoral program. In the statutes of the synod he inserted this norm, revolutionary for Poland in 1972: "All the faithful may participate in the synod if in groups they assume the responsibility to work for the realization of the aims of the synod."[11] At the beginning of the synod there were 325 study groups, but by the end there were 1,000. At the very first assembly of the various groups on October 10, 1972, the Archbishop declared: "We cannot let even a fragment of the great community of the People of God, which is this Church, be lacking."

In 1967, Wojtyła became a cardinal and immediately caught the attention of the Communist secret service. A confidential document from that period reads:

> It can be said with certainty that Wojtyła is one of the few intellectuals in the Polish episcopate. Unlike Wyszynski, he is able easily to reconcile traditional popular religiosity with Catholic intellectualism, and he appreciates them both.... He is not much inclined to engage in activities against the State. It seems that he is not very much interested in politics; his approach is too intellectual.... He lacks organizational ability and command, and this is his weakness in comparison with Wyszynski.... We ought to observe and study the relationship between the two Cardinals and adopt a flexible policy in order to adjust to changing circumstances.... We should encourage Wojtyła's interest in the complex problems of the Polish Church and help him resolve the problems of the archdiocese.... At every opportunity we should manifest our hostility toward Wyszynski, but not in such a way that we force Wojtyła to show solidarity with Wyszynski.[12]

That tactic proved ineffective because Wojtyła remained loyal to Wyszynski and, in his dealings with the government, never took a stand opposite the Cardinal Primate's.

As a cardinal, Wojtyła did not change his manner of life. "He possessed nothing. He had only three threadbare black cassocks, four red ones, his skis and the paddles for the canoe. Everything he received he gave away. He ate little, he did not smoke, he drank very little wine."[13]

Archbishop Wojtyła became well known toward the end of the Second Vatican Council. In the Synods of Bishops, Cardinal Wojtyła became one of the leading participants. When the Communist government refused Cardinal Wyszynski a visa to travel to Rome for the first Extraordinary Synod convoked by Paul VI (Sept. 29 to Oct. 29, 1967), Wojtyła, as a sign of solidarity, also did not attend. He was present, however, for the four other synods held between 1969 and 1977. He was elected to the secretariat of the synod three times.

Wishing to recognize the renunciation Wojtyła had made two years before, Pope Paul VI personally designated him a member of the 1969 Synod of Bishops. At this synod Cardinal Wojtyła urged the bishops to "preserve and increase the energies that flow from collegiality and place them at the service of the primacy of Peter."[14] At the synod of 1971, he said: "We cannot put less importance on the cases of injustice regarding freedom of conscience and religion than on those related to poverty and economic misery."[15] During the 1974 synod, Paul VI assigned Wojtyła as *relator* (the person who drafts the final report on which the Synod Fathers vote) on the topic of the evangelization of peoples. From that experience Wojtyła became convinced of the necessity of proposing "a new evangelization" to humanity as it approaches the third millennium.

Another important assignment Pope Paul VI gave Wojtyła was that of preaching an annual retreat to the Roman Curia during Lent of 1976. The conferences were later published in Italian under the title *Segno di Contradizzione* (Sign of Contradiction). This work casts light upon Karol Wojtyła's dramatic sensitivity, brought to maturity by his own personal experience and animated by the teaching of Vatican Council II. Here is a man who senses that humanity and the Church are living in an exceptional time and that these are years of decisive testing. The end of the second millennium after Christ's coming is a time ripe for the upheaval of cultures, governments, and mentalities on a gigantic scale. At the same time it is an opportunity for a new advent for Christianity. It is a season in which, more than in any other, Christ manifests himself to humanity as a "sign of contradiction"; a time in which "the devil's temptation ['you will become like God'] has found the historical context that suits it. Perhaps we are experiencing the highest level of tension between the Word and the anti-Word in the whole of human history."[16] This exposition of the primordial temptation attains its full development today, "perhaps because humanity as a whole is uncovering and clarifying with ever greater thoroughness the origins of man's existence on earth. And perhaps, too, because today we are on the threshold of a new eschatology."[17]

Global Traveler

Even before becoming pope, Karol Wojtyła was a world traveler. He made a total of fifty journeys outside Poland during his years as bishop and cardinal, most of them to Rome or to other Italian cities.

In December 1964, Cardinal Wojtyła made a pilgrimage to the Holy Land with a group of Fathers from the Second Vatican Council then underway. He spoke of it in a letter to the people of Kraków:

> We felt that since we are working in the Council for the renewal of the Church, we ought to turn directly to the Lord himself, of whom the Church is his Mystical Body. From this came the desire to visit the places where he was born, where he spoke and labored, where he also suffered and died on the cross, and rose from the dead and ascended into heaven. I do not consider my participation in the pilgrimage as something personal or private, but as a grace from Providence granted to me for others.[18]

In 1965 he published the following poem, inspired by his pilgrimage, in the Polish magazine *Znak:*

> *And today, why do I come here?*
> *Do not be surprised!*
> *Every glance, for 1900 years,*
> *Is here transformed into that one immutable glance.*[19]

His first visit to the United States and to Canada took place in 1969; early in 1973 he visited Australia, New Zealand, New Guinea, and the Philippines. From July 23 until September 5, 1976, he was again in the United States, primarily to attend the Eucharistic Congress in Philadelphia, but also to visit other cities including Boston, Detroit, Chicago, Los Angeles, and San Francisco. Cardinal Wojtyła had a very tight schedule but he always managed to greet the Polish communities in each place.

One providential aspect of Wojtyła's numerous journeys was the opportunity they provided him to meet many other ecclesiastical figures and to become acquainted with them. Apart from the Fathers of the Second Vatican Council, Cardinal Wojtyła had an opportunity to meet the following Cardinals: Baum, Bengsch, Cody, Colombo, Cook, Dearden, Freeman, Hoeffner, Koenig, Krol, Manning, Marty, Medeiros, Pellegrino, Poma, Ratzinger, Sin, Suenens, Ursi, and Volk. These contacts not only served to make him well known outside his native Poland, but they also afforded him an opportunity to inform prelates all over the world of the difficult situation of the Church under the Communist regime.

Cardinal Wojtyła's last journey outside Poland before the conclave that elected him pope is of particular significance. Together with a delegation of Polish bishops, he traveled to Germany in September 1978. The purpose of the visit was to conclude the process of a post-World War II reconciliation between the Church in Poland and the Church in Germany. The procedure had been set in motion in November 1965. By means of a letter from the Polish bishops, the German bishops were invited to mutual pardon and reconciliation so that "with a tranquil conscience" the Poles could celebrate the millennium of the Church in Poland (A.D. 966–1966).

> Reverend Brothers, we send out an appeal: Let us try to forget! No polemics; no continuation of the cold war, but the beginning of a dialogue.... In this very Christian and at the same time very human spirit, we extend our hands to you, seated on the benches of a Council that is about to end, forgiving and asking forgiveness.[20]

The German bishops replied with deep emotion on December 5, 1965: "We also ask you to forget; we ask you to forgive"; and there was peace between the two Catholic communities. However, the Polish Communist government instigated a propaganda campaign against the Polish episcopate, one especially directed at Cardinal Wyszynski and Archbishop Wojtyła. The object of the invective was precisely the phrase "forgiving and asking forgiveness." The Communist response to that attitude was: "We shall not forget and we shall not forgive." In fact, the workers of the Solvay factory expressed their indignation in a letter to Archbishop Wojtyła, who had worked there as a laborer during the war. The Archbishop responded in the Polish journal, *Dziennik Polski*, on May 13, 1966, and the workers published a rebuttal: "Poland has nothing for which to ask forgiveness."

During the conclusion of the reconciliation process in 1978, Cardinal Wojtyła visited Germany. He delivered two discourses at Fulda, one of which was to the Conference of German Bishops, and a third discourse at Cologne. During a homily at the cathedral in Fulda, he stated that the meeting had "reinforced" the two churches "in truth and in love." At the moment when the second millennium was drawing to a close, it had helped "to heal the wounds of the past, both ancient and more recent."[21]

During his eleven years as a cardinal, Karol Wojtyła was becoming more widely known. He performed a variety of important functions, such as his participation in the Synods of Bishops held in Rome; his election to the secretariat of the synods; his role as *relator* at the Extraordinary Synod of the Bishops of Europe and at the Eucharistic Congress in Philadelphia; his preached retreat for the Vatican Curia; and his frequent visits to groups of Polish emigrants as well as the meeting in Germany in 1978. These were the principal occasions through which the name and face of Cardinal Karol Wojtyła became known throughout the world and to the members of the College of Cardinals. Later, when the second conclave of 1978 took place, these acquaintances would remember him during the election process for a new pope.

NOTES

1. J. Grootaers, *De Vatican II à Jean-Paul II* (Paris: Editions du Centurion, 1981), p. 132.

2. K. Wojtyła, *Collected Poems* (New York: Random House, 1979), p. 118.

3. M. E. Gervais, *Jean-Paul II, l'homme et l'histoire du XX siècle* (1998), p.133.

4. Ibid., p. 145.

5. A. Frossard, *"Be Not Afraid!"* (New York: St. Martin's, Press 1984), p. 69.

6. Aa. Vv., *Karol Wojtyła, filosofo, teologo, poeta* (Rome: Libreria Editrice Vaticana, 1985), p. 11.

7. J. Grootaers, *De Vatican II à Jean-Paul II* (Paris: Editions du Centurion, 1981), p. 132.

8. John Paul II with Vittorio Messori, *Crossing the Threshold of Hope* (New York: Alfred A. Knopf, 1994), p. 158.

9. Ibid., p. 157.

10. K. Wojtyła, *Alle fonti del rinnovamento* (Rome: Libreria Editrice Vaticana, 1981).

11. K. Wojtyła, *The Diocesan Synod for the Archdiocese of Kraków, 1972–1979* (Libreria Editrice Vaticana, 1985).

12. C. Bernstein, M. Politi, *Sua Santitá* (Milan: Rizzoli, 1996), pp. 119–121.

13. J. Chelini, *Jean Paul II* (Paris: Editions Jean Goujon, 1980), p. 54.

14. J. Sarraf (ed.), *Karol Wojtyła e il Sinodo dei vescovi* (Rome: Libreria Editrice Vaticana, 1980), p. 121.

15. Ibid., p. 180.

16. K. Wojtyła, *Sign of Contradiction* (New York: Seabury Press, 1979), p. 34.

17. Ibid., p. 24–25.

18. A. Boniecki, *Kalendarz zycia Karol Wojtyła* (Znak: Varsavia, 1983), p. 206.

19. K. Wojtyła, *Giobbi ed altri inediti* (Rome: Libreria Editrice Vaticana, 1982), pp. 117–126.

20. L. Accattoli, *When a Pope Asks Forgiveness* (Boston: Pauline Books & Media, 1998), p. 49.

21. Ibid., p. 51.

CHAPTER FIVE

The First Slav Pope

*C*ardinal Karol Wojtyła was elected pope on the eighth ballot by a count of 99 out of 111 votes at 5:20 P.M. on Monday, October 16, 1978. The white smoke signaling a decision was seen at 6:17 P.M., and at 6:43 P.M., Cardinal Pericle Felici announced from the balcony of St. Peter's Basilica: "*Habemus Papam!*" ("We have a Pope!") At 7:35 P.M. the new Pope appeared at the balcony and unexpectedly spoke to the waiting crowd.

It is very unusual for the public to know the number of ballots individual cardinals receive in a papal conclave. But this information comes from a letter written by an anonymous cardinal to Giulio Andreotti, the head of the Italian government at the time. When asked to identify the cardinal, Andreotti said he could not reveal his source, because he had pledged secrecy to the cardinal, "who has died since."

While Andreotti gives a few details about the letter in a book he published in 1980, he mentions no names. On the day after the papal election, a "well-known French journalist" asserted that "because of the defects of the Italian Democratic Christian Party, the cardinals no longer had any confidence in their Italian colleagues," so they elected a non-Italian Pope. Andreotti accused this journalist of "frivolity and pomposity." Then he added, "In fact, it was a cardinal who wrote to me from France to say that there was absolutely no anti-Italian spirit in the conclave: 'So true is this that until and including Monday morning we gave votes to our Italian confreres.' Seeing that it was impossible to reach a consensus, it became evident that the time had come for a different choice. And the choice was made in a remarkably short time: the Archbishop of Kraków received

33

all but the one-hundredth vote in the balloting (Pope John Paul I had received 98)."[1]

No substantiated factual information about the details of the election is available, only conjecture and news leaks. Andreotti spoke in a summary fashion about the proceedings of the conclave in a conversation I had with him on May 31, 1998. During the conversation he shared some particular details which he had received from Cardinal Mario Casariego of Guatemala (perhaps on November 27, 1978, because in Andreotti's *Diary* he records a conversation with Casariego "who has returned from the Vatican").[2]

According to Cardinal Casariego's account, early in the conclave a few Italian cardinals received the following votes:

Benelli 30	Poletti 17
Colombo 5 or 6	Siri 48
Felici 1	Ursi 4
Pappalardo 6	

Presumably Casariego reported the maximum number of votes each of the preceding candidates had received without specifying which ballot had produced those numbers.

Among other things, Casariego confided to Andreotti that at the beginning, he had never heard of Wojtyła who would be elected on the eighth ballot. Not only that, but in the midst of all the whispering going on in the Sistine Chapel, he thought he had heard the name "Botiglia." He wanted to know who "Botiglia" was, but Siri and others hushed him because Wojtyła was sitting nearby. Later, when Casariego approached to greet the newly elected Pope with the other cardinals, John Paul said in an affable manner: "Now you know who 'Botiglia' is."

Karol Wojtyła had received some votes in the previous conclave that elected Albino Luciani—John Paul I. Wilton Wynn, *Time* magazine correspondent in Rome for twenty-four years, gave the following report: "The votes for Wojtyła apparently had come from the German-speaking bloc of cardinals led by the Austrian Franz König. It was the first time in his life that Wojtyła had faced the realistic possibility that he might become Pope, and that looming possibility threw him into a panic.... It was different when he returned for the October conclave."[3]

That August, Cardinal Wojtyła's panic passed quickly because the conclave was of such short duration. Later, he spoke of it when he observed the anniversary of his predecessor's election: "By reason of the number of cardinals present, the conclave was expected to be very different from the previous one [which had elected Pope Paul VI] and to be lengthy and difficult. But, on the contrary, already toward the evening of the first day, at the fourth balloting, the new Pope was elected."

John Paul's statements concerning the four ballots that elected Albino Luciani are evidence of the freedom he felt in speaking about secret matters of the conclave. He repeatedly acted in the same fashion regarding his own election. For example, he revealed the formula with which he accepted the papacy, and the advice he had received from Cardinal Wyszynski not to refuse the election but to take it as a sign that he was to lead the Church into the third millennium.

According to Benny Lai, confidant of Cardinal Siri and another source of information to the public, Cardinal Wojtyła received four votes in the conclave of August 1978. This is based on a statement Cardinal Wojtyła supposedly made to Indro Montanelli: "He told me about being very much surprised when, in the conclave in which Luciani was elected, he had received some votes."[4]

When Wojtyła received a large number of votes in the October conclave, however, he remained calm. This fact has been verified by many present at that conclave. There are several possible reasons why Cardinal Wojtyła did not panic. First of all, after an interval of only 50 days, the same cardinals who had just elected John Paul I were voting again. They would be likely to cast practically the same votes. Interestingly, the same number of votes (that is, 111) were cast in both conclaves, although not all the participants who had been at the August conclave were present now. Luciani, of course, was no longer present, and Cardinal John Wright, who had been absent from the election of Pope John Paul I because of illness, attended the conclave that elected Wojtyła.

It is probable that the cardinals entering the second conclave did so with the supposition that they would elect another Italian pope. The press predicted a race between Cardinal Giuseppe Siri and Cardinal Giovanni Benelli. No one even brought up Karol Wojtyła's name. As Cardinal Joseph Malula of Africa said later, "I never once heard the name of Wojtyła mentioned."[5] *Time* magazine listed Wojtyła's name among the possibilities, but only as a "remote possibility."

The stalemate between Siri and Benelli was evident on the very first day of voting, and the uncertainty continued. Cardinal Franz König described the first evening of the conclave: "We ate supper together, but there was very little discussion. In the cool breeze of the courtyard of San Damaso, we took our evening stroll in silence. There was a strange tension among us. To this day I have no human explanation for the choice on the following day."[6]

According to the testimony of the Pope himself, "I felt the choice resulted from the work of the Holy Spirit, and I know that if the Holy Spirit gives you a role to play, he also gives you the grace and strength to shoulder the burden."[7]

Those who voted for Siri were perhaps seeking a more traditional orientation for the reforms and ecumenical dialogue initiated by John XXIII and Paul VI. Benelli, as substitute Secretary of State for the previous ten years, had been working for reform along the lines marked out by Paul VI. Those who favored him wanted to promote further progress in the areas of reform and dialogue.

According to Benny Lai, Cardinal Siri received 59 votes on the third ballot and Benelli received "a few more than 40."[8] But, according to Jean Offredo, a French journalist of Polish extraction (who gave Wojtyła 97 votes on the eighth ballot), Benelli received 38 votes on the seventh ballot and Siri's followers abandoned him. The result: on the seventh ballot Wojtyła had 73 votes (two less than the number needed for election).[9]

The conclave had convened on Saturday afternoon, October 14. The shift toward a non-Italian would have occurred sometime during the night between Sunday and Monday, with Cardinal König acting as the main impetus behind the change. The German bishops—all of whom knew Wojtyła well—would have supported König. Through the influence of Cardinal Krol of Philadelphia, who was of Polish extraction, the Americans would also turn to Wojtyła. Among the Italians, Cardinals Pellegrino and Poma were definitely pro-Wojtyła.

Historically (in both conclaves) it was the first time that the majority of cardinals came from nations outside Europe, by a ratio of 56 to 55. Also a "first" was the fact that most of the cardinals were *pastoral* prelates, that is, bishops actively working among the faithful of a diocese. This is a decisive factor for understanding how the cardinals, in the space of two months, could have elected two such different men—both of whom could be characterized as *pastoral Popes*. Luciani and Wojtyła both were cardinals personally involved in the administration of a diocese, and neither had any curial or diplomatic experience. It is true that most of the popes in our century were elected out of large cities in Italy; in addition, they had all spent many years in the Roman Curia or in the papal diplomatic corps. The only exception was Giuseppe Sarto, who took the name of Pius X in 1903.

It is also noteworthy that the October conclave was the first time the Italians (who numbered twenty-seven out of 111 cardinals) were not powerful enough to determine the election. In the 1939 election of Pacelli (Pope Pius XII) the Italians had numbered thirty-five out of sixty-two cardinals; in the 1958 election of Roncalli (Pope John XXIII), eighteen out of fifty-three; and in the 1963 election of Montini (Pope Paul VI), twenty-nine out of eighty-two.

Cardinal Wojtyła referred to this change in the number of non-Italian cardinals of power in a homily at Kraków after the election of Pope John Paul I: "In enlarging the sacred college of cardinals, the deceased pontiff, Paul VI, wanted to place greater emphasis on the Church's presence in the contemporary world and on the missionary character of the Church itself. He also wanted to point out that the election of the pope pertains to the whole Church. The beneficial effects of his decision were evident in the election of his successor. One could also sense the influence of the Council, the Synod of Bishops and other gatherings."[10]

Certainly, a decisive factor in Wojtyła's acceptance of his own election was his conversation with Cardinal Wyszynski, which took place possibly on Monday, October 16, between the sixth and seventh ballots. John Paul II himself referred to this conversation in a homily in the Sistine Chapel after the restoration of the paintings by Michelangelo, on April 8, 1994: "In this place the Cardinal Primate of Poland said to me: 'If they elect you, I beg you, do not refuse.'"

The move toward Wojtyła was definitive by the evening of October 16. This was later verified by the Dominican, Cardinal Luigi Ciappi, in an interview with the magazine *Trenta Giorni* (Thirty Days): "The decisive change of mind took place in the room next to the dining room, where they served an appetizer and later coffee. The atmosphere there was always more joyful and relaxed, and it was then that the supporters of Cardinal Wojtyła persuaded the other members of the Sacred College...."

The eighth ballot, which was decisive, ended at approximately 5:20 P.M. on Monday, October 16. Cardinal Jean Villot, the *camerlingo* (papal chamberlain), approached the Cardinal from Poland and asked: "Do you accept the election?"

As he later stated in his encyclical, *Redemptor Hominis* (The Redeemer of Man),[11] Cardinal Wojtyła gave his response: "With obedience in faith to Christ, my Lord, and with trust in the Mother of Christ and of the Church, in spite of the great difficulties, I accept." To what difficulties was he referring? Obviously to the "weight of the keys," in the widest sense of the phrase, which must have been in the minds of all the cardinals as they remembered Albino Luciani. He had accepted his election in that same place some 50 days before. It was commonly believed that this "weight" had caused the unexpected death of Pope John Paul I.

Wojtyła, however, had other, more specific, difficulties. First, he was from a distant country. He and the cardinals who had voted for him feared how the Romans would react to the shock of a "foreigner" being elected pope. The cardinal electors had discussed this, and the Italian electors (who numbered twenty-seven) had urged the Sacred College to take the step which they themselves had voted for by a large majority. But the newly elected Wojtyła still experienced a fear that the rest of the cardinals had overcome. Perhaps this fear prompted John Paul to address the crowd in St. Peter's square immediately. "And so, I present myself to you," he began, adding the enigmatic statement: "I was afraid to accept this nomination."

Anyone who knew Cardinal Wojtyła well surely thought at some time or other that he would make a good pope. Most, if not all, were inclined to dismiss the idea precisely because of his Polish nationality. As the French Jesuit Henri de Lubac stated in a book of recollections published in 1989: "For a long time, in conversations with friends, I was inclined to say: 'After Paul VI, my candidate is Wojtyła.' [The remark] was half-serious and half-jest. Then I would add: 'But he doesn't have a chance.'"

The only person at the conclave who could have shared Karol Wojtyła's sentiments was Cardinal Stefan Wyszynski. Soon after the conclave, he expressed what the election of John Paul II had represented: "The decision of the conclave has crossed the barrier of four centuries of tradition in the Church: the barrier of language and the barrier of nationality. It seemed that it would be difficult for the cardinals and the Roman people to accept the decision. But, on the contrary, the election of a Pole has been natural and simple, and the acceptance by the Romans has been warm and spontaneous!"[12]

NOTES

1. G. Andreotti, *Giovanni Paolo II* (Milan: Rizzoli, 1981), p. 176.
2. Ibid.
3. W. Wynn, *Keepers of the Keys* (New York: Random House, 1988), p. 39.
4. B. Lai, *I segreti del Vaticano* (Rome: Laterza, 1984), p. 279.
5. W. Wynn, *Keepers of the Keys* (New York: Random House, 1988), p. 38.
6. Ibid., p. 39.
7. Ibid., p. 40.
8. B. Lai, *I segreti del Vaticano* (Rome: Laterza, 1984), p. 176.
9. J. Offredo, *Jean-Paul II* (Paris: Editions Carrière-Michel Lafon, 1986), p. 25.
10. M. Malinski, *Le radici di Papa Wojtyła* (Rome: Borla Editore, 1979), p. 261.
11. John Paul II, *Redemptor Hominis* (Boston: Pauline Books & Media, 1979), n. 2.
12. Published in *Tygodnik Powszechny*, n. 44, 1978.

❖ CHAPTER SIX ❖

"I Was Afraid"

*T*he "Petrine service," as theologians like to refer to the papal ministry, has become a dangerous role in our day, as the world learned in the 1981 attempt on the Pope's life. Karol Wojtyła knew the risks he was embracing from the moment he was elected.

He appeared on the balcony of St. Peter's Basilica, still bearing on his face evidence of his struggle to overcome the fear of becoming pope. So much had happened so quickly. First there was the cardinals' remarkably sudden shift of votes in favor of a Pole; then the encouragement from Cardinal Wyszynski to accept if chosen, and the obligation to do so in the name of his fatherland. Indeed, while this acceptance would mean honor for the Polish people, his relentless opposition to Communism would mean possible danger to every Pole as well.

However, John Paul's apprehension was not the same as that experienced by his predecessors, Sarto and Luciani, who had feared the papal ministry was far beyond their powers; at least it was not only that. Wojtyła understood the delicate task of beginning a pontificate that broke the long line of Italian popes. His concern for the people of Rome prompted him to speak to them from the balcony the same night of his election, quickly improvising a short speech in Italian. By so doing, Wojtyła departed from the tradition mandating that the newly elected pope should give a blessing in Latin—and say nothing more.

The Pope realized that neither the use of Latin nor the papal blessing would be sufficient to bridge the distance between the balcony and the great crowd waiting below.

His anxiety over being "from a distant country" made him return to the same theme no less than ten times during the first month of his pontificate. John Paul II seemed unable to believe that his Polish nationality was *not* a problem for the people of Rome.

> May Jesus Christ be praised! Dearest brothers and sisters, we are all still grieved after the death of our most beloved Pope John Paul I. And now the most eminent cardinals have called a new Bishop of Rome. They have called him from a distant country, distant but always so close through communion in the Christian faith and tradition. I was afraid to accept this nomination, but I did it in the spirit of obedience to our Lord Jesus Christ and of total confidence in his Mother, the most holy Madonna.

> I do not know whether I can explain myself well in your...*our* Italian language. If I make a mistake, you will correct me. And so I present myself to you all to confess our common faith, our hope, our confidence in the Mother of Christ and of the Church, and also to start anew on this road of history and of the Church, with the help of God and with the help of men (Oct. 16, 1978).

Between the afternoon and the evening of that first day, everything seemed to go well. The Romans showed an incredible willingness to celebrate with the "foreigner," encouraged by his physically strong figure and his friendly tone of voice. When he had stepped out onto the balcony they had already applauded several times, but the crowd was completely won over when he asked them to correct any mistakes in his Italian.

Everything seemed to be going well, but apparently the new Pope's anxiety was not completely allayed. Two days later, John Paul spoke to the cardinals: "Venerable Brothers, it was an act of confidence and at the same time of great courage to have wished to call a 'non-Italian' as Bishop of Rome. One cannot say any more, but can only bow one's head before this decision of the Sacred College" (Oct. 18, 1978).

The words "trust" and "courage" echo the lesson John Paul had learned from his election: the College of Cardinals had the courage to elect a non-Italian because they trusted the man they had chosen. Wojtyła also understood well "the interplay between hope and fear"; in the drama he had written in his younger days, *The Jeweler's Shop,* he had the character Teresa say: "There is no hope without fear and there is no fear without hope."[1]

Desiring to Be a Roman

In a homily from the beginning of his papal ministry, John Paul stated: "To the See of Peter in Rome there succeeds today a bishop who is not a Roman; a bishop who is a son of Poland. But from this moment he too becomes a Roman. Yes—a Roman!" (Oct. 22, 1978)

Throughout his pontificate the Pope has repeated his desire to "become a Roman." He did so as recently as 1998 when, greeting the crowd at the Campidoglio in Rome, he could acknowledge that he had been a Roman for twenty years. In the early days of John Paul's pontificate he shared this sentiment in a personal letter to Giulio Andreotti. The Pope's letter to the head of the Italian government was never made public, and we know its content only because Andreotti had transcribed a quotation from it into his diary entry for November 4, 1978. One could surmise that John Paul wrote the letter prompted by media speculation concerning the effect a Polish Pope would have on Church-State relations.

> I received a beautiful letter from the Pope. It begins by referring to the faith of the Polish people, which is "lived with the closest bond and deepest union with Rome and with all that this city means to the world." He then says that "the Pope, who comes from far away, feels ardently and profoundly Roman and is desirous of serving in the best possible way the beloved people of Rome, and from Rome, all Italy, which is included in a special way in the duties of the successor of Peter.[2]

Again, in one of his earliest greetings during the Sunday Angelus message, John Paul referred to the fear he had experienced on accepting the election:

> In the enclosure of the conclave, after the election, I thought: What shall I say to the Romans when I present myself before them as their bishop, coming from a distant country, from Poland? The figure of St. Peter then came into my mind. And this is what I thought: Nearly two thousand years ago your ancestors accepted a newcomer; so you, too, will welcome another now. You will welcome John Paul II, as you once welcomed Peter of Galilee.

> It is useless, perhaps, to return to this subject when the succession of circumstances has confirmed with what cordiality you have welcomed a non-Italian Pope, after so many centuries. I wish therefore to give thanks in the first place to God, and then also to you for the great-heartedness shown to me. And today I wish to respond to your welcome in a special way (Nov. 5, 1978).

John Paul expressed amazement at the "cordiality, great-heartedness and kindness" of the people of Rome, although from his first contacts with the people and the city they had given proof of the genuineness of their sentiments. In fact, his first ventures among the people were met with such enthusiasm that there was concern for the Holy Father's security. This was especially true on October 17, when the Pope visited Gemelli Hospital to see his friend, the Polish Bishop Andrej Deskur. The same thing happened on Sunday, October 29, at the Marian shrine, *La*

Mentorella, on Monte Guadagnolo, staffed by the Polish Rogationist Fathers. He had visited the shrine before the conclave and was anxious to return after the election. It took him twenty minutes to travel ten meters, so great was the crowd of people who wanted to see the new Pope. What the poet Elio Filippo Accrocca called "his marvelous mistakes in Italian" endeared him all the more to the crowd.[3]

John Paul continued this theme in the Angelus message on November 5, again comparing his "coming from a distant land" to St. Peter's journey from Galilee, and referring to the ancient ties of the Polish people with Rome. By this time it was apparent that the people of Rome had accepted the new Pope, but John Paul seemed to enjoy this manner of speaking; it gave him assurance that the decision of the College of Cardinals was in keeping with the sentiments of the people.

On that same day, John Paul II visited the tomb of St. Francis in Assisi and soon afterward, the tomb of St. Catherine of Siena in the church of Santa Maria, venerating Italy's two patron saints. At Assisi he said: "Since I was not born in this land, I feel more than ever the need of a 'spiritual birth' in it." And in his prayer to St. Francis he asked for spiritual citizenship: "This is sought of you, holy son of the Church, son of the Italian land, by Pope John Paul II, son of the Polish land. And he hopes that you will not refuse him; that you will help him" (Nov. 5, 1978).

The Pope's prayer in honor of St. Catherine of Siena hinted at a bit of lingering anxiety: "Having been elected by the Sacred College of Cardinals to be successor of St. Peter, I accepted this service with profound trepidation, considering it to be the will of our Lord Jesus Christ. When I thought about not being born here, but about being a foreigner to this land, there came to my mind the figure of St. Peter, who was also a foreigner in this land" (Nov. 5, 1978).

A whole month passed between John Paul's election and his taking possession of his cathedral church of St. John Lateran in Rome. On November 9, he explained to the priests of Rome that he had felt the need to spend some time in preparation, all the more so "since the circumstances are so unusual. The succession of the Bishops of Rome, after 455 years, includes a Pope who comes from beyond the frontiers of Italy" (Nov. 9, 1978). Then, during the ceremony at St. John Lateran on November 12, he spoke with great emotion:

> I, the new Bishop of Rome, John Paul II, Polish by origin, stop on the threshold of this temple and ask you to welcome me in the Lord's name. I beg you to welcome me as you welcomed my predecessors throughout the centuries.... I am not here by my own will. The Lord has elected me. In the Lord's name, I beg you, therefore, welcome me!" (Nov. 12)

John Paul's joy in meeting with the people of Rome was spontaneous, and it has increased through the years. He was determined to be
Bishop of Rome in the fullest sense of the word, although he has frequently lamented that he could not do as much as he desired in that capacity. For example, on October 17, 1993, beginning his fifteenth year as
pope, he visited the parish of the Most Precious Blood in Rome and told
the people:

> Today I cannot fail to recall the first visit I made to the parish of St.
> Francis Xavier at Garbatella. It was in 1978 at the beginning of De-
> cember.... The Cardinal Vicar tells me that we now have more than 200
> parishes, in fact, 331. Thanks be to God for this journey, for so many
> visits, for so many meetings.... In this way, even with a short visit I am
> able to be Bishop of Rome, at least to some extent. The Cardinal al-
> ways gives me great consolation. He tells me that I am doing enough,
> but I say that it is only a little. The Pope could not have this universal
> duty, could not have these visits outside of Rome and outside of Italy, if
> he were not Bishop of Rome.

*A*t the time of this writing, John Paul has made 274 parish visitations;
there can be no doubt that he has become a Roman. Witness his
greeting to the people of Campidoglio on January 15, 1998, during a
visit: "Rome, my Rome! I bless you, and with you I bless all your children and your projects for good!" His initial timid approach to the city
has been transformed into a great love for its people, who have accepted
this Polish Pope as "their own."

> It has been asserted, not without reason, that as Bishop of Rome the
> Pope should belong to the nation of his diocesan bishops. I do not want
> to miss this opportunity of expressing my gratitude to my Roman
> diocesans, who have accepted this Pope from Poland as a son of their
> own country. The charisma of universality must be well anchored in the
> soul of this people whose Christian ancestors had already accepted Pe-
> ter, the Galilean, and with him the message of Christ intended for all
> the peoples of the world.[4]

Notes

1. A. Jawien (K. Wojtyła), *La bottega dell'orefice* (Rome: Libreria Editrice Vaticana,
1992), p. 65.

2. G. Andreotti, *Giovanni Paolo II* (Milan: Rizzoli, 1981).

3. E. Cavaterra, *Il Papa dei giorni futuri* (Rome: Dino Editori, 1981), p. 112.

4. A. Frossard, *"Be Not Afraid!"* (New York: St. Martin's Press, 1984), p. 22.

❈ Chapter Seven ❈

"Do Not Be Afraid"

*S*till deeply moved by his election, John Paul hastened to reassure the world concerning his intentions as Pope. He told the crowd assembled in St. Peter's that he had been fearful about accepting the nomination; six days later, he encouraged them: "Do not be afraid! Open wide the doors to Christ!"

This is Pope Wojtyła—a man acquainted with the drama of the world, the challenge of his priestly mission, the anticipated reaction of the Soviet regime, and the possible resistance of the people of Rome. In the face of it all he acknowledges: "I was afraid." He also senses fear in others—a fear which, in many people, is deeper and older than his own regarding the pontificate and the Church. He would like to dispel this fear, especially the fear that prompts humanity to lose confidence in the power of Christ.

Sunday, October 22, 1978, John Paul celebrated the liturgy in St. Peter's Square to inaugurate his pontificate and to give some indication of the orientation his papal ministry would take in the context of his mission "to the nations." His mission transcends every ideological and geopolitical limitation. He had already stated, in his first radio address the day after his election, that he considered the Second Vatican Council "a milestone in the two-thousand-year history of the Church," and that he intended to base his pontificate on a formal pledge to carry out the directives of the Council. In particular he had emphasized the need to develop a collegial form of government in the Church: "Undoubtedly, this collegiality extends to the appropriate development of institutes—some new, some updated" (Oct. 17, 1978). He had also mentioned ecumenism as one of his priorities. It was a brief statement of his program *ad intra*, addressed to the members of the Church.

Now, from the precincts of St. Peter's, he outlined his program *ad extra*, which goes beyond internal structure and government and is most truly the program of John Paul II.

> Brothers and sisters! Do not be afraid to welcome Christ and accept his power! Help the Pope and all those who wish to serve Christ, and with Christ's power, to serve the human person and the whole of humanity! Do not be afraid! Open wide the doors to Christ! To his saving power open the boundaries of states, economic and political systems, the vast fields of culture, civilization and development. Do not be afraid! Christ knows "what is in man." He alone knows it! (Oct. 22, 1978)

After twenty years of John Paul's pontificate, the development of a more collegial government in the Church has not really taken place in the sense that most commentators had expected. But his program *ad extra* has been fully carried out. The entire pontificate of John Paul has been a follow-up to that missionary call, from his first trip to Poland in June 1979 to his more recent 1998 trip to Cuba; from his confrontation with the dictatorships of the Third World to his challenge to the secularistic and anti-life countries of the northern hemisphere. "Open the boundaries of states, economic and political systems." And in his call, the Pope included specific messages to young people and to women; he also referred to his ecumenical and interreligious ventures.

In gestures and style, John Paul has remained faithful to the words he spoke on that inaugural Sunday. After the liturgical celebration, he descended from the platform to the crowd, laying his hands on the sick, kissing infants, and greeting the assembly by raising his crosier with two hands like a trophy. It was perhaps more the gesture of an athlete than a pope, the gesture of a man who knew intuitively that his actions would find an echo in the hearts of the people and would change the very "iconography" and protocol of the papacy (see Chapter 19). His going down into the crowd that day foreshadowed John Paul's mission to the nations.

The Pope himself once acknowledged the unforeseen significance his words would assume: "When, on October 22, 1978, I said the words 'Do not be afraid!' in St. Peter's Square, I could not fully know how far they would take me and the entire Church."[1]

As a theme and program for his pontificate, John Paul would later develop those words more fully in his first encyclical, *Redemptor Hominis*. In the encyclical letter he shows that Christ is at the very center of the new Pope's ministry and mission. When *Redemptor Hominis* was published, the press and many diocesan chanceries focused on the Pope's challenges to "earthly powers." The encyclical does contain such challenges, but they are mentioned only as corollaries to its central message. Today, it is possible to read the encyclical with greater regard for its original intention.

For John Paul II, Christ is at the center of everything. In the Sistine Chapel when Wojtyła accepted the election, he did so with those remarkable words: "obedient to the faith in Christ my Lord." Two hours later, on the balcony of St. Peter's, his first words were: "Praised be Jesus Christ." Now comes the cry: "Open wide the doors to Christ!" Finally, in the very first line of his first encyclical we read: "The Redeemer of man, Jesus Christ, is the center of the universe and of history." This pontificate's concentration and unity in Christ is truly amazing!

At the very beginning of *Redemptor Hominis*, John Paul speaks of the Jubilee Year 2000 which "is already very close." The Jubilee—that is, the celebration of the presence of Christ some 2,000 years after his birth—enters at the beginning and will also figure into the end of his pontificate, defining his entire ministry.

Redemptor Hominis opens with Christ and then quickly turns to humanity, because "Christ the Redeemer fully reveals man to himself" (n. 10). Therefore, "Jesus Christ is the chief way for the Church. He himself is our way 'to the Father's house' and is the way to each man. On this way leading from Christ to man, on this way on which Christ unites himself with each man, nobody can halt the Church" (n. 13). Conversely, "man in the full truth of his existence, of his personal being and also of his community and social being...this man is the primary route that the Church must travel in fulfilling her mission; *he is the primary and fundamental way for the Church*" (n. 14).

Everything else proceeds from this central and focal point. The encyclical contains a clear warning against programmed atheism, structured into a political system such as Communism, and also against the consumer society which forgets God. It likewise denounces the gigantic weapons investment by the Communist and Capitalist nations, both of which divide and control the modern world.

Time and time again in his pontificate John Paul repeats the message not to be afraid and to open the doors to Christ. In fact, *"Be Not Afraid"* is the title of a collection of conversations between the Pope and André Frossard, published in 1983. A similar theme emerges in *Crossing the Threshold of Hope*, published in 1994, which contains the Pope's written responses to various questions submitted by Italian journalist Vittorio Messori. In this volume, John Paul begins his answer to the very first question: "I state right from the outset: 'Be not afraid!'"[2] Indeed, one of the book's chapters bears the same title. Finally, the call to overcome fear in oneself, in humanity, and in the future is interwoven in John Paul's message to the United Nations in 1985.

"Open the Doors to Christ"

In 1978, John Paul issued the call to open the doors to Christ essentially as a challenge to atheistic regimes under Communist rule. He delivered the same message in Cuba in 1998. But the Pope's call ultimately extends wider than Communism. When he spoke in Vienna on June 20, 1998, after all the Communist countries on the European continent had fallen, he said: "At the beginning of my pontificate I invited the faithful assembled at Rome in St. Peter's Square to open the doors to Christ. Today I repeat my call to the old continent: Europe, open the doors to Christ!"

Later that day he repeated the call, perhaps with less volume then he had twenty years earlier, but with the same ardor, and this time to a worldwide audience: "So many things can be taken from us Christians. But the cross as the symbol of salvation—we will never allow it be taken from us. We shall never let it be excluded from public life!"

When John Paul calls for the opening of economic and political systems, he is implicitly calling for the neutrality of national borders. He expressed himself this way during his visit to Puebla on January 29, 1979: "The Church wants to remain free in the face of opposing systems, in order to choose only in favor of man."

In so many words, the Pope is affirming that it is impossible for the Church to be subject to any earthly power. Later, when told he could not travel to Great Britain because of its war with Argentina over the Falkland Islands, he said to journalists: "No one can say to the Pope: you cannot go!" (May 1982) The phrase "Open the doors" also means that John Paul will go wherever he wants as a missionary to the world, because "the heart of the Pope has a geography as vast as the whole human race!" (May 7, 1988)

But to journey to countries that are at war, to pass through disputed borders, or to speak in prohibited languages—doesn't that expose one to the accusation of political involvement? John Paul simply asks full freedom for his religious mission. He is not interested in any struggle for power. "We leave politics to the politicians, and we let the Pope pursue his religious mission" (flight from Rome to Seoul, Korea, Oct. 6, 1989). He stated this very clearly to Philippine Cardinal Jaime Sin when the latter confronted the country's dictator, Ferdinand Marcos: "The Church does not have civil authority!" (March 6, 1986)

John Paul is not one to be blown about by the winds around him. He reminds himself, as he did the Congregation for the Clergy during a plenary session in October 1993: "It is necessary to be courageous and never retreat!" Perhaps these words sound more like a military slogan than a religious conviction. Here, however, John Paul strategically uses them to bolster the faith and morale of his priests who continue to experience declining numbers.

Pope John Paul also addresses to himself the command: "Be not afraid!" especially when he has to face hostility or resistance. This has happened in the West, but also in Italy itself: "Turin! Be converted! I have no difficulty in saying this, here and elsewhere" (Turin, Sept. 3, 1988). During the same visit he explained to the bishops of Piedmont: "These thoughts came to mind this morning. And I said: 'Lord, let me say it.' I'll say it gracefully and at an opportune moment in order not to offend my hosts."

The following conversation shows the Pope's attitude toward criticism.

"Your Holiness, you are going to Holland. Will there be objections?"

"There were objections to others long before me. St. Paul, and also Jesus Christ" (flight from Rome to Holland, May 11, 1985).

"Woe to the Pontiff if he should be afraid of criticism or misunderstanding" (General Audience, March 10, 1993).

At the same time he never delays in confronting any opposition in the name of humanity: "It is necessary to change something here!" he cried in Haiti (March 9, 1983). He was referring to the dictatorship of Jean-Claude Duvalier, under whose rule people were starving.

If it is necessary to shout, shout he will! John Paul has done so in Nicaragua, Poland, Sicily, and even in St. Peter's Square when he returned from the United Nations (see Chapter 35). As he explained: "I must act this way. Even if the Pope is of a gentle rather than a severe disposition, he must at least be rigid in regard to principles" (March 6, 1994).

During an encounter with the young people of Rome in the middle of the 1990s, the Pope defended his world travels. "There is a Polish song that says: 'One should travel around the world.' It was a dream. How is it possible to go out to the world if it is all closed up, if there are Communists, if there is an iron curtain? On the contrary, the Lord, with his Mother, has brought us here to Rome and from Rome to the world" (April 7, 1995).

For the first few months of his pontificate, John Paul was not yet certain if and how much he would be able to travel. He may even have feared that he was moving from one kind of "prison" to another: "I confess that I would like to travel, to go all over. Instead, quite different from the way it once was, I am located in a definitive place which is Rome, to carry out my far-reaching and evangelical mission as the successor of Peter."[3] But he soon found a solution to this dilemma, and he made it clear that Rome was only the base of his itinerant pontificate.

In his mission to the nations, John Paul has surmounted every barrier or geo-political restriction. And in so doing, he has fulfilled his desire as universal pastor to travel around the world.

NOTES

1. John Paul II with Vittorio Messori, *Crossing the Threshold of Hope* (New York: Alfred A. Knopf, 1994), p. 218.

2. Ibid., p. 4.

3. A. Biscardi, L. Liguori, *Il Papa dal volto umano* (Milan: Rizzoli, 1979), p. 27.

CHAPTER EIGHT

Pastoral Visit to Mexico

I n the first years of his pontificate, John Paul changed the center of gravity for the Catholic Church to the South and to the East with his pastoral visit to Mexico and his return to Poland. In a pontificate well described in terms of the Pope's travels, the visit to Mexico (Jan. 25 to Feb. 5, 1979) marked his initial venture as Pope into the world at large.

This first journey proved his ability to improvise and relate well to the people—even before the plane landed in Mexico. John Paul immediately departed from Paul VI's manner of traveling by granting journalists interviews during flight. In another novel move, which he would repeat many times, the Pope took part in the conference of Latin American bishops at Puebla. This he did despite criticism from the Roman Curia that feared the risk the Pope's involvement might mean in the differences and tensions among the Catholic communities of South America. Ten years later John Paul recalled his decision: "Some persons in the Curia felt that it would be better if I did not go, but it seemed natural to me that the Pope should be present at that important gathering."[1]

His first day in Mexico gave more indications of the new and unique aspects that would characterize his papal journeys. His would be "pastoral visits" to the entire Catholic community, not merely symbolic visits to institutions or nations as was the case with Paul VI. The visit to Mexico showed that, in straightforward exchanges with the local bishops, John Paul is at his best.

The Pope's triumphant reception by the crowds has become legendary. During his passage from the airport to the cathedral in Mexico City, an estimated five million people lined the streets. The following day he encountered swarms of people while making a pilgrimage to the shrine of Our Lady of Guadalupe, whom the Mexicans affectionately call *la Morenita*. The largest crowd by far, however, was assembled at Puebla, estimated at eight to ten million persons. At Guadalajara and Monterrey John Paul received the same fervent welcome. It is estimated that fifteen million Mexicans, one quarter of the total population, turned out to see the Pope.

There was a time, in the not too distant past, when the Masonic and anti-clerical authorities in Mexico would never have permitted the Pope to enter the country as a minister of religion, much less to give his blessing in a public square. But John Paul freely traveled to any part of Mexico and gave his blessing as often as he desired. He went so far as to call for agrarian reform, defend the rights of the Mexican Native Americans, and suggest full liberty for labor unions. The effects of his visit would be seen when the Pope returned to Mexico ten years later, in 1998. Diplomatic relations with the Vatican would be restored by then, making it seem as if a century had passed in the meantime.

Fundamental Option for the Poor

So much for the descriptive details of the pastoral visit. We now want to look at the trip to Mexico as the moment in which John Paul first affirmed his option for the Third World. This choice would be confirmed throughout the succeeding years of his pontificate, but his definitive orientation was made at Oaxaca rather than Puebla.

The meeting of the Conference of Bishops of Latin America was convened on January 28, 1979. In his address to the bishops, John Paul said: "The Church wants to remain free in the face of opposing systems, in order to choose only in favor of man" and to be able to "prevent strong nations from using their power to the detriment of weaker nations."

Unfortunately, the Pope's message at Puebla was misinterpreted throughout the world. In stating his choice "in favor of man," the Pope had also issued an admonition to the radical proponents of the "theology of liberation." The world press focused on this part of the Pope's message, publicizing it without equally emphasizing his option for developing nations and his choice of the poor. On the following day however, at Oaxaca, John Paul clearly restated his preference for the Third World and for the poor; his message in subsequent media coverage was unmistakable.

Oaxaca was the most successful stop of the visit to Mexico. There the Pope met with the Mexican Native Americans and the *campesinos*, relating to them warmly and speaking in their own language. At Oaxaca he formed an alliance with the poor that has continued ever since. The success of that encounter was due to two factors: his direct contact with the people, who kept shouting his name; and the input he had received from the local bishops of that territory, whose center is Oaxaca.

In a document approved and sent to Rome with the preparatory dossier for the papal visit, the bishops had accused landowners and the government of unlawfully dispossessing people of their land; organizing armed groups to spread terror, violence, and death in the region; pillaging the natives of their culture; and using popular religiosity to gain control. "These are the conditions in which the Indians and *campesinos* are living," the bishops explained. "This is what we have found when we went out to them with evangelical sincerity."

The Pope had scarcely arrived in Oaxaca when the bishops presented him with a greeting in writing; Mexican Native Americans repeated it the following day: "You have said that we, the poor of Latin America, are the hope of the Church. Look now at how that hope lives."

The message so moved John Paul that he stayed up late into the night to rewrite the text that had already been prepared. The next day he spoke from his heart. Surrounded by the Mexican poor, he saw in them all the poor of the world, and he reminded them that Paul VI had taken their part during his visit to Colombia in 1968:

> I want to repeat with him—if it were possible, in an even stronger tone of voice—that the present Pope wishes "to be in solidarity with your cause, which is the cause of humble people, of the poor." The Pope is with these masses of the population that are nearly always abandoned at an ignoble level of life and sometimes harshly treated and exploited.

> Adopting the line of my predecessors John XXIII and Paul VI, as well as that of the Second Vatican Council, and in view of a situation that grows ever more alarming—often not better and sometimes even worse—the Pope wishes to be your voice, the voice of those who cannot speak or who are silenced, in order to be the conscience of consciences; to issue an invitation to action in order to make up for lost time, which is often time of prolonged suffering and unsatisfied hopes....

> On your part, leaders of peoples, powerful classes which sometimes keep unproductive lands that hide the bread so many families lack—human conscience, the conscience of peoples, the cry of the destitute and above all the voice of God, the voice of the Church, repeat to you with me: *It is not just, it is not human, it is not Christian to continue with certain situations that are clearly unjust* (Oaxaca, Jan. 30, 1979).

*T*he option for the poor had been proposed to the Church in 1963 by John XXIII's encyclical *Pacem in Terris* (Peace on Earth), and it was further elaborated by Paul VI in his 1967 document, *Populorum Progressio* (The Development of Peoples). John Paul II confirmed their statements in this address at Oaxaca and in numerous other passages in the encyclical he wrote in 1987, *Sollicitudo Rei Socialis* (On Social Concern). He continued along the same path marked out by his predecessors, whose names he had adopted. John Paul called for a new international economic order which would remove the development of poor nations from the control of a market based on inequality which could only increase rather than lessen the distance between rich and poor. During his pontificate John Paul has called for a juridically enforced agreement that would guarantee food for the poor (1985 and 1986); a document on the international debt (1987) and one on the homeless (1988); a proposal for the cancellation, in part or entirely, of international debts owed by poor countries (1994); a document on the use of the earth (1998).

The encyclical *Sollicitudo Rei Socialis* aroused some displeasure in the United States and was a source of controversy in Moscow. But the Church "feels called to take her stand beside the poor," and for that reason it "adopts a critical attitude toward both liberal capitalism and Marxist collectivism." Hence, the Church issues her ecumenical and interreligious call for release of the poor from the unjust domination by these two opposing imperialisms. The encyclical speaks of the idolatry of money and power in paragraph 37, and decisively declares this pontificate's position in relation to the two great world powers.

In Bolivia during May 1988, John Paul mentioned the "inhumane misery" of the Third World resulting from the idolatrous ideologies and practices that permeate the two worldwide systems. At Vienna on June 20, 1998, he invited wealthy countries to bridge the chasm that separates them from poor countries, calling this bridge necessary for a unification of Europe that respects its Christian roots.

The term "idolatrous," which is the strongest expression a reader of the Scripture can use, shows clearly that Pope Wojtyła's primary concern for the Third World is religious. "Be faithful to your rich culture of religiosity," he repeated at each stop in his visits to Asia, Africa and Latin America.

John Paul's preoccupation with the Third World has prompted him to shout, like another Isaiah, at the top of his voice. At Edmonton, Canada, on September 1984, he warned: "In the light of the words of Christ, this poor South [Latin America] will judge the rich North." Several years later in Alice Springs, Australia, the horrible squalor in which the Aborigines lived deeply moved him to confess: "I always feel the tragedy of oppressed people" (Nov. 1986).

In Venezuela he asked the question: "How long must man—and the men of the Third World—unjustly support the primacy of economic processes over inviolable human rights and, in particular, over the rights of the workers and of their families?" (Venezuela, Jan. 29, 1985)

He told the people of Bolivia, on May 14, 1988: "I love this world very much, especially this continent." And referring to the encyclical, *Sollicitudo Rei Socialis,* he said: "It does not speak only of the East and the West, but it speaks especially about the Third World, the majority of the world now and in the future."

On the flight from Rome to Cape Verde, Africa, John Paul told news reporters: "The Pope feels allied to Africa and to the other countries of the Third World; we have to present to the people of wealthy nations the needs of these poor people and push for concrete solutions, worldwide!" (Jan. 25, 1990) During that same pastoral journey, he said at Burkina Faso: "In the name of justice, the Bishop of Rome, the successor of Peter, implores his brothers in the human race not to disdain the hungry on this continent" (Jan. 30, 1990).

Finally, on the flight from Rome to Santo Domingo he stated: "I see that these poor people have understood exceptionally well, and in their own way, the Gospel message. And they have accepted this Gospel message, although they have not accepted the European culture. They have made a distinction between the two. These are things to think about, because the Gospel is always the Gospel of the poor" (Oct. 10, 1992).

Has John Paul's option for the Third World been understood? I believe so, and by both his opponents and his supporters. I quote the following, which will suffice as examples:

The Italian journalist, Indro Montanelli, has always praised Pope John Paul II's anti-Communist stance. But on January 10, 1984, he wrote in *Il Giornale:* "We don't like some of the Third World and anti-Western sentiments of Pope Wojtyła." Another well-known Italian journalist, Eugenio Scalfari, voiced words of appreciation for the Pope's efforts "to offer to the masses of the Third World something different from the European traditions, alternatives and images that are compatible with their culture."[2]

On March 10, 1983, the Conference of Non-Allied Countries met in New Delhi, India, and unanimously approved the motion to applaud the journey of John Paul to Central America which ended that very day. This approval can be understood as positive support for the development of people and their cultural and political independence.

"The visits of the Pope to Mexico, and later to Brazil, and more recently to Central America, have been providential marvels," said the Brazilian Bishop Helder Camara (*Avvenire,* Oct. 29, 1983). And finally, Cardinal Jaime Sin of Manila, Philippines, protagonist of the authentic popular insurrection against the country's dictator, Ferdinand Marcos, asserted: "If the Pope had not been able to come, we would have had less courage to speak out."[3]

NOTES

1. J. Gawronski, "Il Papa, cresci, uomo europeo" *La Stampa,* April 4, 1989.

2. *L'Osservatore Romano,* March 15, 1986.

3. *Famiglia Cristiana,* October, 1983.

❊ Chapter Nine ❊

Return to Poland

N o one will ever be able to say exactly what part John Paul played in the people's movement that led to the fall of the iron curtain. He himself avoids the question because it is not possible to gauge the sudden collapse of a regime by statements made by a pope. That he played a part is certain, even if some people may have downplayed his role.

The election of John Paul II may have thrilled the Poles, but it caused alarm in the Communist government. Poland's euphoria reached its height when John Paul returned to his homeland on June 2, 1979, for a nine-day visit. All during that visit, the Polish people boldly manifested their Catholic faith, which the Communist regime had banned and confined to churches. People resolutely gathered in public despite the obstacles authorities placed in the way. The crowds were much larger than any that atheistic propaganda had been able to assemble during the 60 years of Communist rule. (This was true not only in Poland, but in other Communist countries as well.)

John Paul's return to Poland mobilized crowds that would no longer be dispersed. The movement spread from Church gatherings to labor unions and, finally, to political demonstrations. The Pope's role in preparing for the so-called "revolution" of 1989 unfolded in phases. The first involved his encouragement of the crowds that gathered in violation to the government's prohibition. The second phase consisted in his protecting the movement from any punitive reaction from Moscow; we will discuss this later. For the moment we want to follow the triumphal march of a man returning as Pope John Paul II to the country he had left as Karol Wojtyła.

John Paul always immerses himself completely in whatever he does, as if every act were to be his most important, or his last. But in the case of his "return to the fatherland," as he likes to call it, his emotional reaction was particularly intense. "I do everything possible not to be overcome by sentiment," he told journalists during the flight from Rome to Warsaw on June 2. Nevertheless, his emotions flowed freely at the airport greeting, and they stayed close to the surface all during his visit. This would be true of his six subsequent visits to Poland during the twenty years of John Paul's pontificate.

> Beloved brothers and sisters, fellow-countrymen: I am coming to you as a son of this land, of this nation, and also, by the inscrutable designs of Providence, as a successor of St. Peter in the See of Rome. I thank you for not having forgotten me and for not having ceased, from the day of my election, to help me with your prayers and to show me also such kindly benevolence. I thank you for inviting me. I greet in spirit and embrace with my heart every human being living in the land of Poland (June 2, 1979).

The key to the whole visit, which so amazed the world and alarmed the Kremlin, was the unexpectedly strong bond between the Pope and the people of Poland. As a journalist, I was sent there by the Italian newspaper *La Repubblica*, and my strongest and most lasting impression of the entire nine days was the bond of unity between the people and the Pope. The crowd would immediately surround him, as in an embrace, and they would not let him go. They followed him on the road; they waited for him at every crossing; they greeted him in every town and village. It was late springtime, approaching summer, and Poland overflowed with flowers. Every house, every wayside cross and shrine, was decorated. Even the streets the Pope passed through were strewn with blossoms, and people tossed flowers from windows as he rode by.

Naturally, the nation's embrace reached full intensity when the Pope stood before the crowds. The first, and to some extent the most awesome gathering, took place at Victory Square in Warsaw. Normally the Square is reserved for government celebrations, but that day it was redeemed by the presence of a huge crucifix. From that moment on, Victory Square would be known as the Square of the Pope's Mass. Here John Paul pronounced his first challenge to the atheistic Communism being imposed on his people:

> Christ cannot be kept out of the history of man in any part of the globe, at any longitude or latitude of geography. The exclusion of Christ from the history of man is an act against man. Without Christ it is impossible

to understand the history of Poland.... It is impossible without Christ, to understand this nation with its past so full of splendor and also of terrible difficulties (Victory Square, Warsaw, June 2, 1979).

Before he became Pope, Karol Wojtyła had not been what one might call a "personality" in Poland. He had always stood in the shadow of Cardinal Wyszynski, the nation's Primate. Now, the two men stood together before the people, both deeply moved. It seemed as if one were entrusting the country into the hands of the other. Several months earlier, before a group of Polish pilgrims, John Paul had actually said to Cardinal Wyszynski, "Without your faith, this Polish Pope would not be on the chair of Peter" (Oct. 23, 1978).

After Warsaw, his next stop was Gniezno, the ancient primatial See and one of the great centers of evangelization of the Slav people. From this place John Paul spoke to all Slav peoples—Croatians and Slovenians, Bulgarians, Moravians and Slovaks, Czechs and Serbs—naming them, one after the other, in the historical order of their "baptism."

> Is it not Christ's will, is it not what the Holy Spirit disposes, that this Pope, in whose heart is deeply engraved the history of his own nation from its very beginning and also the history of the brother peoples and of the neighboring peoples, should in a special way manifest and confirm in our age the presence of these peoples in the Church and their specific contribution to the history of Christianity?... Is it not Christ's will, is it not what the Holy Spirit disposes, that this Polish Pope, this Slav Pope, should at this precise moment manifest the spiritual unity of Christian Europe? Although there are two great traditions, that of the West and that of the East, to which it is indebted, through both of them Christian Europe professes "one faith, one baptism, one God and Father of us all" (Eph 4:5–6).... This Pope comes here to embrace all these peoples, together with his own nation, and to hold them close to the heart of the Church, to the heart of the Mother of the Church, in whom he has unlimited trust (Gniezno, June 3, 1979).

For the Pope to emphasize the "spiritual unity of Christian Europe" was an action tantamount to tearing down the iron curtain and the Communist wall. Still, John Paul had only expressed an ardent hope; it lacked a practical program. History, for the time being, would work out a plan; for now, it was only a manifesto. The only possible recourse was to dialogue with the regime, and this John Paul encouraged when he spoke to the bishops. He opened his remarks to them by observing that "with the Polish hierarchy there is today a Polish Pope":

> An authentic dialogue should respect the convictions of believers, guarantee all the rights of citizens and the normal conditions for the

activity of the Church as a religious community to which an immense majority of the Polish people belong. We are fully aware that such a dialogue cannot be easy, because it involves two concepts of the world that are diametrically opposed, but it should be possible and efficacious if it seeks the good of man and of the nation (Czestochowa, June 5, 1979).

The historical significance of Cardinal Wojtyła's election to the papacy emerged during that nine-day visit. And at Auschwitz the world would see how providential was Karol Wojtyła's election.

"Golgotha of the Modern World"

The stage for the Mass in Auschwitz was constructed above the platform, which extended halfway down the railroad tracks running through the camp. Here during the Holocaust, new camp arrivals would be sorted and sent forward in two lines, one to the gas chambers and the other to the barracks for forced labor. In his remarks, John Paul reminded the crowd that he had grown up in that very region (his childhood home at Wadowice was only 30 kilometers from that spot); it had become a "Golgotha of the modern world." He recalled the names of people who were martyred, paused before a stone slab bearing the inscription *"Shoah,"* and spoke about the *Shoah* in words no other pope had ever dared to use. Conscious of his mission as a fellow countryman, John Paul presented himself as "the Pope who has come to the See of Peter from the diocese in whose territory is the camp of Auschwitz." Then he affirmed: "Christ wills that I, who have become the successor of Peter, should give witness to the world of that which constitutes the grandeur of man in our time and his misery as well" (Auschwitz, June 7, 1979).

Listening to him, the world understood that the new Pope would guide it in the difficult task of understanding Auschwitz, or at least of remembering it.

Speaking to the workers at Nowa Huta, John Paul used words that would give life to Solidarity: "The Church has no fear of the world of labor" or of any "system based on labor. Christ will never approve that man should be considered or should consider himself simply a means of production."

At that moment, international observers did not grasp the significance of his words, but the Pope knew how important they were. He knew that his words sharply contrasted the hypocrisy of the Communist regime in its dealings with the workers. In fact, the Pope must have thought it necessary to somehow pacify the authorities with these extemporaneous words:

> No one should be surprised that I speak here in Poland about the dignity of the worker, since I have already spoken so in Mexico, and perhaps more forcefully, using stronger words. For the good of man, the Church wants to come to a common understanding of things, an understanding of every system of labor. The Church only asks of the labor system that it be allowed to speak to man about Christ and to love man as his dignity demands (Nowa Huta, June 9, 1979).

John Paul's pastoral visit ended at Kraków—his city. Here, on the last day, the Pope met the largest and most enthusiastic crowd of the entire visit. For two evenings the young people, in the name of the entire population, serenaded him beneath his window at the archbishop's residence. John Paul stepped out onto the balcony and someone passed him a microphone, but the connection was poor and only those nearby could hear him. So he resorted to gestures to tell the young people that he was going in to eat supper. Then he prayed the Angelus. After supper he returned to tell the crowd that he was going to bed, but no one moved.

The serenade continued for a good part of the night, and then a silent crowd kept vigil under his window, long after the Pope had retired. From the archbishop's residence they proceeded directly to the esplanade along the Vistula River where the final celebration was to take place. Streams of people filled the streets all night long; estimates of the crowd numbered over one million. It was the largest assembly ever gathered together in one place to listen to one person, not only in Poland but also in all the European countries.

And John Paul repeated his theme to that crowd: "Do not be afraid! Open the borders! There is no imperialism in the Church, only service!" Then the sea of people dispersed to line up along the twelve kilometers leading to the airport.

In bidding his homeland farewell from the airport at Kraków, John Paul used language intended to deliver a decisive message to the Soviet regime. His remarks could have been interpreted either as an outstretched hand or as a sword; it all depended on how his hearers received them. One thing was certain, his words could not be interpreted as an acceptance of the present situation. "You must have the courage to walk in the direction in which no one has walked until now. In these times, people and systems cannot approach each other without courage, nor is it possible to work for peace."

CHAPTER TEN

Bonding with the Media

*J*ohn Paul II's excellent relationship with the media began only a half-hour after his election, when from his balcony the new Pope faced the crowd in St. Peter's Square. As far as we know, no pope had ever spoken to the people immediately after the first blessing of the pontificate. John Paul's words were important for another reason, however. Because he was a "stranger" to the people of Rome, Karol Wojtyła wanted to introduce himself. With this action, he changed that first appearance from a traditionally simple ritual to a worldwide media event. In his decision to speak on the night of his election, the Pope seemed to extend to the media the offer of an implicit alliance. John Paul took the opportunity to use the media to encourage his acceptance as Bishop of Rome; he also offered the media the opportunity to be the first recipients and direct channels of an historic papal event.

This alliance with the media deepened during the next few days and entered a new stage because of his spontaneous dialogues with the crowd. The day after his election, the Pope left the Vatican to visit Gemelli Hospital, and a short time later (Oct. 21), he met with journalists for the first time. On November 5 he traveled to Assisi to venerate St. Francis, patron of Italy. In his visit to Gemelli Hospital, the Pope spoke briefly to the crowd in a jovial manner, something Paul VI never did. At Assisi, when a voice from the crowd called out, "Long live the Church of silence!" the Pope promptly retorted: "There is no longer a Church of silence, because she speaks through the Pope!" Journalists quickly grew accustomed to this spontaneous and improvised dialogue, and they appreciated it more and more.

The third stage of this relationship with the media developed during the January 1979 flight from Rome to Santo Domingo (en route to Mexico). It was the Pope's first journey outside Italy, and it was also the first "in flight" dialogue the Pope granted journalists. That first session has grown into a real exchange with international information channels.

Relating to the Media in a New Way

Paul VI had traveled with journalists during his nine international trips, beginning with a flight to the Holy Land in 1964 and ending with his trips to various Asian countries in 1970. He greeted journalists—now and then he would even speak to one or another journalist and ask about his family or his health—but the Pope never really conversed with them or held press conferences. The same regulations established for papal audiences were applied on those flights—it was forbidden to ask the Pope questions.

John Paul instinctively accepted questions and responded to all of them, creating a newsworthy atmosphere that had never before existed at the Vatican. The journalist who asked the first question of the Pope described how it happened: "Perhaps the Pope became animated simply by greeting us, as Paul VI was accustomed to doing. In any case, I asked him directly if he was thinking of visiting the United States and, to my surprise, he answered immediately. 'I think it will be necessary,' he replied in English. 'All that remains is to set the date.' My question broke the ice, and in a short time everyone began asking questions, both simple and complex, and he answered each one clearly and frankly."[1]

The fourth stage of John Paul's relationship with the media became evident during his first visit to Poland in 1979. There the Pope acknowledged that the media had given the return to his homeland a worldwide dimension. From then on his "alliance" with the media would be declared and programmed.

What was new in John Paul's use of the media was similar to the new way with which he introduced his travels. John Paul is not a Pope who makes occasional symbolic journeys. This Pope wants to visit every local church according to a set pastoral plan of missionary journeys. Similarly, we do not have a Pope who broadcasts radio messages only at Christmas and Easter and who authorizes the transmission of solely major liturgical celebrations. We have a Pope who wants to make systematic use of the media so that every significant moment in the life of the Church will be broadcast through every possible communications network.

The Pope's conversations during flight are a classic example of his unique way of acting with the media. There is no sifting of questions; the Pope accepts them all and takes the risk of answering spontaneously because he trusts the media. Moreover, he finds the results of this method beneficial for creating a better media image of the papacy.

He has allowed himself to be photographed on his excursions to the mountains and up ski slopes, holding a koala bear or wearing a sports cap—and even as a patient in Gemelli Hospital. Paul VI also modernized papal journeys, but he limited himself simply to greeting the journalists who traveled with him. He did not accept questions, not because he was old-fashioned with regard to the media, but because he was much more reserved. He was concerned with upholding a lofty image of the papacy.

Previous popes would have considered it inappropriate to answer dozens of questions about Cuba, Castro, and Communism, as John Paul did willingly during the flight from Rome to Havana in 1998. These issues drew the usual wide range of probing questions the press loves. Not long ago, popes only spoke publicly in Latin and then only in a consistory. John Paul's willing acceptance of questions from journalists shows how well he understands that not everything a pope says is a solemn pronouncement.

Another pope might have found it impossible to respond to such a pointed question as, "What do you think of the charge of bank fraud brought against Archbishop Marcinkus?" Wojtyła has never refused to answer questions of this sort, although at times his answer may be a simple yet effective statement, as it was concerning Marcinkus: "We are convinced that one cannot attack another person in such a brutal fashion!" (flight from Rome to Montevideo, March 31, 1987)

Finally, when it comes to the media's role to entertain, the Pope often willingly goes along. "Tonight there is a soccer game between Poland and Italy; which team will you root for?" Journalists asked out of simple curiosity, and John Paul answered with simple humor: "It would be better for me to keep out of sight" (flight from Buenos Aires to Rome, June 14, 1982).

Willingness to adapt himself to a media culture is a basic attitude for John Paul. On one occasion he wanted to repeat, for the sake of those reporters and photographers who had been absent, the Polish labor leader Lech Wałesa's deferential embrace, because "it is necessary to show how Mr. Walesa greets me and how I receive him" (April 21, 1989). Another example was the ease with which John Paul allowed media coverage of his visit with his would-be assassin on December 29, 1983. While some people believed TV coverage of the event was inappropriate, others, including the Pope, maintained that everything that serves as a witness to the Gospel can and should be shown.

Many have tried to explain the media's attraction to the figure of the Pope and John Paul's ability to put the media to such good use. The Pope's visual image—a solitary figure dressed in white—perfectly fits the media's need for symbols of simplicity. A TV news flash of the Pope's condemnation of war, accompanied by a photo of the Pope speaking from a Vatican window, is a far more powerful communication than a newspaper headline declaring that the ecumenical Council of World Churches, assembled at Canberra, Australia, condemns war.

Then there is the Pope's personal attitude toward media. John Paul brings his theater experience to his public appearances and celebrations of the liturgy, making him a marvelous communicator on television. He proves that visibility takes precedence over talk and action over words. Because of television coverage the Pope does not remain a figure from a distant country. At his window in the Vatican or in some ceremony held in St. Peter's Basilica, whether dressed in a white cassock or in colorful liturgical vestments—he dominates the scene, balancing symbolic distance with immediate perceptibility.

Briefly, then, John Paul's use of the media can be summarized as follows:

❖ John Paul is a Pope of action and presence before he is a man of words; he is as much a man of the spontaneous and personal word as he is of the written.

❖ The Pope's preference for action over words, manifested in his journeys and his expert use of the media, enables him to come in contact with a public much more vast than the people he encounters at his papal audiences or through his magisterial publications.

❖ In great part this ability to reach a wider audience is due to a traditional genius for Catholic and papal communication, which has always made use of liturgical, iconographic, and architectural elements. But the Pope's successful use of media also reflects a person naturally gifted with communication skills, experienced in the theater, trained in the fine arts, and well-schooled in Polish religiosity.

Media's Role in the Church

John Paul believes the media have a positive role to play in people's lives. With typical Catholic intuition, he believes that the world is good and the news should be good. To journalists gathered at the United Nations he said: "You promote unity among all nations by the diffusion of truth among all peoples" (Oct. 2, 1979). At the end of that same month, addressing the International Catholic Association of Radio and Television, he surprised one of the delegates by applying his positive media principle to television as a field of mission: "The fundamental motivation of your endeavors is the evangelization of the human race."

He instinctively feels that the media present an epochal opportunity for the Catholic Church: "By these means the Church hopes to promote ever more efficaciously the constructive message of the Gospel" (U.S.A., Oct. 5, 1979).

The Pope does not always distinguish between professional competence and the religious beliefs of those who work in the media. To journalists who accompanied him to Ireland and were not all believers, he said: "The Pope trusts in you to construct here, in the world community, the Kingdom of God" (Sept. 29, 1979). His goal is to establish a world community, and he calls upon journalists to be the first witnesses and first "apostles" in communicating this goal.

The above statements from the first year of John Paul's pontificate demonstrate his trust in the media, a trust he had from the very beginning. At the time of his election, John Paul had not known positive experiences of the media in his own country; there the media were dismal and atheistic. He had great expectations, though, of the media of the free world. It was as if he had been waiting for such an experience of media all his life. Even as cardinal, in his book, *Sources of Renewal* (a commentary on the documents of the Second Vatican Council), he had stated with insight and absolute certainty: "The prophetic aspect of the Christian vocation directs our attention to the mass means of communication."[2]

His hopeful expectations of media in the free world were realized in the worldwide reaction to his election, in the media attention given his pastoral visit to Mexico, and even more so, his visit to Poland. International media coverage of the pilgrim Pope in his homeland signaled Poland's emergence from the geographic and political isolation into which it had been thrust. "I thank you for bringing the whole world to Poland, having it at my side and letting it share in these precious days of prayer and my return home," John Paul told news reporters on June 10, 1979, in Kraków.

One must seriously consider the Pope as a missionary in order to understand his excessive engagements during his journeys (see Chapter 18) and his trust in the media (perhaps excessive at times). He plans his visits as a missionary to the world; his flights are scheduled to allow him to meet with the largest number of people at every stop along the way. At the same time John Paul wants the Church to use "the pathways of the air to bring to the mind and heart of every person the joyful announcement of Christ, the Redeemer of man."[3]

John Paul truly believes the media will enable him to reach the heart and mind of every single person. He has confidence in the medium and in the viewer. He maintains that the advent of media has also increased the possibility of a greater response to the missionary mandate of Christ: "Go and preach the Gospel to all the nations."

Whichever medium he uses—television, radio, or satellite—to touch all people and speak in every language, the Pope considers it not only a great gift, but also a serious obligation. "Great possibilities are open today to social communications wherein the Church recognizes the signs of the creative and redemptive works of God which man should continue. These instruments can become powerful means for transmitting the Gospel."[4] And if they *can* be used for the Gospel, they *should* be— that is the rule of mission.

John Paul's gestures and language can be understood only if we take into account each group to which they are individually addressed. For example, in his Christmas message of 1993, the Pope spoke in fifty-six languages. Such a string of languages contained in one talk would make no sense unless one realized that his was a worldwide transmission addressed to all nations.

John Paul submits to the "tyranny" of television appearances with docility, as is evident in this remark made during a vigil in St. Peter's Square, October 1994: "I am supposed to speak for twenty-five minutes, but I don't know if the twenty-five minutes are up!"

It is common knowledge that reporters are often challenging to deal with, and on occasion they have challenged the Pope. Recalling the day before when reporters had made a point of mentioning how the Pope (suffering from a fractured femur) was visibly pained while ascending to the altar, he said to Vatican spokesman, Joaquín Navarro-Valls: "Ask the journalists if they haven't ever grimaced with pain" (Aug. 22, 1994).

On another occasion he used a bit of irony to answer a journalist who asked the Pope about his health: "I am certainly no longer the age I was in 1979. But perhaps Providence will preserve me. If I want to know anything about my health...I have to read the newspapers" (Jan. 21, 1998, flight from Rome to Havana).

Journalists describe John Paul as a great communicator. Joaquín Navarro-Valls has said that there is "an objective bond between the Pope and the media. We don't know what percentage is due to the Pope or what percentage to the media, but they have established this deep mutual bond." That bond has positively affected not only the papal image, however.

In a conversation with children at a Roman parish, the Pope referred to the decisive role the media played in his visit to Cuba.

"Thanks to radio and television, everyone—even children—knows everything. But do you children know what Fidel Castro and I talked about?"

"Ye-e-e-s!"

"It's really true; everybody knows everything!" (Feb. 8, 1998)

Notwithstanding the deep bond and mutual confidence between the Pope and the media, there exists no naiveté on the Pope's part regarding their relationship. We see this in John Paul's comments in the spring of 1991, after the Gulf War: "This conflict has been carried on not only with the arms of war, but also to some extent through the media."

NOTES

1. K. Del Rio, L. Accattoli, *Wojtyła il nuovo Mosé* (Milan: Mondadori, 1988), p. 4.

2. K. Wojtyła, *Alle fonti del rinnovamento* (Rome: Libreria Editrice Vaticana, 1981), p. 230.

3. From a prayer to Mary, composed in 1992 for *Telepace*, the Italian TV station which televises all papal activities.

4. Message for the Nineteenth World Day for Social Communications, May 1985.

CHAPTER ELEVEN

Visit to the United States

*A*ccording to legend, shortly after his birth Siddhartha Gautama, founder of Buddhism, took four steps: north, south, east, and west. In the early years of his pontificate, John Paul II also traveled in all the directions of the compass. He set out in the name of "the power of Christ which knows no decline," inspired by the missionary mandate which motivates the Church "so that Christ's words of life will reach all people" (Oct. 22, 1978).

Already in 1978, John Paul II concretized this universal orientation of the Church, integrating its ideological and geographical elements in his mission to the nations. He traveled south in his journey to Mexico; east with his triumphal return to Poland; north and west with the joint pastoral visit to Ireland and the United States. The visit to Constantinople, in November 1979, completed the year's scenario and opened his first contact with Orthodoxy and Islam. That particular area of John Paul's mission would increasingly demand his attention. However, his mission of reaching out to all peoples, religions and cultures was already established in his earliest travels.

Of these four symbolic steps, the one to the West was the Pope's most difficult. In the South a drama of hunger was being played on the world's stage; in the East, a drama of tyranny which compelled him to visit Poland as soon as possible. But in the North and the West, from Europe to North America, John Paul found himself at the crossroads of an epoch and at a launching point for the future. He faced the challenge of "freedom"—in a sense, the greatest challenge because of the destiny to which it leads the human person and because of the ancient roots from which it grows. John Paul II—a man who is considered, and who considers himself, a champion of freedom—clearly understood and accepted the challenge.

S tronger and more at ease in his new ministry than ever, the Pope encountered the great American symbols of freedom in New York on October 3, 1979. He spoke in Battery Park, an esplanade at the extreme edge of Manhattan. Behind him stood Ellis Island, the Statue of Liberty rose in the distance, and in front of him lay Wall Street, center of world trade and finance. John Paul positioned himself at the precise place where immigrants coming from the "Old World" arrived at the "New."

As in every "liturgy," so at this meeting with the crowd, symbols and words intermingled to give form and substance to the message, making it at once spectacularly clear and forceful. "My visit to your city would not have been complete without coming to Battery Park, without seeing Ellis Island and the Statue of Liberty in the distance. Every nation has its historical symbols.... The Statue of Liberty is such a symbol in the United States" (Oct. 3, 1979). He paid sincere and unreserved homage to this symbol of the New World, describing at length the positive characteristics of the nation Americans had constructed on the foundation of liberty.

But, after speaking of the Statue of Liberty which personifies the American ideal, John Paul suggested for his audience's reflection two other symbolic words: justice and truth. Regarding justice, he spoke of the plight of the poor in the Third World; addressing the issue of truth, he spoke of objective moral law. The Pope challenged the West to look closely at these two areas.

John Paul linked liberty with justice. He stated that in order for the United States to be faithful to its history as a nation founded on liberty, it must support the search for justice today. True freedom cannot exist without justice. "The freedom that was gained must be ratified each day by the firm rejection of whatever wounds, weakens or dishonors human life." It was not acceptable, for example (as he would insist again in Washington, D.C.), that freedom should be used "to dominate the weak, to squander natural resources and energy, and to deny basic necessities to people" (Oct. 7).

He spoke again of liberty and justice in his homily at Logan Circle in Philadelphia. He also paid homage to the history of the United States by recalling its Declaration of Independence: "Your attachment to liberty, to freedom, is part of your heritage." He then went on to say:

> Christ himself linked freedom with the knowledge of truth. "You will know the truth and the truth will make you free" (Jn 8:32). Freedom,

therefore, can never be construed without relation to the truth as revealed by Jesus Christ and proposed by his Church, nor can it be seen as a pretext for moral anarchy, for every moral order must remain linked to truth.... This is especially relevant when one considers the domain of human sexuality. Here, as in any other field, there can be no true freedom without respect for the truth regarding the nature of human sexuality and marriage. In today's society, we see so many disturbing tendencies and so much laxity regarding the Christian view of sexuality. They have all one thing in common: recourse to the concept of freedom to justify any behavior that is no longer consonant with the true moral order and the teaching of the Church.... Free indeed is the person who models his or her behavior in a responsible way according to the exigencies of the objective good.... Divine law is the sole standard of human liberty and is given to us in the Gospel of Christ, the Gospel of Redemption (Oct. 3, 1979).

Years later, John Paul would treat of the possibility of a conflict between freedom and truth in his 1993 encyclical, *Veritatis Splendor* (The Splendor of Truth). He would also return to the question of freedom and justice during his visit to Cuba in 1998. But for now, in Philadelphia, he called upon the United States not to forget justice; in Cuba, he would remind people that they must not sacrifice freedom (see Chapter 37).

John Paul's challenge to the West, which he formulated here for the first time, would become a challenge he would raise again and again in other countries as well; this theme would also recur every time he returned to the United States (1987, 1993, 1995, 1998). In fact, the Pope's challenge would dominate his address to the anti-life proponents at the United Nations in the mid-90s (see Chapter 35).

John Paul can accept the call for public and private freedom. He cannot, however, accept a distinction that seems especially important to contemporary society, namely, *unrestricted personal freedom* which allows an individual to determine the extent of his or her own freedom without any regard for objective moral standards or the laws of God. Speaking on the feast of St. Francis of Assisi to religious brothers in Chicago, the Pope said: "The freedom of which I speak is a paradox to many; it is even misunderstood by some members of the Church" (Oct. 4, 1979). It is precisely his lack of ambiguity concerning the Catholic teaching on freedom, as well as his personal witness and credibility, that highlights the "scandal" of a Pope who acknowledges the limitations of freedom to people whose "religion" is freedom without limits.

Even as cardinal, Karol Wojtyła had spoken of freedom as being at once the greatest gift and the greatest temptation that could be offered a person. When it comes into conflict with God, freedom constitutes the "primordial temptation," the same that addressed our first parents in the Garden of Eden when the serpent deceived them with the enticement: "You will be like gods" (Gen 3:5). That temptation, says John Paul, has found an answer in the historical context of our times through unrestricted license.

*I*n his visit to Ireland, which preceded his journey to the United States, the Pope described that historical moment as a marvelous time for the Church. He told Irish priests and religious: "You must work with the conviction that this decade of the 1980s we are about to enter could be crucial and decisive for the future of the faith in Ireland.... To all of you I say this is a wonderful time in the history of the Church. It is a marvelous time to be a priest, to be a religious, to be a missionary of Christ" (Oct. 1, 1979).

This dramatic sentiment, together with an apocalyptic vision of our times, prompted the Pope to appeal to all persons in secular society. He called for an irrevocable "No" to every form of violence. He recalled people to the primacy of ethics over politics, vigorously reaffirming traditional morality. He could not have chosen more challenging themes!

Accepting the Pope's Challenge

In his first lengthy discourse after arriving in America, the Pope warned his Boston audience that they might find his talk hard to accept, but that he could not water down the Gospel message to make it more "palatable." "Real love is demanding. I would fail in my mission if I did not clearly tell you so" (Oct. 1, 1979). At the same time, he framed his appeal as an invitation to dialogue, not as a declaration of hostility. "I hope that this entire journey can be seen in the light of [the Vatican II document] *The Constitution on the Church in the Modern World.*" And rightly so, since the United States personifies modernity.

Despite his challenging message, John Paul's first pastoral journey to the United States was a huge success. American media reports were unanimous in their positive evaluation of the Pope's visit. According to the *New York Times*, the press corps that had mobilized itself for the seven days of the papal trip (journalists, photographers, television crews, etc.) was perhaps the largest in history. As for general media coverage, the space and time dedicated to reports on the Pope were unprecedented. For John Paul's reception at the White House, a record 10,000 persons were invited to attend, and the *Washington Post* stated that the number of people who poured out to see him during his week-long stay was the largest in American history.

One newspaper report described the Pope as "severe in the pulpit and cordial in the street." Americans liked him immensely, but the most overwhelming response he received was from young people. They gathered at Madison Square Garden on October 2, and at Catholic University of America in Washington, D.C., on October 7. In New York the young people greeted him with waves of cheers: "John Paul II, we love you!" which he playfully returned from the microphone four times: "John Paul II loves you too!"—causing pure delirium to ensue in his young audience. At Catholic University the young people made gestures as if they were throwing confetti or flowers. To their delight, the Pope enthusiastically returned the gestures. By the end of the visit, these young people had undoubtedly found their hero.

John Paul told reporters who had followed his journey to the five major U.S. cities: "You Americans have been very supportive of me." Indeed, America had wonderfully accepted this great Polish priest, who, to win their affection, had not sacrificed any of the doctrinal or disciplinary patrimony of which he is the depositary.

※ CHAPTER TWELVE ※

First Ecumenical Ventures

*B*eginning with the second year of his pontificate, John Paul traveled to three major religious centers: Constantinople (1979), Canterbury (1982), and Geneva (1984). These three visits in some way shed light on his ecumenical dream. On numerous occasions he voiced his desire to visit a fourth and for him perhaps most important site: Moscow.

John Paul speaks passionately about the Church's commitment to ecumenism, but Catholic progress in the area of Christian unity has met numerous delays and obstacles during his pontificate. In great part this is due to new difficulties that cropped up in the East after the fall of the Communist regime, and in the West over the issue of admission of women to priestly ordination in the Anglican Church. To a lesser degree, misunderstandings between the Roman Catholic and Orthodox Churches have contributed to failed attempts to reach unity.

This failure of the ecumenical movement in the East dramatically culminated in the refusal of the Orthodox Churches—except for Constantinople—to send delegates to the special European Synod in 1991. Difficulties with the Anglican Church, on the other hand, arose during the mid-80s and led to a stalemate during the 1996 visit to Rome of the Archbishop of Canterbury.

The Pope has suffered because of these difficulties; one might even speculate they have baffled him. With statements and symbolic gestures fully in accord with those of his predecessor, Paul VI, John Paul II has not only tried to reopen initiatives aimed at promoting unity; he has never failed to use every occasion to do so. In fact, he has extended himself beyond the Montini heritage in three different ways:

❖   by promoting, after the ecumenical failure in 1991, the *mea culpas* of the Catholic Church for the Jubilee Year;

❖   by expressing in 1994 the idea of a worldwide Christian ecumenical assembly to take place either in Jerusalem or Bethlehem for the year 2000;

❖   by inviting all the Christian Churches, through the 1995 encyclical *Ut Unum Sint*, to suggest new ways for the Bishop of Rome to exercise his "Petrine ministry."

It is uncertain just how the Pope's suggestion for a world-wide Christian assembly in the Holy Land in the year 2000 will turn out. But the self-examination which the Catholic Church has begun at the end of the second millennium, as well as the search for new ways of exercising the Petrine ministry while entering the third millennium, are already two fruitful ecumenical legacies of the Wojtyła pontificate.

*I*n November 1979, John Paul arrived in Constantinople. Patriarch Dimitrios I greeted him warmly: "I bid you welcome to this historic meeting. Blessed be the name of the Lord who brought you here." John Paul responded in French: "This meeting is a divine gift." The welcoming ceremony took place within a small garden inside the Patriarch's residence in the Byzantine Quarter of Istanbul. Wearing a violet stole, Dimitrios advanced to embrace John Paul, whose stole was red. At that meeting of the Orthodox Church with the Church of Rome, the Pope expressed his hope for the future: "May the dawn of the new millennium break upon a Church which has regained full unity" (Nov. 29, 1979).

Looking back over his pontificate, this has been one of the most courageous statements John Paul made in reference to the "ecumenical dream," one he has repeated several times. In the 1990s he expressed it as a hope that "during the Great Jubilee we shall be able to present ourselves, if not completely one, at least much closer to overcoming the divisions of the second millennium" (*Ut Unum Sint,* 1995).

The very day John Paul set foot in Turkey (Nov. 28, 1979), the Turkish newspaper *Mylliet* printed a letter on the front page. The terrorist and murderer Ali Agca, who had recently escaped from a military prison, addressed the Pope:

> John Paul II, the Commandant of the Crusade, has been sent to Turkey by the Western imperialists because, at this critical time, they are afraid of the Turks who, together with their Islamic brothers, threaten to gain greater economic and military power in the Middle East. If this meeting is not cancelled, it is certain that I shall kill the Pope.[1]

The only critical events prior to the attempt on John Paul's life in May 1981 are this letter and the confrontation between the Pope and the Soviet regime when he visited Poland (see Chapter 14). This may possibly shed some light on the attack. Perhaps Agca's public threat to kill John Paul was being used by the secret service of a world power that feared the Polish Pope. Or perhaps others, who put blame on the secret service of the East, were using Agca. After numerous investigations only two possible hypotheses exist: that the attacker acted on his own or was used by the Bulgarian secret service. We may never know which is correct.

*A*fter John Paul's visit to Constantinople, equally solemn in gesture and compelling in content was his meeting with the Archbishop of Canterbury, Robert Runcie, on May 29, 1982. Paul VI had already traveled to Constantinople and Geneva, but this was the first time a pope had paid a visit to Canterbury. There, on the bishop's throne which St. Augustine of Canterbury had once occupied, the book of Gospels was set. The Pope and the Archbishop took their places at a lower level in front of the altar, seated on identical chairs and facing each other at a slight angle. To emphasize that this meeting was not simply a ceremony staged to address past wounds of an ancient Christian Europe, the Pope and Archbishop met in a chapel dedicated to the saints and martyrs of the twentieth century. Seated with them were four other persons who represented the principal Christian denominations. Each member of the group placed a candle in a candelabra close to the altar while pronouncing the name of a martyr of the twentieth century. Pope John Paul was first in line, and he dedicated his candle to St. Maximilian Kolbe. Archbishop Runcie then followed, pronouncing the name of Oscar Romero, Archbishop of San Salvador. Other names proposed were Dietrich Bonhöeffer and the Ukrainian Sister Maria Skobotsova (both of whom, like Kolbe, had been victims of the Nazis); Reverend Martin Luther King; and the Anglican bishop from Uganda, Janami Luwun, martyred by the dictator Idi Amin. Perhaps it was this ceremony that would later prompt John Paul to propose a "contemporary martyrology" for the Great Jubilee and an ecumenical commemoration of the new martyrs, to be held on May 11 in the year 2000.

Finally, at Geneva on June 12, 1984, John Paul met with the ecumenical World Council of Churches. John Paul recalled the Catholic Church's "conviction" about the role of the Bishop of Rome, that "he is the visible bond of unity" which "our fidelity to Christ does not permit us to renounce." Rather, it was necessary to discuss the papacy "in a spirit of openness and friendship. We know," the Pope acknowledged, "that this poses a difficulty for most of you, that it is a source of painful memories, and for this my predecessor Paul VI asked forgiveness" (Geneva, June 12, 1984).

At this time John Paul did not ask pardon in his own name. He would do so later, and with even greater energy than his predecessor (see Chapter 39). He would also respond positively to the suggestion of the secretary general of the World Council of Churches, Jamaican pastor Philip Potter, to go beyond formalities to the actual performance of "shared concrete acts of obedience to the Gospel." John Paul would act by convening a day of prayer and fasting at Assisi, and by making plans for the Great Jubilee.

The Pope's expectations in the area of ecumenism vary according to the individuals with whom he dialogues. For example, in a letter to James R. Crumley, President of the Lutheran Church of America, the Pope wrote: "Should we not hope that the dawn of the third millennium will mark the advent of a time especially dedicated to the search for full unity in Christ?" (July 22, 1985)

One aspect of John Paul's ecumenical dream is the extent to which he has searched, at Constantinople and at Geneva, for every possible development of the basic points laid down by Paul VI. In *Tertio Millennio Adveniente*, John Paul wrote:

> Papal journeys have become a regular occurrence, taking in the particular churches in every continent and showing concern for the development of ecumenical relationships with Christians of various denominations. Particularly important in this regard were the visits to Turkey, Germany, England, Scotland, and Wales, Switzerland, the Scandinavian countries and, most recently, the Baltic countries (n. 24).

During the 1990s, when the Catholic Church's emphasis on ecumenism was overshadowed by its penitential path to unity (see Chapter 29), John Paul constantly affirmed the importance of focusing on the goal of church unity. As he stated in an ecumenical meeting held in the Baltic republic of Estonia: "To achieve the unity of all believers in Christ could constitute, and certainly will constitute, one of the major events in human history" (Sept. 10, 1993).

The road of penance that John Paul announced at the very beginning of his pontificate has been long. Less than a month after his visit to Constantinople, he called for a re-examination of the Galileo case. This action clearly reinforced the Pope's willingness to settle accounts with history.

NOTES

1. L. Accattoli, "Io ho avuto paura a ricevere questa nomina" (Turin: SEI, 1993), 147.

❖ CHAPTER THIRTEEN ❖

Reopening the Galileo Case

*P*ope John Paul II has already made history by courageously combating Communism. It is also likely he will be remembered for yet another act of courage, namely, his call to examine the "dark pages" in the Church's history—its "deviations from the Gospel"—and his petition for God's pardon. Pope Wojtyła refers to this great undertaking as "an examination of conscience at the end of the millennium," and it became an explicit program of his pontificate with the publication of *Tertio Millennio Adveniente* in November 1994.

To start off the "examination," John Paul announced the reopening of the Galileo case at a meeting of the Pontifical Academy of Sciences during a commemoration of Albert Einstein on November 10, 1979. Galileo, the Florentine mathematician, astronomer and physicist, had held and taught Copernicus's theory of the sun as center of the solar system. The Church condemned Galileo for his teaching and forced him to publicly retract his views. Centuries later, this issue remained a "sore" point, not only with regard to the Church's relationship with science, but also for certain people who would bring up the Galileo case when any controversy arose involving Catholics in political, social or intellectual spheres.

In the document *Gaudium et Spes*, the Second Vatican Council had made implicit reference to Galileo, although he was never mentioned by name. The Pope's decision to look again at his case indicated John Paul's dissatisfaction with the ambiguity contained in *Gaudium et Spes* and with the insufficient attention that had been paid to the whole issue. It also revealed John Paul's great confidence that the matter could be clarified and much of the misunderstanding corrected.

The greatness of Galileo, like that of Einstein, is known to everyone, but unlike the latter, whom we are honoring today before the College of Cardinals in the Apostolic Palace, the former had to suffer a great deal—we cannot conceal the fact—at the hands of men and organisms of the Church. The Second Vatican Council recognized and deplored certain unwarranted interventions:

"We cannot but deplore"—it is written in number 36 of the Conciliar Constitution *Gaudium et Spes*—"certain attitudes (not unknown among Christians) deriving from a shortsighted view of the rightful autonomy of science: they have occasioned conflict and controversy and have misled many into thinking that faith and science are opposed."

To go beyond this stand taken by the Council, I hope that theologians, scholars and historians, animated by a spirit of sincere collaboration, will study the Galileo case more deeply and, in loyal recognition of wrongs from whatever side they come, will dispel the mistrust that still opposes, in many minds, a fruitful concord between science and faith, between the Church and the world. I give all my support to this task, which will be able to honor the truth of faith and of science and open the door to future collaboration (Nov. 10, 1979).

As a follow-up, the Pope instituted a pontifical commission to study the Galileo controversy. Plans for the commission were announced on July 3, 1981, and placed under the supervision of Cardinal Gabriel-Marie Garrone. Four distinct groups of the commission held responsibility for certain areas of study. Cardinal Carlo Maria Martini headed the exegetical section; Cardinal Paul Poupard the cultural section; Carlos Chagas, President of the Pontifical Academy of Sciences, and Father George Coyne, S.J., Director of the Vatican Observatory, were in charge of the scientific and epistemological section; and Father Michele Macarrone, President of the Pontifical Commission for Historical Sciences, headed the historical and juridical section.

The members of the commission were as convinced as the Pope of the necessity and importance of their investigation. In 1984, Cardinal Garrone formally presented one of the most important publications of the commission: the documents compiled by the Pontifical Academy of Sciences covering the trial of Galileo. Then, in 1986 and under the care of Cardinal Martini, the Pontifical Academy of Sciences published a volume on the exegetical orientations of Galileo's time. It seems, however, that projects outside the traditional practice of the Curia, even when entrusted to Curial officials, meet with resistance. As a result, the work of the commission begun in 1979 was not concluded until 1992. Cardinal Poupard delivered the final report during a papal audience granted to the

Pontifical Academy of Sciences on October 31, 1992. The most important statement of the lengthy document appears in the fifth paragraph:

> Certain theologians, Galileo's contemporaries, being heirs of a unitary concept of the world universally accepted until the dawn of the seventeenth century, failed to grasp the profound, non-literal meaning of the Scriptures when they described the physical structure of the created universe. This led them unduly to transpose a question of factual observation into the realm of faith.

> It is in that historical and cultural framework, far removed from our own times, that Galileo's judges, unable to dissociate faith from an age-old cosmology, believed quite wrongly that the adoption of the Copernican revolution, in fact not yet definitively proven, was such as to undermine Catholic tradition, and that it was their duty to forbid its being taught. This subjective error of judgment, so clear to us today, led them to a disciplinary measure from which Galileo had much to suffer. These mistakes must be frankly recognized, as you, Holy Father, have requested (*L'Osservatore Romano*, Nov. 1, 1992).

The substance of the report is clear, although its language remains somewhat minimized. "Some theologians" and "the judges of Galileo" are expressions that do not fully indicate what happened in the palace of the Holy Office and in papal Rome of 1633. Everyone in the papal ambience of that time shared the opinion condemning Galileo and the Copernican theory, and Galileo's judges acted in literal obedience to the directives of Pope Urban VIII. The Pontiff's personal involvement in the decision regarding Galileo, and in the regulations issued against him on June 16 of that same year, might have been acknowledged in a document of this type.

Nevertheless, the meaning is clear and the Church's admission of such mistakes is courageous. No less important is what Pope John Paul said on October 31, 1992:

> A twofold question is at the heart of the debate of which Galileo was at the center. The first is of the epistemological order and concerns biblical hermeneutics.... Paradoxically, Galileo, who was a sincere believer, showed himself to be more perceptive in this regard than the theologians who opposed him.... The upset caused by the Copernican system thus demanded epistemological reflection on the biblical sciences, an effort which later would produce fruit in modern exegetical works and which has found sanction and a new stimulus in the Dogmatic Constitution *Dei Verbum* [On Divine Revelation] of the Second Vatican Council.... The pastoral judgment, which the Copernican theory required, was difficult to make insofar as geocentrism seemed to be a part of scriptural teaching itself. It would have been necessary all at

once to overcome habits of thought and to devise a way of teaching capable of enlightening the people of God. Let us say, in a general way, that the pastor ought to show a genuine boldness, avoiding the double trap of a hesitant attitude and of hasty judgment, both of which can cause considerable harm....

From the beginning of the Age of Enlightenment down to our own day, the Galileo case has been a sort of "myth," in which the image fabricated out of the events was quite far removed from reality. In this perspective, the Galileo case was the symbol of the Church's supposed rejection of scientific progress, or of dogmatic "obscurantism" opposed to the free search for truth. This myth has played a considerable cultural role. It has helped to anchor a number of scientists of good faith in the idea that there was an incompatibility between the spirit of science and the rules of research on the one hand and the Christian faith on the other. A tragic mutual incomprehension has been interpreted as the reflection of a fundamental opposition between science and faith. The clarifications provided by recent historical studies enable us to state that this sad misunderstanding now belongs to the past....

Another lesson which we can draw is that the different branches of knowledge call for different methods.... The error of the theologians of the time, when they maintained the centrality of the earth, was to think that our understanding of the physical world's structure was, in some way, imposed by the literal sense of Sacred Scripture.[1]

By October 1992, John Paul had at last become firmly convinced that all the "dark pages" of the history of the Church should be brought out into the open. It might have seemed as if the commission's delay, coupled with resistance by the Curia, had caused the Pope to drop the plan he had announced at the beginning of his pontificate: to "acknowledge the errors" of the Church. In fact, the contrary was true: throughout the eleven years of the Commission's labor, John Paul was carrying out a vast judicial investigation of individual dark pages in the Church's history. He did this during travels that brought him in contact with crucial spokesmen. None of those years is without its particular pronouncement based on self-examination.

Looking at the Church's "Dark Pages"

At Madrid, for example (Nov. 3, 1982), the Pope spoke about the Spanish Inquisition, reputedly the most terrible chapter of Church history and which even today is the most fiery of topics in Spain. "In certain moments such as those of the Inquisition, there were tensions, errors and excesses—facts which the Church today can consider in the objective light of history."[2]

At Vienna (Sept. 10, 1983), the Pope faced the question of wars that have dotted the history of Europe—wars fought by baptized Christians against one another—especially in cases where those wars arose as the result of unjust oppression. "We have...to confess—and ask forgiveness for the fact—that we Christians have burdened ourselves with great guilt in thoughts, words and deeds, and by not standing up against injustice."[3]

Initially, Pope Wojtyła's statements were more or less motivated by the fact that historically, popes were somehow responsible for errors of the past. But, very soon, John Paul would extend this self-examination beyond the responsibility of popes or ecclesiastical structures. He would address questions of slavery, the mistreatment of indigenous peoples by European colonists, and the lawlessness and violence of the Mafia in Italy. In such cases, the confession of sin would be made, not in the name of the Roman Pontiff or of the Catholic hierarchy, but in the name of baptized Catholics.

The first and perhaps most significant case took place in the southern Italian region of Calabria, and involved organized crime. On October 6, 1983, the Pope celebrated an outdoor Mass. During the homily he enumerated a list of Mafia crimes and exhorted the community to take responsibility to remedy the situation. "We, who are the vineyard of the Lord—how many wild grapes we have produced instead of good grapes! How many feuds and vendettas, thefts, robberies, kidnappings, and injustices; and how much shedding of blood and violence of every kind!"[4]

From Santo Domingo, on October 12, 1984, John Paul acknowledged the Catholic Church's responsibility for the mistreatment of the indigenous population. "The Church does not intend to deny the interdependence of the cross and the sword which characterized the first phase of the missionary penetration of the New World." John Paul went to Santo Domingo to launch a "novena of years" in preparation for the celebration of the fifth centenary of the evangelization of Latin America. Throughout the nine years that followed, he returned time and time again to the same theme in countries outside Latin America (e.g., Canada, Australia, the United States) until 1992, when he brought the novena of years to a close.

Two years later Pope Wojtyła visited Cameroon in Africa. He addressed the country's intellectuals on August 13, 1986, recalling that the Church bore some responsibility for the inhumane treatment of Africans. He first reminded his audience that Christianity promotes and defends freedom as well as the inalienable rights of the human person; then the Pope said: "In the course of history, men belonging to Christian nations unfortunately have not always acted in this way, and we ask forgiveness from our African brothers and sisters who have suffered so much, for example, because of the slave trade."⁵ This was the first time that John Paul referred directly to a "dark page" in the history of the Church and then concluded with a formal request for pardon from those who had been victimized.

In 1985 Pope Wojtyła addressed Islamic youth at Casablanca, Morocco, asking their forgiveness for the enmity of the past. On April 13, 1986, he visited the Jewish Synagogue in Rome, where he deplored the persecution of the Jews "at any time and by anyone; I repeat, by anyone" (which would include any of his predecessors in the papacy). Then, on the day for peace at Assisi (Oct. 27), he stated: "I am ready to acknowledge that Catholics have not always been faithful to this affirmation of faith. We have not always been peacemakers." (A more detailed treatment of these events follows in Chapters 21, 22 and 23.)

In September, 1987, John Paul referred to the colonists' mistreatment of Native Americans. His comments were more pointed and more vehement than they had been in Santo Domingo: "The cultural oppression, the injustices, the disruption of your life and of your traditional societies must be acknowledged.... Unfortunately, not all the members of the Church lived up to their Christian responsibilities."⁶

Beginning in 1987 the Pope's self-criticisms on behalf of the Church became more numerous and, in 1988, he delivered at least two in Strasbourg, France. The first, which took place on October 8, was an admission that the Church had not preached energetically enough against injustice. "There should not be special privileges for the rich and powerful, and injustice for the poor and the handicapped. Does the Church proclaim this with sufficient force? We are the Church, you and I." John Paul did not specify instances or persons responsible; here he preferred to call everyone to a sense of *community responsibility*, as he had in Calabria.

In his second pronouncement at Strasbourg, the Pope gave an address to the Parliament of Europe; his words this time were much more significant: "Medieval Latin Christendom, to mention only one example, while theoretically elaborating the natural concept of the State, following in the great tradition of Aristotle, did not always avoid the integralist temptation of excluding from the temporal community those who did not profess the true faith."⁷

In spite of his statement at Strasbourg, the Pope himself would be accused of "integralism," and precisely during his journey to Poland in 1991. He would once again make a declaration against such a stance during a discourse in defense of life. "The Church wants to participate in the life of society only as a witness to the Gospel. Today the tendency to ingratiate itself with any particular sector of public life is foreign to the Church. It is not possible to reconcile with Christian truth such a fanatical and fundamentalist attitude" (Olstyn, June 6, 1991).

In 1989, the Pope issued a statement on the participation of Christians in European wars. John Paul had already taken up this theme in 1983 and 1985, but this time he outlined his reflection in a document which commemorated the fiftieth anniversary of the outbreak of World War II. "We have just recalled one of the bloodiest wars in history, a war which broke out on a continent with a Christian tradition. Acknowledgment of this fact compels us to make an examination of conscience about the quality of Europe's evangelization."[8]

John Paul composed a lengthy "confession of sin" in the statement he made at the Orthodox Cathedral in Bialystok, Poland, on June 5, 1991: "We cannot fail to admit in all humility that in the past the spirit of evangelical brotherhood has not always prevailed.... There is fault on all sides, regardless of the degree, and it can be overcome by the acknowledgment of one's own culpability before the Lord and by mutual forgiveness."[9]

Finally, John Paul expressed his strongest request for pardon on his return from Santo Domingo in October 1992. In his statement he used the phrase, "act of atonement," words he had never used before.

> Through my pilgrimage to the place where evangelization began, a pilgrimage characterized by thanksgiving, we wanted at the same time to make an act of atonement before the infinite holiness of God for everything which, during that advance toward the American continent, was marred by sin, injustice and violence.... We do not cease asking these people for forgiveness. This request for pardon is primarily addressed to the first inhabitants of the new land, the Indians, and then to those who were brought from Africa as slaves to do heavy labor. "Forgive us our trespasses." This prayer is also part of evangelization.[10]

Thus, in the thirteen years from the reexamination of the Galileo case to the celebration marking the fifth centenary of the evangelization of America, John Paul made some twenty announcements of self-examination in the name of the Church.

Pope Wojtyła was following in the wake of the Second Vatican Council and Paul VI, making explicit what the Council had implied (as in the Galileo case); repeating the messages which the Fathers of the Council had addressed to various groups (Jews, Muslims, Orthodox and Protestant Churches); or adding new material (the Inquisition, integralism, the

Native Americans, the Africans, the Mafia, etc.) which had already been treated in general.

The Pope formulated practically all of the pronouncements during his journeys. This missionary Pope was taking responsibility in the name of the Church for the actions of those who had preceded him as the first evangelizers, carrying the same message to the nations. Perhaps if the Pope had not traveled, he would not have asked pardon on behalf of the Church.

*B*eginning with the year 1993, the evangelical self-examination, which the Pope called for at the end of the millennium, would no longer have a missionary tone. Instead, his appeal would be directed toward the Great Jubilee, and its theme would be penitential. This self-examination would not attempt to clear up the misunderstandings that grew out of the early preaching, or the mistakes of past history; it would instead concentrate on preparing, in a spirit of penance and reconciliation, for the passage from the second to the third millennium.

NOTES

1. L. Accattoli, *When a Pope Asks Forgiveness* (Boston: Pauline Books & Media, 1998), pp. 133–135.

2. Ibid., p. 172.

3. Ibid., p. 140.

4. Ibid., p. 202.

5. Ibid., p. 240.

6. Ibid., p. 161.

7. Ibid., p. 178.

8. Ibid., p. 142.

9. Ibid., p. 223.

10. Ibid., pp. 158–159.

❋ Chapter Fourteen ❋

Attempted Assassination

*B*lood shed as a result of violence is always a startling and traumatic event, but the most startling thing about the attempt on the Pope's life was that it took place in the midst of the usual crowd of people gathered in St. Peter's Square. The shocking image of the Holy Father lying prostrate, his white cassock stained with blood, has become symbolic of these times of international terrorism. It was the first time in modern history that a pope had become the target of physical violence. It was also the first time photos appeared in newspapers and magazines showing the Pope as a hospital patient in a dressing-gown or in his hospital bed, a bottle of water on the table beside him. As a result, people began to sense the dramatic nature of John Paul's pontificate, and they understood better the Pope as a man intimately connected with the turbulence of the times.

Wednesday, May 13, 1981, precisely 5:17 P.M. John Paul was warmly greeting and blessing some 30,000 pilgrims and tourists assembled in St. Peter's Square for the weekly papal audience. He moved slowly through the crowd in an open automobile that allowed him to reach out occasionally, to clasp an outstretched hand or take an infant in his arms. John Paul was completing his second tour around St. Peter's Square, and had just passed a two-year-old infant, Sara Bartoli, back into her mother's arms, when the unimaginable happened.

Present in the crowd at St. Peter's was Mehmet Ali Agca, a single twenty-three-year-old man, born in southeastern Turkey. A criminal condemned to death for murder, Agca had escaped from a military prison in Istanbul and was well known by police around the world as a professional terrorist. While the crowd in St. Peter's continued to reach out excitedly to touch the Pope, two shots rang from a nine-caliber Browning, hitting John Paul directly in the abdomen.

The gunshots drove the pigeons into the air. Before the terrified crowd had time to comprehend what had happened, the Pope's white car surged forward to one of the Square's exits. The Pope, bleeding heavily, was supported in the arms of his secretary, Father Stanisław Dziwisz, and now was surrounded by a protective wall of security officers. Reaching an emergency ambulance stationed nearby, the wounded Pope was quickly moved into the waiting ambulance; it then sped through the gate of Santa Ana. Attending the Pope were his personal physician, Dr. Renato Buzzonetti, a nurse, and Father Stanisław. It took eight minutes to reach Gemelli Hospital. The Pope remained alert and lost consciousness only when he was transferred to a stretcher at the hospital entrance.

Amid the confusion that ensued, the Pope was mistakenly taken to the tenth floor of the hospital and then rushed to the operating room downstairs. John Paul's pulse was barely perceptible. Father Stanisław began to administer the Anointing of the Sick, while an anesthesiologist slid the Pope's ring from his finger—6:00 P.M.

Surgeons began their work, which would last some five hours. When they opened the Pope's abdomen, they found blood everywhere. They had to cut and shorten the gastroenteric canal in the area damaged by the bullet, a classic case of military surgery. Chief surgeon Dr. Francesco Crucitti later told André Frossard: "There were perhaps six pints of blood. The bullet had gone through the sacrum after entering by the front wall of the abdomen.... But the essential organs, damage to which would have caused death, had only been grazed."[1]

By means of radio and television the world received fragmentary reports on the Pope's condition. A worldwide vigil began that lasted until the following Sunday, May 17, when Vatican Radio transmitted to the crowd waiting in St. Peter's Square a message recorded by the Pope. Speaking slowly, his voice clearly weakened, he said: "Pray for the brother who shot me and whom I have sincerely pardoned. United to Christ, Priest and Victim, I offer my sufferings for the Church and for the world."

Forensic experts of the Roman tribunal later concluded that Ali Agca had fired two shots from a distance of no more than 3.5 meters. He was standing to the right and slightly in front of the Pope's vehicle. The first bullet had struck the Pope in the abdomen, passing through his sacrum and then going on to strike an American tourist, Anne Odre, in the throat. The official report stated that if the bullet had not first passed through the Pope's abdomen, decreasing its velocity, it would certainly have killed Odre instantly.

A second bullet, which was fired at a higher trajectory than the first, fractured the Pope's index finger of his left hand as it was brought toward his abdomen. The bullet grazed the Pope's right arm above the elbow. It then struck the left arm of Rose Hall—another American tourist—who was standing to the left of Anne Odre.

The two women were rushed to a hospital near St. Peter's Square. The Pope, however, had been taken on the longer journey to Gemelli Hospital. Despite the Pope's condition, as Father Stanisław told André Frossard: "After his election, the Holy Father had said that if he ever needed medical attention, he was to be taken to a hospital like anyone else, and that the hospital could be the Gemelli."[2]

After the operation, the Pope spent the next few weeks confined to a small apartment, with a bedroom and a small waiting room, on the tenth floor of the hospital. By June 3, an apparently recovered John Paul was pressuring doctors to release him. Three days later, on June 6, the Feast of Pentecost, the Pope was back at St. Peter's Square to greet an ecumenical delegation which had come to Rome to celebrate the anniversaries of the Councils of Constantinople and Ephesus. The following week, however, the Pope was running a high fever caused by an infection from a blood transfusion. A medical bulletin, dated June 24, stated that it would take at least six weeks for the Pope to be rid of the infection.

On August 5 the Pope underwent a second surgery to close the temporary colostomy performed the day he was shot. A week later, John Paul left Gemelli Hospital to continue his convalescence at the papal summer villa at Castel Gandolfo. By October 4 John Paul's doctors declared him sufficiently recovered to celebrate Mass in St. Peter's Square.

The Pope's voice was as strong and clear as before the assassination attempt; his step was firm and energetic. John Paul was once again in charge, showing no sign of fear of another attempt on his life. Or at least he was determined not to let such a fear hold him back. After the liturgy, the Pope went down into the crowd as usual, shaking hands, caressing infants, consoling the sick, and blessing everyone. He had been advised against close contact with the crowd because of the possible danger, but he did not heed the advice. Perhaps he wanted to prove to himself and to the world (the Mass was televised worldwide), that despite the events of May 13, he was the same John Paul II.

On October 7, prior to the first papal audience since the attack, it was announced that, for security reasons, the audience would be held in one of the Vatican's halls. John Paul refused this precaution. Not only did he have the audience in St. Peter's Square; he also entered the square in his white Popemobile and toured it exactly as he had on May 13.

Was There a Conspiracy?

Meanwhile, after a trial in which the assailant's motives were never discovered, Mehmet Ali Agca was sentenced to prison on July 22, 1981, 70 days after the attack. Article 8 of the Concordat between Italy and the Holy See states that any attempt on the life of the pope is considered legally equivalent to an attempt on the life of a Head of State. Agca's sentence was read on September 24, stating that the attack was not the work of a single fanatic or a lone gunman. Rather, the crime was considered a complex plot orchestrated by unknown persons who were interested in "creating destabilization." However, the State has admitted that even to this day, insufficient evidence exists to prove others were involved in such a conspiracy.

Within the Vatican, many believed from the outset that the attack had been planned by a group of foreign agents and was not the work of one terrorist. Speaking at the Vatican on the feast of Saints Peter and Paul in 1981, the Secretary of State, Cardinal Agostino Casaroli, said:

> A heart (or is it hearts?), a hostile heart—and we pity it all the more in that we are not able to condemn it, seeing it so closed to the light of a love that has illuminated and warmed the world—armed, a hostile hand to strike, in the Pope (in *this* Pope!), the very heart of the Church; to try to silence a voice that was raised only to proclaim, with a courage born of love, the truth; to preach charity and justice; to announce peace! (June 29, 1981)

A great deal of speculation has arisen regarding possible accomplices of Mehmet Ali Agca. A British television station went so far as to assert that Vatican officials believed the Russian KGB had been involved in a plot against the Pope. According to this theory, the Polish Solidarity Movement, well known as being publicly supported by the Polish Pope, created a serious enough disturbance in Communist-dominated countries to lead the KGB to decide that John Paul must go. But Pierfrancesco Pastore, vice-director of the Vatican Press office, publicly denied the theory in a statement he made on September 5: "The Holy See has never expressed any hypothesis regarding any organization or country that may have ordered the attack on the Pope."

In the first investigation, Ali Agca claimed he had acted alone. Later, he admitted that three accomplices were present with him in St. Peter's Square: Oral Celik, Omer Ay, and Sedat Kadem. This group, the so-called "Bulgarian track," became the subject of a second investigation. And although this investigation never yielded sufficient proof to indict anyone else, the Italian public minister declared: "Agca did not act alone; he could not have acted alone. There was an accomplice, an organization that had recruited Agca and protected him."

NOTES

1. A. Frossard, *Portrait of John Paul II* (San Francisco: Ignatius Press, 1990), p. 237.

2. Ibid., p. 226.

CHAPTER FIFTEEN

Gratitude to the Madonna

*U*nder Pope Wojtyła, the Roman pontificate distanced itself from the regulations and structures of centuries-old traditions and returned to the spirit of adventure inherent in its "mission to the nations." John Paul II would like to see the entire Catholic Church swept up in this adventure. The missionary adventure also involves encountering the world, and mysteriously, the attempt on the Pope's life facilitated such an encounter. In a sense, the assassination attempt signifies a drama that summarizes his entire pontificate.

The preceding chapter followed John Paul to Gemelli Hospital after he was shot by Mehmet Ali Agca. Now, we return to the scene of the shooting to look more closely at what happened in St. Peter's Square.

Not a single trace or reminder of the attempted assassination remains in the Square. When John Paul returned there five months after the shooting, he celebrated the Eucharist. In a sense, with this gesture he "repossessed" the Square and removed from it any lingering sense of taboo.

On the anniversary of the attempt on the Pope's life, *L'Osservatore Romano* recalled the event in solemn tones and with rhetoric that did not echo Pope Wojtyła's sentiments. In fact, John Paul often spoke with irony when directly or indirectly referring to the attack. For example, Cardinal Albert Decourtray of France told the Pope that people in France were talking about the prophecies of *Nostradamus*—and warning against the Pope's trip to Lyons planned for October 1986. The Pope responded: "I assure you, Your Eminence, there is no place more dangerous than St. Peter's Square!"

An official Vatican report on the assassination attempt does not exist, and there has been no attempt to investigate it. The Pope has always spoken of the event from a spiritual perspective. Documentation of the case issued by the Italian court includes this official statement promulgated at the conclusion of the court proceedings:

> By a sentence handed down on July 22, 1981, the *Prima Corte di Assise* at Rome condemned the Turkish citizen, Mehmet Ali Agca, to life imprisonment, with solitary confinement for a period of a year, for having committed an act of terrorism in St. Peter's Square on May 13, 1981, by an attempt on the life of the Sovereign Pontiff John Paul II, shooting him several times with a nine-caliber Browning pistol, inflicting wounds on the person of the Pontiff and, through an error in the use of the gun, wounding also two citizens of the United States, Anne Odre and Rose Hall.

Agca's attempt led the Vatican to take greater security measures for John Paul's safety, and this heightened security was evident on October 4, 1981, when the Pope first returned to St. Peter's Square. The entire perimeter of the colonnade was secured; people had to pass through metal detectors to enter the Square; media representatives had to identify themselves to the police. Still, the Pope refused to be kept at a safe distance from any crowd. John Paul not only resumed his custom of moving freely around the Square, but he continued to travel in and out of Rome, and even around the world.

One of the most obvious changes to the Pope's public audiences was the use of a new Popemobile—a special vehicle equipped with bulletproof windows—which the Pope has been using for outdoor transportation since 1981. It has been said that the Popemobile is like a modern-day papal throne, and like the papal throne, the Popemobile makes it difficult for the Pope to mingle with the people. While John Paul is effectively shielded from possible threats of terrorism, he is also separated from the crowds he loves.

The attempted assassination has heightened the awareness that the Pope faces constant danger each time he leaves the Vatican. Certainly, the threat existed before, at least theoretically. Paul VI ran the risk of being crushed by the crowd in Jerusalem in 1964, and was also the target of an attack in Manila in 1970. But no one would ever have imagined a life-threatening incident occurring in St. Peter's Square. At least this was the opinion Vatican personnel expressed. In an interview with the newspaper *Messaggero*, Cardinal Carlo Confalonieri, dean of the College of Cardinals, stated: "The predominant reaction was one of shock at such a deed: violence to the Pope!"

The attack has also increased the Pope's already overwhelming popularity. Because he has shed his blood, John Paul's words and actions seem to hold even more weight. Consider, for example, the magnified impact of his words when he speaks out against terrorism and violence. Paul VI had written a letter to the Red Army Brigade in April 1978, and John Paul had spoken against violence during the Christmas season of 1980 ("men of violence—they are also my brothers"). Perhaps what was still needed for the Church's message to be taken seriously and become even more relevant was for a pope to give testimony in blood.

The attack had yet another effect: it confirmed John Paul's teaching with respect to our responsibility to share in the suffering of others. The Pope continually visits hospitals and the sick, both when in Rome and during international travels. But it must have been an intensely emotional moment when, as a patient himself, the Pope visited the sick of Gemelli Hospital. After he was discharged the second time, John Paul could say: "Now I know better than before that suffering is a dimension of life in which, more profoundly than ever, the grace of redemption takes hold of the human heart" (Aug. 14, 1981). One of the most personal documents the Pope ever composed is the apostolic letter *Salvifici Doloris* (On the Christian Meaning of Human Suffering), which he promulgated on February 11, 1984.

*J*ohn Paul's stay in Gemelli Hospital gave him ample time to reflect on doctor/patient relationships, and he would occasionally return to this topic in later addresses to the sick and to doctors. Interestingly, during the 77 days he spent in the hospital, there were at least two occasions when the Pope disagreed with his medical team. Both times he managed to persuade doctors to consent to his wishes: first, when John Paul wanted to leave the hospital on June 3 and they advised against it; and second, when he rejected their plan to postpone a second operation until October. Dr. Crucitti recounted the Pope's insistence on undergoing the operation sooner. John Paul reminded the medical team: "Don't forget that although you are the doctors, I am the patient, and I must make known to you my medical problems, above all this one: I should not return to the Vatican until I am completely cured. I feel I am absolutely in a position to endure another operation."

The effects of the attack on the person of Karol Wojtyła are unfathomable to the observer. When he resumed his public activity, the Pope dedicated his first five General Audiences to "the content of my meditations during that period in which I participated in a great divine trial."[1] During the first General Audience of Wednesday, October 7, John Paul described the incident recorded in the Acts of the Apostles. The scene in Acts takes place while St. Peter is imprisoned and an angel of the Lord is sent to rescue him from the hand of Herod (cf. Acts 12:3–11). The Pope then explained:

> I have quoted this passage...because of the words which we find in it and which gave me so much support in that period. While "Peter was kept in prison...earnest prayer for him was made to God by the Church" (Acts 12:31). I experienced, dear brothers and sisters, in a way similar to Peter who was confined and destined for death, the efficacy of the prayers of the Church.... For this prayer I am grateful to my brothers and sisters. I am grateful to Christ the Lord and to the Holy Spirit.... With deep gratitude to the Holy Spirit, I am thinking of the weakness which he deigned to let me experience on the thirteenth of May, believing and humbly trusting that it has served for the strengthening of the Church and of my human person.

There can be no doubt that John Paul received a strengthening of faith and the grace for an even greater dedication to his mission, far beyond the mere limits of human prudence. We can glimpse something of this strengthening of faith when John Paul visited Ali Agca in maximum security prison on December 27, 1983. The visit expressed in action the pardon which the Pope had already verbally extended. It also gave a sense of closure to the final scene of the attempted assassination drama.

Images from that unprecedented meeting flashed across television screens around the world. Agca, with his black hair closely cropped and stubble on his face, wore a pale blue sweater. On the right side of his small cell there was a cot; on the left, standing opposite the doorway, were placed two chairs.

Mehmet Ali Agca greeted the Pope by bowing deeply—in a manner nearly resembling a genuflection—before John Paul. The Pope offered his right hand; Ali Agca took it and bent over to kiss it. Then, in an Islamic gesture signifying respect and trust, Ali Agca pressed his forehead against the back of the Pope's hand.

During the brief meeting the two men sat closely together. At the beginning of the visit, John Paul lightly tapped Ali Agca's knee with his right hand and nodded his head as if to say: "Now, let's talk." The guard left them alone and returned after 20 minutes, signaling the visit's end. When journalists later questioned him about the meeting, the Pope replied: "What we spoke about is a secret between us. I spoke to him as I would to a brother whom I have pardoned and who enjoys my trust."

Looking back on the assassination attempt, John Paul revealed to André Frossard that he had not been afraid that he would die on the way from St. Peter's Square to Gemelli Hospital. This confidence stemmed "not from courage, but because at the very moment when I fell in St. Peter's Square, I had this vivid presentiment that I would be saved. This certainty never left me, even at the worst moments, after the first operation and during the virus infection. One hand fired, but another one guided the bullet."[2]

The Mercy of God, the Nearness of Mary

The hand that saved him was the hand of God's mercy; and for John Paul, God's mercy has a personality and is experienced as nearness to God. As soon as the Pope was able to leave Rome, he visited the Sanctuary of Merciful Love at Collevalenza in Todi to give thanks. "My personal experiences this year, together with the events on May 13, make me cry out: We owe it to the mercy of God that we are not dead."

The mercy of God has taken on a maternal face as well, the face of Mary. John Paul made two pilgrimages of thanksgiving to the Madonna on both the first and the tenth anniversaries of the attack, and both pilgrimages were to Fatima.

> ...When I was wounded by gunshots fired in St. Peter's Square, at first I did not pay attention to the fact that the assassination attempt had occurred on the exact anniversary of the day Mary appeared to the three children at Fatima...and spoke to them the words that now, at the end of this century, seem to be close to their fulfillment.[3]

Mary is always present in John Paul's spiritual life, and there is always a Marian dimension to his prayer. This in no way conflicts with the strong Christocentric focus in his theology, however. His primary focus on Christ emerges clearly in the statement John Paul made when he accepted his election, in the discourse at the beginning of his pontificate, and in the theme of his first encyclical, *Redemptor Hominis*.

The Pope explained to author Vittorio Messori how his thought has developed: *"Totus Tuus.* This phrase is not only an expression of piety, or simply an expression of devotion. It is more. During the Second World War, while I was employed as a factory worker, I came to be attracted to Marian devotion. At first, it had seemed to me that I should distance myself a bit from the Marian devotion of my childhood, in order to focus more on Christ. Thanks to St. Louis de Montfort, *I came to understand that true devotion to the Mother of God is actually Christocentric; indeed, it is very profoundly rooted in the mystery of the Blessed Trinity* and the mysteries of the Incarnation and Redemption."[4]

The autobiography, *Gift and Mystery*, contains a complete summation of John Paul's Marian piety; in it John Paul refers to the Marian thread that has run through and united the phases of his spiritual formation. And in his book, *Crossing the Threshold of Hope*, the Pope refers to chapter 8 of *Lumen Gentium* (The Dogmatic Constitution on the Church) as an excellent statement of the Christological orientation of Marian devotion: "When I participated in the Council, I found reflected in this chapter all my earlier youthful experiences, as well as those special bonds which continue to unite me to the Mother of God in ever new ways."[5]

The fruitful results of integrating Marian elements within the Christological focus of his spirituality can be seen in the innovations the Pope introduced to his papacy during its early years:

❖ At the weekly Angelus message on October 29, 1978, John Paul described the rosary as "my favorite prayer," and five months later he began reciting the rosary on Vatican Radio every first Saturday of the month;

❖ On December 2, 1981, he inaugurated perpetual adoration in the Blessed Sacrament chapel of St. Peter's Basilica;

❖ For Christmas that same year, he had a huge Christmas crib set up inside the Basilica and, in 1982, he had an outdoor crib placed next to the Christmas tree in St. Peter's Square.

The Pope also introduced the following:

❖ He placed a plaque of the Madonna on a wall in the courtyard of St. Damasus, visible from St. Peter's Square. On June 28 he said to the Curia: "Starting this year, a beautiful Marian image looks down from the Apostolic Palace on the crowds who come to this center of Christianity to pray and to 'see Peter'";

❖ On March 25, Feast of the Annunciation to Mary, he began the custom of ringing the bell in St. Peter's every day at noon to invite pilgrims and tourists to pray the Angelus;

❖ He restored the feast of Saints Peter and Paul, co-patrons of the city of Rome, to June 29 rather than on the following Sunday;

❖ He restored the practice of a *Corpus Christi* procession in Rome, which makes its way from the basilica of St. John Lateran to the basilica of St. Mary Major, to the day of the feast rather than on the following Sunday.

These are a few of the Pope's initiatives during the years 1978 to 1982, but they suffice to illustrate John Paul's spirituality as well as his pastoral commitment to combine the liturgical changes introduced by Paul VI with traditional popular devotion. Also worthy of mention are the Extraordinary Holy Year of Redemption in 1983 and the Marian Year of June 1987 to August 1988.

The phrase *Totus Tuus* also expresses John Paul's spontaneous desire to entrust everything to Mary's intercession. The following prayer to the Mother of God, which the Pope gave at the end of his 1988 Easter message, reinforces this:

> Pray for the whole world, for all of humanity, for all peoples! Pray for peace in the world, for justice! Pray for the rights of man, especially for freedom of religion for every man, Christian and non-Christian! Pray for the solidarity of people of the whole world, the First and the Third, the Second and the Fourth!

The Pope made these extemporaneous remarks during the closing days of the Marian Year; they sum up the entire pontificate of John Paul. When a particular thought predominates in a person's life, it manifests itself in spontaneous outbursts such as these. And here we see a concrete expression of Pope Wojtyła's Mariology: everything can be entrusted to Mary because she is the "sign of the woman" spoken of in the Book of Revelation. She is the sign of salvation for the history of the world.

John Paul continually refers all things to Mary, to the "sign of the woman" which should dominate history and especially our own times. This reference to Mary is not only expressed in words; it is also expressed in the Pope's many acts of piety. Oftentimes, John Paul's invocations reflect a language of poetry more than of prayer. Perhaps a study of the unique language John Paul uses in his prayer is called for, a study which no one, to my knowledge, has attempted thus far.

In suggesting such a study I rely, above all, on a declaration Cardinal Ratzinger made when he presented the encyclical *Redemptoris Mater* (Mother of the Redeemer) to the media and announced the Marian Year:

> The Marian Year signifies that the Pope wishes to maintain within our present historical moment "the sign of the Woman" as the essential "sign of the time"; on the path indicated by this sign we proceed in the footsteps of hope towards Christ, who leads history through her who indicates the way.

It is possible that even Cardinal Ratzinger finds it difficult to understand John Paul's profound intuition.

"The sign of the woman"—that is, the sign promised to our first parents in the words addressed to the serpent, "I will put enmity between you and the woman" (Gn 3:15)—is more fully revealed in the Book of Revelation. This prophetic text speaks of the "sign of the woman" as a great sign in the sky; the woman is pursued by the devil but is ultimately victorious over him. Cardinal Ratzinger continues: "The last book of the New Testament speaks expressly of 'the sign of the woman,' who, at a determined moment of history, rises above it, to reconcile heaven and earth from that moment onwards. The sign of the woman is the sign of hope. She is the one who shows us the pathway of hope."

The Pope intends to direct us toward this hope. The Marian Year and John Paul's continual invocations to Mary; his *Totus Tuus*; the consecration to Mary and the pilgrimages; the emphasis on Fatima and Jasna Gora—all of these are meant to highlight for our era "the sign of the woman," that is, the hope of victory over the serpent; the triumph of blessing over curse and of good over evil. John Paul communicates this by blending new words and ancient gestures, in conformity with Catholic pedagogy handed down in the Roman tradition. The Marian Year was meant to reemphasize for everyone the message of the encyclical, *Redemptoris Mater*.

*T*he "sign of the woman" also refers to *woman*, to the women of our time. It directs our attention to woman as the guardian of love and the fruit of love; to woman who gives birth to man and to whom man is entrusted. And here we touch another level of depth in John Paul, although somewhat obscure and implicit. The topic is discussed more fully in Chapter 20 when we speak of the "theology of the body" and the "theology of woman."

NOTES

1. *Catechesi della sofferenza*, "I testi delle prime cinque udienze genereali successive all'attentato del 13 maggio 1981." Libreria Editrice Vaticana, 1982.

2. A. Frossard, *Portrait of John Paul II* (San Francisco: Ignatius Press, 1990), p. 251.

3. John Paul II with Vittorio Messori, *Crossing the Threshold of Hope* (New York: Alfred A. Knopf, 1994), p. 221.

4. Ibid., pp. 212–213.

5. Ibid., p. 214.

❧ CHAPTER SIXTEEN ❧

Promotion of Solidarity

*F*or ten years John Paul defended Poland against the Soviet threat—from the first trip back to his fatherland in 1979 to the elections of 1989—and his efforts finally helped to bring about a Polish government under the direction of Tadeusz Mazowiecki, a Catholic. Mazowiecki received the congratulations and best wishes of Soviet President Mikhail Gorbachev. But before signing any congratulatory message, Gorbachev—during a tumultuous meeting of the leaders of the Warsaw Alliance—had to reject the Romanian proposal for a military intervention in Poland similar to that used in Czechoslovakia in 1968.

The ten-year struggle leading to the fall of Communism was, in great measure, thanks to the influence of John Paul II. Wojtyła lived out the drama of a man who as Pope undoubtedly had the power to help his country. But he had to keep his distance so as not to involve the Church in a Polish question that was not, strictly speaking, its concern.

As painful as that drama may have been for Wojtyła, it provided a providential historical circumstance, which hastened Eastern Europe's peaceful exodus from Soviet domination. Moreover, it restored to the papacy the right to love one's native country—something Italian popes always renounced as a long-standing tradition of papal asceticism and neutrality. In fact, when addressing his fellow Italians, Pius XII had even reached the point of referring to Italy as "your fatherland."[1]

Only rarely did John Paul display any signs of the personal anxiety he was living. Rather, he always gave the impression of strongly identifying with the destiny of his fatherland and of firmly resolving not to abandon Poland in its hour of need. In the early 1980s, he showed impatience with the expression "the Polish Pope," when some used it as a reproach for his passionate patriotism. I recall a meeting with workers at Livorno, Italy, in 1982, when he began by saying: "I am not going to speak to you about Poland!"

On another occasion he received in private audience his friend Tadeusz Mazowiecki, the first Catholic to head the Polish government after World War II. In response to the gratitude Mazowiecki expressed "for the support you have given us in recent years," John Paul responded: "I think that if I have done anything in this regard, I have done it as part of my universal mission; and that is the way it should be seen."

Years of Suffering and Prayer

A number of key moments reveal John Paul's broad influence (both direct and indirect) on Poland's political liberation from Communism.

- ❖ August 31, 1980: The signing of the protocol of Danzig, from which the Solidarity Movement officially emerged. That day, as on all the other days of the strike, the Liturgy was celebrated in the morning. A huge picture of Our Lady of Czestochowa, and a poster of Pope John Paul, were hanging on the fence.

- ❖ December 25, 1980: When leaving the church after midnight Mass in Warsaw, groups of young people shouted in unison: "Long live John Paul II, king of Poland!"

- ❖ January 19, 1981: John Paul received in audience Lech Wałesa, the leader of Solidarity, and stated publicly: "There does not exist and there should not exist any contradiction between an autonomous social initiative such as Solidarity and the structure of a system that pertains to labor."

- ❖ March 28, 1981: At the peak of a season dominated by the threat of Soviet intervention, John Paul sent a telegram to Cardinal Wyszynski, who was critically ill. The message contained this statement: "The Polish people have an inalienable right to solve their problems by themselves, by their own power." On the following day, at the Angelus message, John Paul repeated this same principle and he referred to the Helsinki Charter, which rejects all forms of interference in another nation's affairs—a document signed by Russia and the Holy See. That day, John Paul sent a letter to Soviet leader Leonid Brezhnev. Although the contents were never publicized, it is commonly believed that the message was a reminder to Brezhnev of the Helsinki agreement.[2] A little over a month later, the attempt was made on the Pope's life, and Cardinal Wyszynski died on May 28.

❖ Finally, on December 13, 1981, a state of siege was declared in Poland and John Paul spoke about it in his Angelus message: "The events in the last few hours now induce me to ask everyone once more to pray for our country. I recall what I said in September: no more Polish blood can be shed because too much has already been shed, especially during the Second World War. Everything possible must be done to construct the future of our country peacefully. In view of the forthcoming jubilee of Our Lady of Czestochowa, I recommend Poland and all my fellow countrymen to her who is given to the nation as its defense."

❖ August 26, 1982: The six-hundredth anniversary of the shrine of Our Lady of Czestochowa was celebrated. An empty seat marked the Pope's absence. His second planned visit was postponed upon the insistence of the Polish government.

❖ October 10, 1982: Pope John Paul canonized Maximilian Kolbe as a martyr in St. Peter's Square. Back in Poland the celebration was intense, almost as if to make up for martial law restrictions. Just four days before the canonization, the government officially dissolved Solidarity.

❖ December 29, 1982: The Soviet news agency *Tass* accused John Paul of fomenting subversive activity in Communist countries, being responsible for the political crisis in Poland, and promoting anti-Communist propaganda on a vast scale.

❖ June 16–23, 1983: John Paul's second visit to Poland took place, which he began with these words: "My cry will be the cry of the entire fatherland!" The country was still under martial law and his every word had to be carefully chosen. Each time the Pope used the word "solidarity," there was enthusiastic applause, tantamount to a public demonstration. In addressing government officials, John Paul clarified his attitude as a Pole and as Pope: "I will continue to consider as my own every true good of my homeland, as though I were still living in this land, and perhaps even more, because of the distance. With the same strength I shall also continue to feel the effects of what could threaten Poland, what could do her damage, or bring her dishonor, what could signify stagnation or a depression" (June 16, 1983).

❖ June 8–14, 1987: The Pope's third visit to Poland. The situation was more peaceful because, during the preceding two years, Gorbachev had introduced much needed reforms. John Paul greeted the people as follows: "O land of Poland! Land severely tested! Beautiful land! My land! Blessed may you be! Accept my greeting! I salute you, my fellow countrymen, you who know the joy and the suffering of living in this land!" On the last day of his third visit, John Paul addressed the episcopate and explained how the Church had reacted to the challenge of Communism and what he personally had done:

> After a thousand years, Christianity in Poland ought to accept the challenge that is contained in the ideology of dialectic Marxism, which classifies every religion as an alienating factor for man. We know that challenge. I myself have experienced it here in this land. The Church is experiencing it in various places around the globe. It is a very profound challenge.... It can also be a destructive challenge. But after years of experience, we cannot fail to note that it could also have been a challenge that has deeply prompted Christians to integrate their efforts to find new solutions. In this sense it becomes in a certain way a creative challenge, of which the Second Vatican Council is an eloquent witness. The Church has accepted the challenge and has seen in it a providential sign of the times. By means of this sign, with a new depth and strength of conviction, the Church has given witness to the truth about God, about Christ, and about man, against all the reductionism of an epistemological or systematic nature, against all dialectical materialism (June 14, 1987).

To have some idea of the determination with which John Paul carried on this ten-year struggle, it suffices to recall the courage he showed by visiting Poland in June 1983, while the country was still under martial law. Back in December 1981, on the day after the declaration of a state of siege, the French newspaper *Le Monde* had criticized the Vatican's cautious reaction and insisted that the Pope should have gone to Poland. Contrary to all the rules of papal diplomacy, John Paul's second visit took place during the state of siege. This time, the Pope's courage measured up to the media's demand.

John Paul certainly did not expect the fall of Communism to occur during his pontificate; he admitted as much on several occasions. Once the Holy Father told André Frossard a joke which reflects this:

> The Pope was praying, and he asked God:
> "Lord, will Poland regain her freedom and independence some day?"
> "Yes," said God, "but not in your lifetime."

Then the Pope asked: "Lord, after I'm gone, will there be another Polish pope?"

"Not in my lifetime," said God.[3]

However, the Pope had no doubt that eventually Communism would indeed meet its end. After the iron curtain finally fell, the Pope spoke of Communism as "an incident lasting fifty years," one that could never compare with "the thousand years of Slav Christianity." And, in another remark he made some eight years before, he said: "The military regime has existed since December; the Virgin of Czestochowa, for 600 years."

We know very little even today about the Communist regime's reaction to the election of John Paul II. We can imagine it contradicted the Russian author Aleksandr Solzhenitsyn's enthusiastic response: "The election of Pope Wojtyła is the only good thing that has happened to humanity in the twentieth century!"[4]

The "Bogomolov Report" (commissioned by the Soviet Politburo and submitted November 4, 1978, nineteen days after the conclave) offered advice regarding official relations with the new Pope:

> According to Catholics at a high level, the election of a Polish cardinal will do much to promote the worldwide impact of the Church; that is, its activity in all the socio-political systems, and especially the socialist types.... It is possible that, on the Vatican's part, this dialogue will take on a more systematic and aggressive character than it had under Paul VI. It can be predicted that Wojtyła will be less disposed to compromise with socialist governments, especially in matters pertaining to local churches.[5]

The Kremlin lost no time in its evaluation, but the suggestions Oleg Bogomolov submitted were not implemented. As far as negotiations went between the Polish government officials and the Vatican pertaining to John Paul's first visit to Poland, Brezhnev told Edward Gierek, secretary of the Communist Party in Poland, to "close the borders" to the Pope. It is said that Gierek objected, asking how he could refuse to receive a Polish pope when the majority of his fellow citizens were Catholic. Brezhnev, showing that he failed to grasp the significance of a Polish pope, replied: "Wladyslaw Gomulka [former Communist leader in Poland] was a far better Communist than you, because he did not permit Paul VI to enter Poland, and nothing terrible happened."[6]

One year after Bogomolov offered his advice to the Communist government, the central committee of the Soviet Communist Party adopted devious measures. The "Suslov Resolution" concentrated on the actions

of those in Vatican circles working for peace and on dissemination of
material denouncing the "dangerous tendencies" of John Paul II. These
and other schemes yielded no more results than similar tactics employed
during the time of Pope Pius XII.[7]

NOTES

1. J. Offredo, *Jean-Paul II* (Paris: Editions Carrière-Michel Lafon, 1986), p. 352.

2. C. Bernstein, M. Politi, *Sua Santità* (Milan: Rizzoli, 1996), pp. 252, 267; and M.
Malinski, *Le radici di Papa Wojtyła* (Rome: Borla Editore, 1979), p. 221.

3. A. Frossard, *Portrait of John Paul II* (San Francisco: Ignatius Press, 1990), p. 46.

4. L. Di Schiena, Karol Wojtyła (Rome: Editalia, 1991), p. 54.

5. *La Stampa,* Turin, Italy, April 23, 1993.

6. C. Bernstein and M. Politi, *Sua Santità* (Milan: Rizzoli, 1996), p. 199.

7. *La Stampa,* Turin, Italy, April 23, 1993.

❖ Chapter Seventeen ❖

The Missionary Pope

*D*uring the first twenty years of his pontificate, John Paul made over eighty-five trips outside and 132 within Italy. He visited 116 different countries and 252 distinct localities in Italy. His constant traveling is the most visible and original aspect of his pontificate. Perhaps it is also the most widely discussed, for John Paul uses his pastoral visits and pilgrimages to communicate with the masses, and as a way of governing the Church.

First of all, there is John Paul's visibility. The time and energy this Pope spends in traveling certainly speaks for itself. To date, he has spent nearly one year and a half of his pontificate on international trips alone. These journeys are impressive signs of the Catholic Church's presence both in the media and on the world scene. No other man in the world has been seen in person by so many people and in such vast crowds as John Paul II. And no other man or woman in the world has been able to attract and hold the attention of the media, both international and national, as has this traveling Pope.

Then, there is the originality of his travels. Although papal journeys around the world are not unique—Pius VI and Pius VII traveled extensively during the Napoleonic era; Pius IX traveled in an effort to prevent the dissolution of the Papal State; Paul VI traveled widely after the Second Vatican Council—John Paul's methods are quite different. He is not merely an occasional traveler; he travels methodically and as if by vocation. With the pastoral intention of visiting every local church, John Paul has systematically scheduled missionary journeys throughout the worldwide Catholic community. Pope Paul VI's nine international journeys were symbolic and intended as the beginning or resumption of contacts and dialogue with our separated brethren, with the Jewish people, with the international community, and with diverse peoples and continents. The eighty-five international journeys of John Paul, on the other hand, are part of his universal mission to all nations, his way of exercising his "Petrine ministry" and of promoting the re-evangelization of the world.

T he independent nations of the world now number 200, and the Pope has visited three out of every five of these countries. Between 1978 and 1998 he visited thirty of these countries more than once. He has gone twice to Argentina, Australia, Belgium, Benin, Cameroon, Canada, Croatia, El Salvador, Guatemala, Nicaragua, Nigeria, New Guinea, Peru, Philippines, Portugal, Slovakia, South Korea, Switzerland, Hungary, Uruguay, Venezuela, Zaire. Three times he has traveled to Austria, Brazil, Czech Republic, Dominican Republic, Ivory Coast, Germany, Kenya, Mexico. Finally, he has gone four times to Spain, five times to the United States, six times to France, and seven times to Poland.

In Italy, the Pope has gone once or twice to Brescia, Genoa, Milan, Naples, Reggio Calabria, Siena, Treviso; three times to Bologna; four times to Loreto and Turin; and five times to Assisi.

The longest international journeys the Pope made were to Uruguay, Chile and Argentina in 1987, and to the Far East (Bangladesh, Singapore, Fiji, New Zealand, Australia, Seychelles) in 1986. His longest stay in any one nation was in Brazil, which has the largest number of bishops and baptized Catholics; John Paul spent thirteen days there in 1980. His longest visits to local churches in Italy were in Emilia-Romagna (five days in 1988) and Naples (five days in 1990). On an average, John Paul has made four international journeys each year, although none were made in 1981 due to the injuries he sustained during the attempt on his life, and in 1994, because of a fractured femur in his right thigh.

In forty-four European journeys Pope Wojtyła has visited almost all of the countries in Western Europe, including Liechtenstein, Malta, and San Marino. He has yet to visit Andorra, Gibraltar, and Monaco. He has not been able to visit the Eastern European countries of Belarus, Bulgaria, Greece, Romania, Russia, Serbia, or the Ukraine. John Paul has been to the Americas nineteen times and has visited all the countries except Guyana, Suriname, and some small countries in the Antilles. He has made twelve trips to Africa and seven to Asia and Oceania.

John Paul has traveled around the world the equivalent of twenty-five times, but thus far he has not been able to visit Jerusalem, Moscow,

China, Vietnam or Northern Ireland. In the Middle East he has visited only Lebanon, but he plans to go to Bethlehem and Jerusalem for the Great Jubilee and, beyond that, he would like to include Iraq and Syria, Egypt and Jordan, in his pilgrimage to the biblical lands of Abraham, Moses, and Jesus.

The Pope had hoped to go to Northern Ireland in 1979 when he visited Catholic Ireland. He actually got as far as Drogheda in Ulster, but was advised to go no further lest his visit provoke violence instead of peace. As for the countries under Communist domination, he has visited some small African countries under Marxist-Leninist rule (1980 and 1982), and Cuba (1998). Since the fall of Communism, he has been able to visit Albania (1993), Lithuania and Estonia (1993), Croatia (1994 and 1998), the Czech Republic and Slovakia (1995), Slovenia (1996) and Sarajevo (1997). Perhaps one day he will visit Moscow.

Of course, at present the Pope is also unable to visit China and Vietnam, although when he was in Manila and Seoul he did "knock on the door," where there was no answer. Perhaps one of his greatest disappointments has been the restriction from entering Vietnam, an Asian country with the largest Catholic population after the Philippines.

All types of things have happened during the Pope's travels. Several times he has found himself in the midst of a state of siege: Argentina (1982), El Salvador (1983), Guatemala (1983), Timor (1989), Sarajevo, and Beirut (1997). He entered into discussion with the Sandinistas at Managua, Nicaragua. A traditionalist priest tried to attack him at Fatima (1982). During a Mass in Santiago, Chile, there was a disturbance in which teargas fumes reached the altar (1987). In São Paolo, Brazil (1980), and at Asunción, Paraguay (1988), a meeting with workers evolved into a demonstration against the dictatorships of these two countries.

Sometimes the weather has inadvertently caused some excitement or anxiety. During a flight from Botswana to Lesotho, Africa, the plane was forced to land at Johannesburg, and the Pope then traveled 4 hours across the savanna by car. In 1984, a snowstorm in Canada prevented a landing at Fort Simpson (located near the Arctic Circle), where the Pope was scheduled to meet with Eskimos. Returning from India in 1986, the Pope's plane landed at Naples because a heavy snowstorm had forced the airport in Rome to close. The Pope reached Rome on the following day—by train.

On a flight from Puerto Rico to Rome in 1984, when John Paul was asked how he could stand such a grueling traveling schedule, the Pope replied: "It's better not to think about it and just do it." In spite of the removal of a tumor from his colon in 1992, and the onset of a tremor in his left hand the following year, the Pope still recovers quickly from the fatigue of traveling.

During the long flight from Lima, Peru, to Rome in 1985, a journalist asked the Pope how he managed not to feel exhausted after such a trip. John Paul simply replied: "It's a wonder to me also."

John Paul told the children of a Roman parish that it has always been the most natural thing in the world for him to travel: "Ever since I was a boy I was a great hiker. Then I became a great traveler, and I hope to continue to be one" (Feb. 18, 1996).

Once, during a visit to St. Benedict's Parish in Rome, an altar boy named Alessandro Monno asked the Pope: "Why do you always travel around the world?" The Pope replied: "Because the whole world is not here! Have you read what Jesus said? 'Go and evangelize the whole world.' And so I go to the whole world."

In *Redemptoris Missio* (Mission of the Redeemer) John Paul says: "I feel that the moment has come to dedicate all the forces of the Church to the new evangelization and the mission to the nations." And during a General Audience on March 10, 1993, he said: "Since the Bishop of Rome is the primary herald of the faith, he has the primary responsibility for the spread of the faith throughout the world."

Among the members of the Roman Curia, the most common criticism of the Pope's journeys at the beginning of his pontificate had to do with their number and frequency. Some Curia members considered such trips excessive. John Paul acknowledges their objection, and even considers it a reasonable one, but, as he affirms, his traveling is an excess "suggested" by divine Providence.

John Paul II enroute....

A customary gesture of John Paul II
upon arrival at each country he visits.

PILGRIM OF THE GOSPEL

☙

Pastoral Visits of John Paul II

1979
Dominican
  Republic
Mexico
Bahamas
Poland
Ireland
United States
Turkey

1980
Zaire
Congo
Kenya
Ghana
Burkina Faso
Ivory Coast
France
Brazil
Germany

1981
Pakistan
Philippines
United States
Japan

1982
Nigeria
Benin
Gabon
Equatorial
  Guinea
Portugal
Great Britain
Brazil
Argentina
Switzerland
San Marino
Spain

AZ, PERO NO A COSTA DE LA

Pastoral Visits of John Paul II

1995
Philippines
Papua-New
  Guinea
Australia
Sri Lanka
Czech
  Republic
Poland
Belgium
Slovakia
Cameroon
Republic of
  South Africa
Kenya
United States

1996
Guatemala
Nicaragua
El Salvador
Venezuela
Tunisia
Slovenia
Germany
Hungary
France

1997
Bosnia–
  Herze-
  govina
Czech
  Republic
Lebanon
Poland
France
Brazil

1998
Cuba
Nigeria
Austria
Croatia

1999
Mexico
United States
Romania
Poland
Slovenia
India
Georgia

The opening of the Holy Year on March 25, 1983.

CLEMENS·X·PONT·MAX·
ANNO·IVBILEI·MDCLXV·

The Pope listens to the concerns of mine workers in Bolivia.

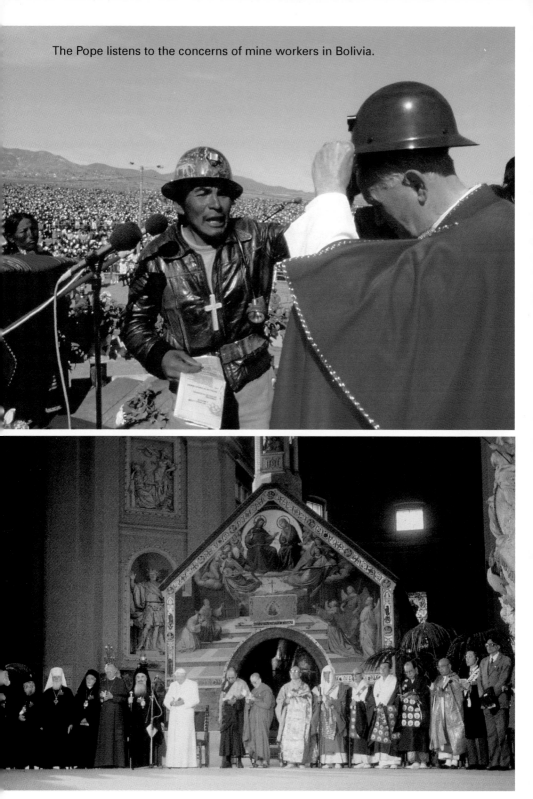

Assisi, 1986. The Pope and representatives from various world religions gather for the first time in history on the occasion of the World Day of Prayer for Peace.

The Pope draws crowds of young people wherever he goes (Sicily, 1993).

CHAPTER EIGHTEEN

The Pope's Frequent Travels

*J*ohn Paul II goes far beyond the boundaries dictated by Vatican tradition, and this has created an image that lies at the very heart of his pontificate. He steps beyond these boundaries with full awareness. He justifies what some view as excess, daring, risk, and provocation (words used to describe John Paul's "departure" from the path of his predecessors) by referring to the particular situations or needs of the moment. In occasional disagreements with members of the Curia, who encourage him to follow the "golden way" of the Italian popes, he always invokes the "suggestion of divine Providence."

Significantly, the first conflict between the Pope and the Curia arose precisely because of the frequency of his trips. Since that time, the Pope has often defended his decision in interviews and in discourses to the Curia. He responds to their criticism by indicating the importance of his journeys in the light of the apostolic constitution for the reform of the Curia, and by referring to the apostolic letter, *Tertio Millennio Adveniente.*

Of all the available texts on this topic, the best organized and the lengthiest is the Pope's discourse to the Curia in June 1982. But perhaps the one that best reveals the spirit of John Paul is an interview broadcast by Vatican Radio and published in *L'Osservatore Romano* on June 13, 1980. The interview took place shortly after the Pope's return from a visit to France, a month after his ten-day visit to Africa. He was in the process of preparing to leave for a thirteen-day visit to Brazil. Critics claimed that by making such frequent trips, John Paul was neglecting the government of the Church. In essence, the Pope replied:

> Many people say that the Pope travels too much, and at too close intervals. I think that, humanly speaking, they are right. But it is Providence

that guides us and sometimes prompts us to do something *per excessum* (excessive). Indeed, St. Thomas teaches us that *in medio stat virtus* (virtue lies in the middle of two extremes). However, for some time a kind of appeal had been coming from France, a kind of invitation, not expressed formally, which came to me as a surprise.[1]

To do something "excessive" seems to be a maxim of this pontificate—which also seems to contradict the thinking of the Curia. The Pope's excessive travels bothered Curia officials for some time. Their intense criticism paused after the assassination attempt of May 13, 1981. Then, when John Paul resumed his travels, the criticism returned as a concern for the Pope's health. That same year, he set a new record for pastoral visits, rescheduling the trips cancelled from the previous year! In addition to concern over the frequency of his pastoral visits, the Curia questioned the prudence of such trips as, for example, the Pope's visit to Great Britain and Argentina at the time of the Falkland War.

Again, the Pope justified his travels in an address to the Curia on the eve of the feast of Saints Peter and Paul in 1982. He stated that his travels were "an application of the charism of Peter on a universal scale," and he gave as a theological basis the fact that "the service of the Pope today has emphasized the universal dimension." In an analogous circumstance two years before, he had attributed his travels to "consciousness of his mission."

> In this perspective the Pope travels to announce the Gospel, to strengthen the brethren in the faith, to consolidate the Church, to meet the people.... They are voyages of love, of peace, of universal brotherhood.... In these meetings with souls, in view of the immensity of the crowds, the modern-day charism of Peter at the crossroads of the world manifests itself (June 28, 1980).

A Sense of Urgency

Concerning his travels, John Paul confided something very interesting, from a purely human point of view, to André Frossard. The French author had asked the Pope "why he was in such a hurry to travel the world, as if little time were left to gather the flock of people of good will before a storm broke, as if some 'state of emergency' had been declared." The Pope answered:

> First of all, it was not I who started this practice. It was started by two great predecessors, the Popes of Vatican II, especially by Paul VI. But John XXIII had already let it be understood that the Pope must not

only be visited by the Church but that he himself must visit the Church.... If God permits, I shall accept most of the invitations I have received.... The more difficult the life of men, of families, of communities and of the world becomes, the more necessary it is for them to become aware of the presence of the Good Shepherd.... It even seems to me that the life of the post-conciliar Church has changed this need into an imperative that is both a command and a moral obligation.... You may point out that I have said nothing of the state of emergency of which you spoke. In my view, it would be better to speak of an "urgent situation." This would be closer to St. Paul and the Gospel.[2]

The Curia's criticism has not ended, but neither has it stopped the Pope from traveling. He believes that his travels are, in themselves, sufficient proof of their necessity. As he commented during his first pastoral visit to Africa:

Some people in Europe think that the Pope should not travel, that he should stay in Rome, as was always done. I read these things in the newspapers, and I get advice of the same kind. But I want to say that it is a grace of God to be able to come, because by coming here I can get to know you. Otherwise how can I know who you are, how you live, and what your history is? And this strengthens my conviction that the time has come for the Bishop of Rome—that is, the Pope—not to think of himself exclusively as the successor of Peter, but also as the heir of St. Paul who, as we well know, never stood still; he was always traveling. And what is true for him is true also for those who work with him in Rome and accompany him.[3]

There is a Roman proverb which states that "he who perseveres, conquers." John Paul, in fact, has prevailed over criticism from the Curia. One could almost say that the criticism ceased when the number of assignments and meetings called for by the Pope left little time for such talk.

During the flight back to Rome from Lima, Peru, on February 6, 1985, a reporter asked the Pope:

"Your Holiness, are you aware of the criticism regarding your travels?"

"I know that there are many who understand and request them, because they consider them to be efficacious. But I also know that there are some persons who are not pleased with them, and that very fact convinces me they should be made."

"But do you consider the trips efficacious?"

"As regards their efficacy, one cannot use this term as an absolute criterion. Even the message of the Gospel is rarely 100 percent efficacious. But even if the efficacy were only ten percent or fifteen percent, such trips would be worthwhile."

M ight John Paul interpret the strong criticism of Curia officials as prejudice against a non-Italian pope? Possibly. Several times John Paul has recalled the image of St. Catherine of Siena reprimanding the pope who abandoned Rome for Avignon: "What do you say, what do you tell me, Catherine? Should I travel more or less? And the response that comes to me: Yes; you may travel, but you may never transfer the Holy See from Rome. Travel, yes; but always come back" (Roman Seminary, Feb. 17, 1996).

The Pope made this reference shortly after he returned from his sixty-ninth international journey. His health had begun to deteriorate; consequently, his light tone not only responded to critics but also addressed those concerned about his health.

There are some individuals in Rome who think the Pope should travel only in cases of urgent necessity, hearkening back to a time when the pope always spoke in Latin and rarely in public, except on official occasions and with great care to avoid saying anything "dangerous." Obviously, John Paul thinks quite differently; for him, the pope's words and actions must have the same value—furthermore, he introduces a bold vocabulary into the pontificate: "I have expressed a desire to go to China," he told journalists on January 24, 1994, "because sometimes the pope should use bold words." On the same occasion he said: "It is also necessary to speak courageously. Words are as true a witness as actions."

This Pope is fully conscious of his claim to freedom with respect to other pontifical models. John Paul is a man of excess and risks; he is a man of courage and of quick reactions, even of angry outbursts. When he sees an injustice or senses a need, Pope Wojtyła does not hold back his heart.

One might think that his boldness applies only to his impromptu remarks to the press, but that is not at all the case! He addressed the clergy during the Synod of Rome on March 1, 1990 thus: "In what way could this synod be more of a challenge? Perhaps it would be helpful if it *could* become more of a challenge, because many are asleep!" "Many are asleep," is a phrase taken from St. Paul's writings, but the word "challenge" is 100 percent Wojtyła.

Courage is another word the Pope frequently uses in his preaching to stir up missionary zeal. On the 1996 World Day of Prayer for Vocations, he asserted: "To face the challenge of the contemporary world calls for a measure of evangelical courage."

The Motives Behind John Paul's "Excesses"

When there is an accusation of evident excess (that which goes beyond the norm, or is unreasonable), an explanation is needed to determine the cause. And John Paul's "excesses" are explained by his depth of missionary zeal and his profound desire to respond to pressing needs. Among those needs is the missionary revival of all local churches so that they can better address the challenges of the third millennium. Hence, what some consider excessive is, in reality, simply John Paul's intense zeal to fulfill his mission as pope. Similarly, one can understand other aspects of this pontificate which have been criticized, but which John Paul also sees as having been "suggested by divine Providence."

Besides traveling, critics have questioned the "excess" in Pope Wojtyła's discourses, synods, beatifications and canonizations. To this list, we can add the following: the numerous visits to Poland, his comments on the Gulf War, his defense of life and conjugal morality, and his *mea culpas*. But I repeat: to judge these so-called excesses correctly and fairly, one must understand the missionary thrust which lies at the heart of this pontificate. Seen in this light, John Paul's discourses aim at catechizing everyone during his pastoral visits. The synods inspirit the Catholic communities on every continent with a sense of mission and evangelization. The beatifications and canonizations provide models of Christian holiness for the faithful. And the requests for forgiveness serve to promote a much needed reconciliation because of the misunderstandings and injuries that have multiplied throughout the centuries.

A critical evaluation of John Paul's departure from the papal norm requires making a distinction between its *quantitative* element (such as the frequent traveling) and its *ideological* element (such as the *mea culpas*). The quantitative element includes *traditional papal activities* such as discourses, beatifications and canonizations, as well as such *new and contemporary activities* as pastoral visits and the various synods. Similarly, the ideological element comprises topics already accepted as proper for papal discussion: world peace, marital ethics, defense of life; and those which are new: the requests for forgiveness and opposition to the death penalty.

Whenever John Paul's excess has been criticized, whether quantitatively or ideologically, the Curia has tried, in turn, to apply the brakes. Historically speaking, and this includes recent history, the Curia has sometimes prevailed, and popes have not always been able to do or to say what they wanted. On some occasions, however, the popes prevailed. This is especially true of John Paul. Moreover, during John Paul's pon-

tificate there has been an extensive development of teaching on particular moral questions, but even here the Curia has sometimes stubbornly
held on to past practices and pronouncements. This resistance helps us
to understand the spirit of a pontificate. John XXIII's suggestion for an
ecumenical council met resistance, but the Second Vatican Council was
convened nonetheless. Paul VI was accused of distorting the liturgy; and
now John Paul is reproached for not respecting historical papal traditions
in both word and deed.

John Paul's excessive amount of discourses during papal visits merits some attention here. In the past, popes seldom gave public discourses.
During the pontificate of Pius XII, the increase of papal audiences called
for more public speeches on a wide variety of topics. Paul VI requested
that the *Libreria Vaticana* (Vatican Press) publish an annual volume of
papal discourses. Typically, these volumes would exceed a thousand
pages, but John Paul has broken that record. Each year his discourses fill
two volumes, and every year the size of the volumes increases. Earlier in
his pontificate John Paul published more than ten times the number of
discourses and documents issued by Pius XII, whose pontificate spanned
twenty years. According to the Italian journal, *Trenta Giorni* (July 1989),
Pius XII delivered an average of seventy discourses annually, filling 478
printed pages. John XXIII gave an average of 182 discourses a year that
averaged 777 pages. Paul VI generally gave 347 discourses and 1,255
pages annually, and John Paul has exceeded this with 746 discourses and
3,626 pages—each year! Thus, all the popes of this century, from Pius
XII to John Paul II, have multiplied the occasions and volume of their
messages. John Paul has arranged a systematic method for visiting the
parishes of Rome and has greatly increased the number of international
pastoral visits with numerous daily meetings. In Geneva, for example
(June 15, 1982), he gave ten talks in twelve hours!

The vast increase of commitments in John Paul's pontificate is due
largely to his personality. He animates the Christian community, and he
often governs by persuasion and example rather than by legal norms.

Another, though paradoxical, hypothesis is that the Curia persuades
John Paul to make journeys in response to various "crises" in Catholicism. However, when the Italian journal, *Panorama,* interviewed Vatican
spokesman, Joaquín Navarro-Valls (Feb. 7, 1993), he energetically rejected this speculation. "No one has ever urged the Pope to do what he
does. He acts because he believes he ought to. On one occasion I heard
him say: 'We shall have all eternity to rest.'"

John Paul gave the same reason when explaining the number of discourses and journeys he makes:

The daily preoccupations, the concern for all the churches, as well as the desire to be close to the entire human race entrusted to me, with its needs and aspirations, call for an alert and attentive response to the needs and capacity of all, on every occasion, whether convenient or not (May 24, 1983).

The number of John Paul's written texts is so great, no one preson in the papal household can manage to read them all. Customarily, thirty individuals are assigned to read the collection of papal texts; in addition, they are read by a Dominican theologian belonging to the papal household, Vatican spokesman Navarro-Valls, and selected journalists considered experts in Vatican information. But only a computer database could hold all the information concerning what the Pope has said on a particular subject for the fifth, tenth or twentieth time he discussed it.

There is an element of risk in this, but risk and method exist together in John Paul's pontificate. The Pope's passion for the Gospel prompts his missionary excess, but his study of Latin and ecclesiastical discipline dispose him to follow Curia methods. The Pope may come from a distant country, but he understands his Vatican surroundings and he knows how to govern both methodically and in keeping with his naturally adventurous spirit. Rather than govern the Church through the Curia, Pope Wojtyła follows his own spirit of initiative; and his pontificate keeps in step with events and trends without being led entirely by them.

*T*hus far, the inevitable physical weakness due to age and illness has not caused John Paul's governing ability to wane. Nevertheless, since the middle of the 1990s he has turned over to others a good part of the activity he formerly handled personally: synods that have been held in rapid succession, international discussions, and interreligious meetings. Even the preparations for the Great Jubilee—which had been under the direct control of John Paul and meant handling logistics for pilgrimages and ecumenical events—were entrusted to a Jubilee committee. In this way continuity was assured.

There is an unpredictable element to John Paul's pontificate. A pope who is meticulously faithful to tradition can put all his decisions and methods safely under an "umbrella of precedent." But such a criterion is meaningless if, as in the case of Pope Wojtyła, a pope is willing to risk and to go beyond established norms. Twenty years after his election, John Paul's unexpected decisions in government and in missionary initiatives are self-evident. No one could have foreseen the "examination of conscience" he proposed for the end of the millennium, the ecumenical and interreligious activities he planned for the Great Jubilee, or the invitation he extended to the sister-churches to discuss new forms for exercising the Petrine ministry.

Not only is unpredictability a characteristic of Pope Wojtyła's decisions and initiatives; there is also an element of risk in his magisterial statements. I believe John Paul is at his best when he leaves the harbor of papal tradition and ventures out on the open sea. He did this with his theology of the body (Chapter 20), his theology of woman (Chapter 28), and his ideas regarding reconciliation and penance in the life of the Church (Chapter 39). Just as he is the first pope not to be restricted in his governing of the Church to the directions received from the Curia, so he is also the first to free his teaching from a strictly "Roman theology." Although two other popes were also somewhat outside the traditional *Roman* theology—Pope John XXIII, who tried to restore the patristic and synodal traditions, and Pope Paul VI, who was greatly influenced by the French school of theology—only Pope Wojtyła has freed himself from the Roman use of language. He has made bold statements, does not fear to hypothesize, and enjoys complete freedom of expression.

This pontificate of personal initiative and activity prevails over institutional tradition, and it is marked with John Paul's unique charism. In word and deed, he has made use of a freedom that will provide a wonderful opportunity for whoever succeeds him.

NOTES

1. S. Trassatto, R. Tucci, "Intervista a Giovanni Paolo II," *L'Osservatore Romano*, June 13, 1980.

2. A. Frossard, *"Be Not Afraid,"* (New York: St. Martin's Press, 1984), pp. 193–197.

3. M. Malinski, *Le radici di Papa Wojtyła* (Rome: Borla Editore, 1979), p. 168.

※ CHAPTER NINETEEN ※

An Athletic Pope

*I*t is August 16, 1985, and the Pope is traveling through Africa. His first stop was Lubumbashi in Zaire; now he is in the Congo. A cloud of dust hovers over the crowd of 200,000 people, and smoke from the incense rises from the papal platform. The standing crowd assembles in horseshoe formation around the altar.

The Pope ascends the long stairway leading to the altar; reaching the top, he turns to face the people. They respond with staccato shouts as they clap their hands against their mouths. The Pope raises the crosier in his left hand and slants it toward the crowd. His red chasuble flutters behind him on the breeze so that the Pope's body seems to incline itself with the crosier. The Pope stretches out toward the crowd, the golden miter moving back and forth as John Paul nods his head in greeting. He raises and lowers his right arm over each section of the crowd in a collective caress. The people know very little French, so they cannot understand the homily he later gives. In fact, out of everything the Pope came to say and do, what they comprehend best is this initial fatherly greeting.

Twenty young girls in white dresses dance the *Gloria* of the Mass with delicate movements. The Pope follows their gestures and the music by slightly swaying back and forth. He is happy, and the people clap their hands. Someone has said that in Africa the Mass is a festival, and if it is not danced, it is made rhythmical by moving one's shoulders. Once, when speaking about the Africans, John Paul said: "This people lives with the heart, and also with their bodies."[1] Perhaps the Pope and the Africans are beginning to understand each other through this language of the body.

J ohn Paul's body has served him well in suffering and in health, and he has taken good care of it. During the past twenty years his excellent physique has been visible in St. Peter's Square and at the window for the Sunday Angelus messages. John Paul has not wanted to depersonalize himself, as some popes before him may have done. Instead, he has purposely shown his private side.

This Pope takes time out to go skiing in the mountains or swimming in the pool at Castel Gandolfo. In his writings and discourses he uses such phrases as, "In my opinion" or "It seems to me."[2] He does not use the traditional *sedia gestatoria* (papal throne). In fact, early in his pontificate someone cried out from the crowd in St. Peter's Square: "We want you in the *sedia gestatoria*!" John Paul turned around, pointed his finger—a gesture he used later when addressing Ernesto Cardenal in Managua, Nicaragua, and when speaking to the Mafia in Sicily—and said: "No! Not in *sedia gestatoria,* no!"[3]

John Paul doesn't stand on ceremony. He speaks of his election as pope—at one time described as the "elevation to the throne of Peter"—as if it were just another stage in his priestly ministry. In fact, he has referred to it very simply as: "my election to the See of St. Peter"[4] and "the very day of the inauguration of my papal ministry."[5]

This is John Paul, the first pope to function as Bishop of Rome in his day-to-day ministry. He has radically changed the public perception of the pope, bringing himself closer to the common people. His has been perhaps the only authentic renovation of the papacy that was achieved without a reform.

These are a few of the qualities that best portray Pope Wojtyła: he is fearless and tireless, creative and without regret. Yet, he has known fear and fatigue, difficulty in making himself understood, and perhaps a bit of sadness for what was missing in his life. But when it comes to the question of whether the image of the pope has prevailed over the image of the man, one cannot deny that in the making of Pope John Paul II, the man, Karol Wojtyła, has not been extinguished! As one author put it: "Karol Wojtyła has never completely become John Paul II."[6]

One could look for significant and grand plans beneath John Paul's plain and simple bearing, and certainly these exist. Yet, John Paul projects an image of purpose combined with humility. During the flight from Brussels to Rome (May 21, 1985), a journalist asked the Pope about the risk of exposing himself to public criticism and objections. John Paul responded: "Even the Pope can learn something."

Sometimes even in the Pope's banter there is a purpose, as is evident in this exchange with young people in Manila:

"We love you, Pope Lolek!"

"Lolek is a name for a baby, but I am an old man..."

"No! No!"

"...But *John Paul* is too serious. Call me Karol" (Jan. 14, 1995).

He has a strong tendency to put himself on the same level as his audience. When a crowd at Castel Gandolfo shouted: "Long live the Pope! Long live the Pope!" he retorted: "Long live everyone!" (April 17, 1995)

There is purpose in John Paul's simplicity and openness. Yet he also exhibits, on occasion, a certain firmness that contrasts with his affability and indicates his determination to remain himself, in spite of the pontifical robes. At times, in fact, he controls a crowd with his seriousness. This is true in public confrontations, like the one that occurred at Managua, Nicaragua, on March 4, 1983, when he repeatedly shouted to the Sandinistas, "Silence!" It is also true of General Audiences like the one in which a group sang without stopping; finally the Pope said rather sharply: "Enough!"[7]

John Paul's simplicity becomes most apparent when he is responding to the innocence and simplicity of children. In Melbourne, Australia, the Pope visited an elementary school, and one child asked him what his favorite music was. A complete answer is found in the comments he made after a concert by Bob Dylan in Bologna on September 27, 1997:

> Perhaps I prefer classical music, but I also like modern music. I am not a man of the past, no. I am very interested in contemporary music. I am also supportive of...what is it called? ...Of Rock! I can distinguish various kinds of music. But most of all I prefer music with depth, like liturgical music and Gregorian chant."

Love for the Great Outdoors

As a youth, Karol Wojtyła would go out to the mountains and write poetry. He loved swimming, good food, and performing plays with his high school companions. He had a passion for hiking with his friends— something he continued to do with young people even as a bishop. In fact, John Paul continued all of these practices, as best he could, after his election as pope.

At one time in the history of the papacy a clearly defined separation existed between the pope's private living quarters and public offices and meeting rooms. No one knew anything about a pope's private life; in public, popes observed a strict protocol. John Paul abolished this separation by admitting outsiders to his private chapel and even to his dining room.

Very early in his pontificate, John Paul had a swimming pool installed in the summer villa at Castel Gandolfo. Some Curia officials felt they had to defend the Pope's use of a swimming pool by saying he had it built for medical reasons. They cited in particular Karol Wojtyła's childhood bout with mononucleosis and his need to keep himself in good physical condition. But it is more probable that an athletic man like John Paul simply desired to maintain some form of physical exercise in an otherwise confined and uninterrupted official role. When he was once asked about the human side of his life as pope, he acknowledged: "It lacks contact with young people, and therefore it lacks sports and athletic activity."

Perhaps the swimming pool also serves to lessen the tedium of summers at Castel Gandolfo, but that is not enough for John Paul. He needs to leave the immediate confines of his villa, and he has done so. In July 1987, while the Pope traveled in the company of reporters, one of them referred to the Vatican as a prison. The Pope commented: "You have to have experienced *that* prison in order to enjoy *this* freedom."

John Paul inaugurated the custom of breaking his summer stay at Castel Gandolfo with two weeks in the mountains. He is also the first pope to be photographed in skiing and hiking clothes. In July 1984, such photos appeared in Italian newspapers before the Vatican newspaper, *L'Osservatore Romano*, had the courage to report that the Pope had actually gone skiing and hiking in the mountains.

Castel Gandolfo served very well as a vacation spot for more sedentary popes, but the Italian Alps are much more suitable for an athletic, traveling pope like John Paul. He himself once said: "The mountains have always held a special attraction for my spirit." His first trip to the mountains took place in 1984. In time, the Pope was able to go to the mountains on an average of two or three times a year, but he had to give them up after his fall in November 1993. The most he is able to do now is an occasional one-day excursion outside Rome.

Many officials in the Curia have never been pleased with the physical liberty John Paul exercises. We have already seen some of their objections to his activities. So, naturally, the objection to the Pope's skiing was even more vehement. Here is a statement by Cardinal Siri, an ardent disciple of Pius XII and the recipient of the second highest number of votes in the conclave that elected John Paul:

> John Paul II has revived the religious sense of the world, and that is no
> small thing. He has become a great moral authority to whom everyone
> looks. But enough now! There is the Curia and there is government;
> and in order to govern, one must be at his desk. Do you know what it

means to entrust a Vatican dicastery to someone from another continent? I have a tremendous fear...that if tomorrow the parish priest of Pentema (the furthest northwest region of Liguria) were to invite him, the Pope would go. Sometimes I think that divine Providence wanted this kind of pope—an excellent person, understand, with his personal qualities—so that the Church could be on guard against many dangers. Many persons are upset that he has gone to ski on Terminillo and on Mount Adamello. I am not upset, because I have said that the popes who come in the future will understand that this should not be done.[8]

Pope Wojtyła also tries to spend a day or even a few hours in the countryside when he is traveling. In his first visit to Canada (1984), he made a trip to the Rocky Mountains. He did something similar during his pastoral visits to Kenya, Poland, the Asturias in Spain, and the United States.

Such extensive travels are at once an indication of his missionary zeal and his energetic spirit. We must respect the human side of this Pope: his eagerness to travel, to get out into the open, to see the world and its peoples. After all, he travels so much because he also has such a healthy curiosity about life and a warm, outgoing spirit.

NOTES

1. S. Trassatti, R. Tucci, "Intervista a Giovanni Paolo II," *L'Osservatore Romano,* May 14, 1980.

2. Cf. *Redemptor Hominis,* n. 4.

3. M. Sansolini, *Io sediario Pontificio,* Libreria Editrice Vaticana, 1998, p. 104.

4. John Paul II with Vittorio Messori, *Crossing the Threshold of Hope* (New York: Alfred A. Knopf, 1994), p. 98.

5. Ibid., p. 125.

6. G. Baget Bozzo, *Ortodossia e liberazione* (Milan: Rizzoli, 1981), p. 65.

7. M. Sansolini, *Io sediario Pontificio,* Libreria Editrice Vaticana, 1998, p. 113.

8. B. Lai, *Il Papa non eletto* (Rome: Laterza, 1993), p. 290.

CHAPTER TWENTY

A Theology of the Body

*W*hen it comes to a theology of the body, John Paul's sentiments are far more extensive than his words. One has the impression that he withholds words and—saying what he thinks—does not say all he feels. I believe that to understand what this courageous Pope feels regarding human love and the body—subjects so often passed over by theologians—could be a great gift for the Church.

It would be marvelous to really go beyond his words and probe the content of John Paul's feelings, but that is not possible. We can only rely on our intuition, and to do that, we must not only listen to his words but observe his actions; for example, his physical nearness and affection toward others, including children. And we should also keep in mind his contacts with young married couples as a parish priest and a bishop. In his book, *Crossing the Threshold of Hope,* John Paul said: "As a young priest I learned to love human love."[1] That statement reveals a defining quality about this Pope: he is enamored of human love.

When John Paul speaks of love, his language is forthright even if sometimes obscure. He does not speak only of a theology of the body, but of a theology of sex: "The theology of the body...becomes also, in a sense, a theology of sex, or rather, a theology of masculinity and femininity" (Nov. 14, 1979).

Such a theology can help us understand "the reason for and the consequences of the Creator's decision that the human being should always and only exist as a woman or a man."[2] The basis for that statement is the relational characteristic of human beings which is expressed in the nuptial union, that is, "in the capacity of the body to express love."[3] It finds its fulfillment in the union of masculinity and femininity, thus forming a "unity of two" in which nuptial love is fully expressed in sexual union as a "reciprocal giving." This teaching can be found in the book, *Man and Woman He Created Them,* although if the Pope had chosen the title, he might have called it *Masculine and Feminine He Created Them,* or perhaps *Catechesis on the Theology of the Body.*[4]

The Pope has not confined his treatment of this subject to the Wednesday General Audiences. John Paul has constantly spoken on the theology of the body throughout his pontificate. Recall especially his *Letter to the Youth of the World* (1985); the apostolic letter, *Mulieris Dignitatem* (1988), particularly chapters 3 and 4; the *Letter to Families* (1994); his homily at the celebration for the restoration of the Sistine Chapel (1994); and the *Letter to Women* (1995).

John Paul II's most beautiful tribute to human love is contained in *Mulieris Dignitatem*: "In the biblical description, the words of the first man at the sight of the woman who had been created are words of admiration and enchantment, words that fill the whole history of man on earth."[5]

In his *Letter to Families,* John Paul says that in using the image of "spouse" in speaking of God, Jesus shows how much the fatherhood and love of God are reflected in the love of a man and woman who are united in matrimony. Prior to that, in *Familiaris Consortio* (1981), he had pointed out that the biblical teaching that God loves his people is reflected in the conjugal love of a man and woman. And in *Love and Responsibility* he had said: *"Amor concupiscentia* [concupiscent love] is present even in man's love of God, whom man may and does desire as a good for himself."[6] In this context John Paul's most open-minded statements are found in his *Letter to the Youth of the World:*

> Yes, through that love which is born in you—and wishes to become a part of your whole plan of life—you must see God who is love.... When Christ says "Follow me," his call can mean: "I call you to still another love"; but very often it means: "Follow me," follow me who am the bridegroom of the Church who is my bride; come, you too become the bridegroom of your bride, you too become the bride of your spouse.... Christ as spouse..."gave himself" and teaches all husbands and wives how to "give themselves" in the full measure of each one's personal dignity. Christ teaches us married love. To set out on the path of the married vocation means to learn married love day by day, year by year; love according to soul and body (March 31, 1985).

In the homily at the re-opening of the Sistine Chapel, John Paul referred to the nude figures by Michelangelo as "a sanctuary of the theology of the human body." He then added, "Only in the sight of God can the human body be naked *and* still preserve its beauty intact" (April 8, 1994).

But what sense does it make to speak of a theology of the human body? To answer this question, the Pope turns to the central mystery of Christianity, the Incarnation: "Theology is that science whose subject is divinity. Through the fact that the Word of God became flesh, the body entered theology through the main door" (April 2, 1980).

And here is his commentary on masculinity and femininity from God's viewpoint:

> Masculinity and femininity are two different incarnations, that is, two modes of being "body" in the self-same human nature created in the image of God. The function of sex is a constitutive element of the person and not merely an attribute of the person. This shows that human nature is deeply rooted in the body as "he" or "she." The presence of the feminine element alongside the masculine and conjoined with him signifies an enrichment for the man in every aspect of his history, including the history of salvation.[7]

But perhaps the following is John Paul's most compact statement on the theology of the body: "Male and female he redeemed them."[8]

This is the way the Pope interprets the "language of the body," beginning with the perception that lovers have of each other at the moment of their mutual giving to each other. He explains that words of love spoken by the couple focus on the body not only because in itself it is the source of reciprocal fascination, but also and especially because that attraction for the other person, the other "I," whether feminine or masculine, activates the interior impulse of the heart that generates love.[9]

John Paul says that the words, "they were both naked, yet they felt no shame" (Gn 2:25), should be understood as a revelation concerning the freedom that makes possible and qualifies the meaning of bodily spousal love.[10] In *Love and Responsibility*, one of his early works, he had spoken of "the absorption of shame by love" (cf. pp. 181–186).

John Paul manifests the same anthropological and psychological depth when he comments on sexuality as the language of love. For example, at the Angelus on June 26, 1994, he said: "Sexuality is a language in the service of love and therefore it cannot be seen as something purely instinctual."

An Appreciation of Tenderness

In contemporary theology, the phrase "theology of the body" refers to the restoration of a positive appreciation of sexuality and a promotion of tenderness in the sexual relationship. Both of these elements are abundantly evident in Wojtyła's teaching, but they are more fully manifested in his actions and gestures. The closeness and tenderness that characterize John Paul's contacts with individuals are not only natural gifts, but are the result of a lengthy discipline in self-control as well as a reflection of his theology of the body. We should interpret Pope Wojtyła's behavior in light of his writings, and we should read his writings in light of his behavior.

We will begin with a passage that discusses tenderness and sensuality in *Love and Responsibility* and end with his 1995 letter to priests on the role of women in the life of a priest.

> Genuine human love—love "for" a person and love "between" persons—must combine two elements: tenderness and firmness.... We must not forget that love for a human being must also contain certain elements of struggle.... Tenderness has no *raison d'être* outside of love.... Tenderness is the ability to feel with and for the whole person, to feel even the most deeply hidden spiritual tremors, and always to have in mind the true good of that person.... Tenderness, then, springs from awareness of the inner state of another person...and whoever feels it actively seeks to communicate his feeling of close involvement with the other person.... Sentiment naturally brings people closer together. Hence also the need actively to communicate the feeling of closeness, so that tenderness shows itself in certain outward actions: ...pressing another person to one's breast, embracing him, putting one's arms around him...certain forms of kissing.[11]

How frequently we have seen this tenderness in John Paul! When he speaks of "certain forms of kissing," we can recall how he paternally kisses young children on their foreheads, or hugs those who come up to greet him. I remember seeing John Paul leaning over the balcony of the nunciature in San José, Costa Rica, in March 1983, and reaching out toward a young guitar player who had leaped up to touch the Pope. I also recall how, twelve years later, in New York's Central Park, John Paul lightly patted the head of a singer who had performed in the celebration. But of all the recollections of his warmth and friendliness, perhaps the most touching took place in Sydney, Australia, on November 26, 1986. In the stadium he kissed the forehead of the young girl who gave the welcoming speech, holding her face in his two hands. Then, singing and moving back and forth to the music, he took the hands of two other girls who were members of the choral group. When the song ended he hugged them both affectionately.

We have noted that in his relationship with women the Pope has always been natural, free and respectful. John Paul does not fear physical closeness, rather he welcomes it, valuing it as a means of pastoral contact. To a group of parishioners in Rome he said, "Pastoral visits are a privileged moment because I can touch and embrace you!" He would like all priests to exhibit the same freedom and tenderness. To this end, he wrote a letter to priests in 1995 in much the same vein as Paul wrote to Timothy, advising him to treat "older women as mothers and younger women as sisters, with absolute purity" (1 Tm 5:2). John Paul concluded by saying that older priests should treat young women as daughters, because their "ministry of authentic spiritual fatherhood gives them sons and daughters in the Lord."

Every year John Paul writes a letter to priests for Holy Thursday, but this particular letter is perhaps the most engaging and personal of all. Notice, for example, the following excerpt:

> In order to live as a celibate in a mature and untroubled way, it seems particularly important that the priest should develop deep within himself the image of women as sisters.... Certainly "woman as sister" represents a specific manifestation of the spiritual beauty of women; but it is at the same time a revelation that they are in a certain sense "set apart."...The figure of woman as sister has considerable importance in our Christian civilization.... When a woman remains single, in her "gift of self as sister" by means of apostolic commitment or generous dedication to neighbor, she develops a particular spiritual motherhood.[12]

The letter reveals that John Paul is able to have a special love for every woman, although, after his mother's death, there was no significant woman in his life at home or during his adult years. His concept of woman has always been that of "sister."

Perhaps we may say that in the case of Pope Wojtyła, his actions are much more revealing and convincing than his words alone. There we see his theology of the body enacted. And perhaps it is permissible to think that John Paul's behavior is a prelude to what we can expect in the teaching and behavior of his successors. We could never have imagined that some twenty years after Pius XII, the "angelic pastor" who seemed not even to have a body, we would have a pope who embraces a young person as a father embraces a child.

In spite of the difficulty in expressing the content of this chapter, I have reason to believe that here we are touching upon a most intimate and profound aspect of Pope Wojtyła's personality. At the same time, this may be one of his greatest legacies to us. John Paul's actions can be viewed as a homily, and we can interpret his homilies by his actions. More than anything else he says or does, this is what has made John Paul II so universally loved.

NOTES

1. John Paul II with Vittorio Messori, *Crossing the Threshold of Hope* (New York: Alfred A. Knopf, 1994), p. 123.

2. John Paul II, *Mulieris Dignitatem* (Boston: Pauline Books & Media, 1988), n. 1.

3. *Uomo e donna lo creò*, 3a ed., Libreria Editrice Vaticana, 1982.

4. John Paul II, *The Theology of the Body: Human Love in the Divine Plan* (Boston: Pauline Books & Media, 1997).

5. John Paul II, *Mulieris Dignitatem* (Boston: Pauline Books & Media, 1988), n. 10.

6. K. Wojtyła, *Love and Responsibility* (New York: Farrar, Straus, 1981), p. 82.

7. Ibid.

8. John Paul II with Vittorio Messori, *Crossing the Threshold of Hope* (New York: Alfred A. Knopf, 1994), p. 49.

9. *Uomo e donna lo creò*, 3a ed., Libreria Editrice Vaticana, 1982, p. 70.

10. Ibid.

11. K. Wojtyła, *Love and Responsibility* (New York: Farrar, Straus, 1981), pp. 202–207, *passim*.

12. John Paul II, "1995 Letter to Priests for Holy Thursday," *L'Osservatore Romano*, April 12, n. 15.

✸ CHAPTER TWENTY-ONE ✸

Casablanca

*T*he challenge Islam poses to the Catholic Church runs throughout the entire pontificate of John Paul II. This challenge is not
to be understood as a competition—at least, not in John Paul's
mind—but as an approach toward one another for the purpose of mutual
growth in understanding, which is just as difficult. In carrying out
Vatican II's mandate for dialogue with non-Christian religions and for
lessening the ever-growing uneasiness of Catholic communities in Muslim countries, the Pope uses a direct approach with the Islamic world.

His first action was an event known as the "preaching to Islamic
youth" and it took place at Casablanca in August 1985. A little more than
a year later, John Paul hosted the World Day of Prayer for Peace at Assisi.
Muslims accepted the Pope's invitation to world religions to observe a
day of fasting and prayer in the interests of peace (see Chapter 23). The
Pope's outreach attempts to Islam also include a week's visit to Indonesia
in 1989 and his seven-hour visit to Tunisia in 1986.

Even more important than these meetings, however, are his interventions in the wars in Lebanon, the Persian Gulf, and Bosnia. John Paul
was radically opposed to the armed attack on Iraq, approved by the
United Nations and carried out by the United States and England in January–February 1991. His strong vocal opposition signaled to Islam that
the Catholic Church does not identify itself with the interests, cultures,
and wars of the West (see Chapter 32).

Finally, in Chapter 33, we will speak of the Pope's visit to Khartoum
in February 1993. It was the most daring of all his ventures into the world
of Islam, and John Paul made the journey precisely to ask for a minimum
amount of freedom for the Christian communities in that country.

These actions are some of the most creative and original of his pontificate. For the first time a pope directly addressed Muslim crowds. For the first time a pope called Muslims "brothers," recognizing them not only as members of the human family, but as brothers in Abraham and as adorers of the one true God worshiped by the patriarchs. For the first time a pope invited Muslims to pray with him, and he admitted that the wars the Crusaders had waged were not in keeping with the spirit of the Gospel (Feb. 12, 1995).

This courageous attempt to approach Islam directly—an approach the Pope carried out tenaciously in spite of modest results—is not yet finished. John Paul has proposed to both Jews and Muslims a meeting on Mount Sinai to take place in the year 2000 in the name of Abraham and Moses. He has also repeated his desire to follow the biblical itinerary of Abraham, Moses, and Jesus, which would take him from Iraq to Syria, Jordan, Egypt, Israel, and Lebanon. If he is able to complete the itinerary, it would bring John Paul into contact with six Muslim nations, only one of which he has previously entered: Lebanon (see Chapter 36).

The beginning of the Pope's contacts took place on August 19, 1985, at the invitation of King Hussein II of Morocco. John Paul was invited to speak to 50,000 young Muslims in the stadium at Casablanca. It was the first time in history that any pope had made this risky journey, though St. Francis of Assisi had preached briefly in Morocco in the thirteenth century.

Fifty thousand young people were assembled in the middle of the stadium. At a given signal they released thousands of colored balloons bearing the pictures of King Hussein and Pope John Paul. The king introduced the Pope to the crowd as "an educator and a defender of values that are shared by Islam and Christianity." John Paul spoke simply in this first encounter with people unknown to him: "It is as a believer that I come to you today, simply to give witness to what I believe, what I wish for the well-being of my brothers and sisters, for humanity, and what, through experience, I consider to be useful to all."[1]

The Pope did not introduce anything new in his remarks; he simply repeated what Vatican II had said about dialogue with the Muslims. But he personally carried this message to his intended listeners, and that was no small thing. It gave the Pope an opportunity to plea for an end to wars and the beginning of dialogue:

> Christians and Muslims—generally we have understood each other badly. Sometimes in the past we have opposed each other and even exhausted ourselves in polemics and wars. I believe that God is calling us

today to change our old habits. We have to respect each other and
stimulate each other in good works upon the path indicated by God....
In a world that desires unity and peace, but which experiences a thousand tensions and conflicts, believers should foster friendship and
union among humanity and the peoples who comprise a single community on earth.[2]

This close contact with Muslims also gave John Paul a chance to
emphasize the need for mutual pardon, a theme that would dominate his
statements in the 1990s. But for the Pope to speak as he did in 1985, and
in a Muslim country, was quite extraordinary. In his concluding remarks
John Paul invoked "the good God, infinitely merciful," words contained
both in the Bible and in the Koran. He begged for Christians and Muslims the "sentiments of mercy and understanding, of pardon and reconciliation, of service and collaboration."

Calling Muslims "Brothers"

There is something very moving in this frank expression of trust between "brothers" with which John Paul makes his appeal to the Muslims.
He speaks in the name of their common membership in the human family,
but he also calls upon their common descent from Abraham, the father of
all believers. This was a creative use of the term "brothers" that John Paul
extended to Muslims, unprecedented in the language of the popes. Addressed to Muslims, that word holds the promise of a new relationship,
and it was used in the invitation John Paul sent to Muslims to attend the
days of fasting and prayer at Assisi in 1986 and 1993. The invitation and
the use of the word "brothers" was very likely John Paul's personal decision. He may have thought that if Muslims and Christians could pray
together, perhaps they would stop waging war against one another.

His use of the word "brothers" goes back to the early days of the
pontificate of Pope Wojtyła. On December 10, 1978, only a few months
after his election, in an appeal from the Vatican for peace in Lebanon, the
Pope invoked Mary as Queen of Peace: "We know that the Mother of
God is greatly venerated also by our Muslim brothers."

Three years later he again used the title normally reserved for our
brothers in the faith, namely, all the baptized. This time he was not
speaking from the Vatican but extended his hand to them in a land illumi-
nated by the sun of Islam. The Pope was at the airport in Kaduna, Nigeria, but the persons to whom his prepared discourse was addressed were
not present. Most likely they absented themselves because of internal

disagreement, although some journalists attributed it to their remembrance of the Crusades. However, the government officials who welcomed the Pope on his arrival were also Muslims, so John Paul was able to read his discourse to them.

> All of us, Christians and Muslims, live beneath the sun of the one merciful God. We all believe in one God, the Creator of man. We acclaim the sovereignty of God and we defend the dignity of man as a servant of God. We adore God and we profess total submission to him. In this sense we can call each other brothers and sisters in the faith in one God (April 14, 1982).

Seven years later, John Paul would again use the words, "Muslim brothers" in his letter to bishops regarding the situation in Lebanon (Sept. 26, 1989). On the same day he would issue an appeal to Muslims as brothers in faith: "How can we believers, sons of the merciful God, our Creator, our Guide and our Judge, remain indifferent before an entire people that is dying under our very eyes?" (Sept. 26, 1989)

The most important text in which John Paul refers to Muslims is a prayer that he inserted in the ceremony for peace in Europe, over which he presided at Assisi on January 10, 1993. He referred to Jews, Muslims, and Christians as brothers since they are all sons of Abraham. Historically, the Muslims come later than the Jews, so the Pope calls them our *fratelli minori* (younger brothers) born in Abraham; and since the Jews are older than Christians he refers to them as *fratelli maggiori* (older brothers). But on that particular occasion, perhaps with his gaze fixed on Bosnia where Muslims were being persecuted by Serbs and Croatians, the Muslims were first in his thoughts, and John Paul read the prayer in Arabic.

In Christian usage the word "brother" connotes love and pardon, and Pope Wojtyła does not hesitate to use that term in addressing Muslims. He even used that word when speaking to Ali Agca in prison (see Chapter 15). On that occasion the Pope told journalists: "I have forgiven him as one forgives a brother in whom one has confidence" (Dec. 27, 1983).

Could this be perhaps a futile attempt to win over with words those who have been deeply offended? No. It is much more than that, as is evident from the Pope's remarks after seven Trappist monks were murdered in Algeria by an armed Islamic group. This is how John Paul spoke about the news when it reached the Vatican:

> Despite our deep sorrow, we thank God for the witness of love given by those religious. Their fidelity and constancy honor the Church, and they will certainly be a seed of reconciliation and peace for the Alge-

rian people with whom they were in solidarity. May our prayers also reach their families, the Cistercian Order, and the small ecclesial community in Algeria. In this tragic trial may they never lack the courage of forgiveness and the strength of hope based on Christ, who has conquered death.[3]

To speak of forgiveness in the face of Islamic fundamentalism would not make any sense were it not for the fact that the Gospel teaching on forgiveness has been so amply manifested in recent years by Christians living in Islamic countries. A remarkable document on this spirituality of forgiveness has come to light since the murder of the French Trappists in Algeria. It is contained in a last testament, dated January 1, 1994, written by the superior of the group to his family in France.

> If they seize me some day (and it could happen today) to become a victim of the terrorism which seems to threaten all the foreigners who live in Algeria today, I would want my community, my Church and my family to remember that I have given my life to God and to this country.... I have lived long enough to consider myself an accomplice in the evil which, alas! seems to prevail in the world and also in that which can unexpectedly happen to me. If that moment comes, I would like to have the spark of lucidity that would enable me to ask pardon of God and of my brothers in humanity, and at the same time with all my heart to pardon him who has struck me.[4]

For Pope Wojtyła the Islamic problem has proved difficult. But in spite of a limited response, John Paul continues to extend his hand with the message of brotherhood and forgiveness.

NOTES

1. *L'Osservatore Romano*, August 1985.

2. Ibid.

3. L. Accattoli, *When a Pope Asks Forgiveness* (Boston: Pauline Books & Media, 1998), p. 189.

4. Ibid., p. 190.

❈ CHAPTER TWENTY-TWO ❈

The Synagogue in Rome

*T*he Pope's visit to the Synagogue in Rome on April 13, 1986, lasted an hour and fifteen minutes. John Paul twice embraced the Chief Rabbi and addressed his hosts as "Hebrew brothers." The Pope also recited a psalm in their language. In his remarks he deplored the oppression of the Jews by his predecessors in the papacy, and he recalled with emotion the genocide Hitler had decreed. In each of these instances the Jews applauded with fervor.

It was the first time a pope had ever entered the Synagogue in Rome. The ceremony was televised internationally, and few other gestures by the Pope have been as warmly received throughout the world.

Two Jewish representatives welcomed the Pope: Giacomo Taban, President of the Jewish Community of Rome, and Elio Toaff, the Chief Rabbi. Taban referred to the silence of Pius XII regarding the persecution of the Jews during the Second World War, and he asked John Paul to recognize the State of Israel. Toaff made the same request, but in a religious rather than a political context. The Pope did not explicitly refer to Israel, and he indirectly defended Pius XII by pointing out the hospitality and protection numerous religious houses and the Vatican itself had offered the Jews during World War II.

Taban recalled popes who had ordered that Hebrew books be burned, and he mentioned Paul IV who had instituted the ghetto in 1555, thus putting the Jews in a state of "economic and cultural poverty and depriving them of their basic human rights." On this point John Paul stated emphatically: "The acts of discrimination, unjustified limitation of religious freedom, oppression also on the level of civil freedom in regard to the

Jews were, from an objective point of view, gravely deplorable manifestations. Yes, once again, through myself, the Church, in the well-known words of the declaration *Nostra Aetate* (Declaration on the Relation of the Church to Non-Christian Religions), 'deplores the hatred, persecutions and displays of anti-Semitism directed against the Jews at any time and by anyone,' I repeat, *by anyone.*"[1]

Prolonged applause followed this statement. The phrase "by anyone" indicated that John Paul expressly wanted to "deplore" the oppression individual popes and their collaborators had practiced. Then he continued: "I would like once more to express a word of abhorrence for the genocide decreed against the Jewish people during the last war, which led to the holocaust of millions of innocent victims." More vigorous applause greeted these words, as it did again when the Pope affirmed: "You are our dearly beloved brothers, and in a certain way it could be said that you are our elder brothers."

The Pope and the Chief Rabbi were both dressed in white and seated on matching chairs. They recited a psalm together and professed a common resolution to collaborate further. Many of the Jews in the Synagogue were in tears, and the Pope himself was deeply moved.

There was little or nothing said that could really be called new regarding the change of attitude toward the Jews that Vatican II had called for, but it took courage to put the Council's teaching into practice. Prompted by his pragmatic spirit, John Paul was showing Catholics around the world how they should relate to the Jews. With the simplicity of a gesture understood and gratefully received by all, the visit to the Synagogue in Rome reconfirmed John Paul's previous initiatives to improve relations with the Jews. We should recall that earlier, John Paul had paid homage before the memorial plaque at Auschwitz on June 7, 1979, during his first visit to Poland: "The very people who received from God the commandment 'Thou shalt not kill' experienced in a special measure what is meant by killing. It is not permissible for anyone to pass by this inscription with indifference" (June 7, 1979).

That gesture served as a prelude to John Paul's visit to the Synagogue in Rome. Using an expression from his discourse at the Synagogue, we can say that the visit was most appropriate for "a Pope who has come to the See of St. Peter from a diocese in whose territory is located the concentration camp of Auschwitz." Pope Wojtyła was already well acquainted with the Synagogues of Kraków and Wadowice since his childhood days.

The embrace John Paul gave to "our elder brothers" in the Roman Synagogue was destined to lead to other gestures. The following year the

Pope met with the Jewish community in Miami, Florida (Sept. 11, 1987); the meeting was scheduled by the National Conference of Catholic Bishops of the United States. During that visit the Pope made a general but explicit act of repentance for persecutions in the past. "There can be no doubt that the sufferings the Jewish people have endured are also for the Catholic Church a motive for sincere sorrow, especially if we recall the indifference and resentment that, in particular historical circumstances, have divided Jews and Christians. Surely this calls for a stronger resolve to work together for justice and true peace."

*A*t the beginning of 1990, two other occasions mark specific moments when words were accompanied by action, as is typical of Pope Wojtyła. Relations with our Jewish brethren made several important advances because of these initiatives. The first was a penitential service in St. Peter's Basilica at the conclusion of the Synod for Europe on December 7, 1991. It was an exceptionally important event and we will return to it in Chapter 29, when we discuss the examination of conscience scheduled by John Paul for the end of the millennium. When the Pope called for a confession of sins during the service, an invocation was read, asking forgiveness for the passivity of Christians in regard to the *Shoah*. It was the most explicit text that the Pope had approved thus far:

> Lord, our Liberator, in the Christian communities of Europe we have not always obeyed your commandment, but relying on purely human forces, we have followed worldly logic in religious wars, struggles of Christians against Christians, passivity in the face of persecution and the Holocaust of the Jews, with savage attacks against so many innocent persons. Forgive us and have pity on us!

The second important occasion was the fiftieth anniversary of the Holocaust, and it was observed on April 18, 1993 with a fervent greeting in St. Peter's Square to our "beloved Jewish brothers":

> In deep solidarity with that people, and in communion with the whole community of Catholics, I would like to commemorate those terrible events, so remote in time, but etched in the minds of many of us. The days of the *Shoah* marked one of "history's darkest nights," with unimaginable crimes against God and humanity. How could we not be with you, dear Jewish brothers and sisters, to recall in prayer and meditation such a tragic anniversary? Be sure of this: you are not alone in bearing the pain of this memory: we pray and watch with you, under the gaze of God, the holy and just one, rich in mercy and pardon.

The most important results of the Pope's visit to the Jewish Synagogue were:

❖ the accord with Israel on December 30, 1993, establishing diplomatic relations with the Vatican which were finalized on June 15, 1994;

❖ the document on the *Shoah,* promulgated on March 16, 1998;

❖ the insertion of a reference to the Jews in the penitential service scheduled for the year 2000 (see Chapter 38).

The document on the *Shoah* was published in March 1998, under the title, *We Remember: A Reflection on the "Shoah."* It was accompanied by a cover letter composed by John Paul who describes the *Shoah* as "an indelible stain on the history of the century that is coming to a close." The document opens with a quotation from the apostolic letter *Tertio Millennio Adveniente:*

> It is appropriate that as the second millennium of Christianity draws to a close the Church should become more fully conscious of the sinfulness of her children, recalling all those times in history when they departed from the spirit of Christ and his Gospel and, instead of offering to the world the witness of a life inspired by the values of faith, indulged in ways of thinking and acting which were truly forms of counter witness and scandal.[2]

The document itself contains passages that are not only significant, but unusual for a Vatican publication. It states that the Church's relation to the Jewish people is unlike its relation to any other religion, but it admits that the history of that relationship has been a "tormented one." Unfortunately, Christians have been guilty of sentiments of mistrust and hostility toward the Jews. After a rapid survey of the persecution of the Jews throughout the centuries, the document comes to the persecution of various groups by the Nazis:

> Did Christians give every possible assistance to those being persecuted, and in particular to the persecuted Jews? Many did, but others did not. Those who did help to save Jewish lives, as much as was in their power, even to the point of placing their own lives in danger, must not be forgotten.... Alongside such courageous men and women, the spiritual resistance and concrete action of other Christians was not what might have been expected from Christ's followers. We cannot know how many Christians in countries occupied or ruled by Nazi powers or their allies were horrified at the disappearance of their Jewish neighbors and yet were not strong enough to raise their voices in protest. For Christians, this heavy burden of conscience of their brothers and sisters during the Second World War must be a call to penitence.

We deeply regret the errors and failures of those sons and daughters of the Church.... This is an act of repentance *(teshuva),* since as members of the Church we are linked to the sins as well as to the merits of all her children.... We wish to turn awareness of past sins into a firm resolve to build a new future in which there will be no more anti-Judaism among Christians or anti-Christian sentiment among Jews.... The spoiled seeds of anti-Judaism and anti-Semitism must never again be allowed to take root in any human heart.[3]

John Paul has taken many steps toward the Jews, but his journey is not yet finished. Ideally, his efforts should culminate in a request for forgiveness for the persecution suffered by Jews throughout history. The time is ripe, and it could bring an end to the dissatisfaction some Jews have expressed whenever a papal pronouncement or a Vatican document is issued on the subject. In fact, an appropriate time for this request for pardon would be Ash Wednesday of the year 2000, when a penitential service will be celebrated in the *Circo Massimo* in Rome. This could be an appropriate occasion for asking forgiveness of our Jewish brothers and sisters, and it seems to be the direction in which John Paul is moving.

NOTES

1. *L'Osservatore Romano,* April 1986.

2. John Paul II's "Regina Caeli Message," *L'Osservatore Romano,* April 21, 1993, n. 16.

3. Vatican Commission for Religious Relations with the Jews, *We Remember: A Reflection on the Shoah* (Boston: Pauline Books & Media, 1998).

※ CHAPTER TWENTY-THREE ※

World Day of Prayer for Peace at Assisi

*T*hrough a series of initiatives in the middle of the 1980s, John Paul extended the horizon of his pontificate under the theme of "mission to all the nations." This missionary outreach can be summarized in the call to "open the doors to Christ." In his encyclical *Dominum et Vivificantem* (The Holy Spirit in the Life of the Church and the World), John Paul explains: "Within the perspective of the Great Jubilee, we need to look further and go further afield, knowing that 'the wind blows where it wills.'"[1] The steps leading to this phase of his pontificate include his journey to Africa in August 1985, and his trip to India in January and February 1986. These pastoral visits were followed by the visit to the Synagogue in Rome (April 1986) and by the day of prayer and fasting for peace at Assisi in October 1986. All these initiatives culminated in the publication of the encyclical, *Redemptoris Missio* (Mission of the Redeemer), which the media practically ignored because the Gulf War was then in progress. Consequently, even "experts" on this pontificate have, for the most part, forgotten the encyclical.

In a sense the day of prayer for peace at Assisi was a very creative aspect of John Paul's missionary endeavor. In the two preceding chapters we saw how, for the first time (for the Pope and the papacy), John Paul preached directly to Muslims and visited the Jewish Synagogue in Rome. Assisi also marked a first, as representatives of the major religions of the world surrounded the Pope. The actual event took place in October, but the Pope had already mentioned the idea at an ecumenical service held the previous January 25. This is what he said on that occasion:

> The Holy See desires to contribute to and promote a worldwide move-
> ment of prayer for peace that, going beyond the confines of a single
> nation and involving the beliefs of every religion, comes to embrace
> the entire world.

The project was new, but the announcement fell on prepared ground. A World Conference of Religions for Peace, begun in 1968, had been sponsoring periodic meetings with an ever-increasing membership. In 1986 the Ecumenical Council of Churches at Geneva began preparations for a worldwide conference of Christian churches on the theme, "Justice, Peace and the Preservation of Creation," scheduled to take place at Seoul, Korea, in 1990. On December 12, 1985, the Anglican primate Robert Runcie had announced that he was preparing for a religious summit for peace. And as early as June 1977, the Russian Orthodox Church had hosted a world conference at Moscow on the theme, "Religious Men for a Lasting Peace."

So the time was ripe to stage a major event on the theme of world peace. John Paul seized the opportunity and did not meet with any major negative reaction. The gathering took place as planned and had a great impact throughout the world, far surpassing any ecumenical gathering to date.

Never before had an ecumenical meeting included such diverse membership and so many high-ranking persons (160 people had been of-ficially invited, thirty-two of whom belonged to Christian churches, two from the Jewish tradition, and twenty-six from non-Christian religions; all together, sixty delegations took part). Not all the non-Christian del-egations were considered representatives of a specific religious organiza-tion, because some of the Islamic and Hindu delegates lacked a central organization. As for the Christian delegations, however, there had never been an ecumenical gathering in which all the churches were present.

The Catholic Church was represented by the Pope, by various cardi-nals, and by bishops from countries such as Argentina, Canada, the United States, Great Britain, Czechoslovakia, Zaire, Lebanon, Italy, Aus-tria, and India. Representing the Orthodox Church were the Ecumenical Patriarch of Constantinople, the Greek Orthodox Patriarch of Antioch, the Metropolitan of the Russian Orthodox Church, and Orthodox repre-sentatives from Romania, Georgia, Bulgaria, and Finland. Worldwide Christian churches were represented as follows: Old Catholic, Anglican, Lutheran, Dutch Reformed Church, Methodist, Disciples of Christ, Bap-tist, the Ecumenical Council of Churches, Mennonite, Quakers, YMCA and YWCA.

The Jews were represented by B'nai Brith and by Rabbi Elio Toaff of the Synagogue in Rome. Registered within the non-Christian delegations were the Dalai Lama; Buddhists from India, Thailand, Korea, and Japan; Hindus from India and Great Britain; Zoroastrians from India; Sikhs from India; Muslims from Morocco, Pakistan, Turkey, India, Bangladesh, Ivory Coast, Kenya, Saudi Arabia, and Mozambique; traditional African religions from Kenya, Ghana, and Togo; North American Indian traditions; and Japanese Shintoists.

The day was divided into three sections. First, the delegates gathered at the Church of St. Mary of the Angels in Assisi and were welcomed by the Pope. Then the gathering was divided into twelve different assemblies so that each group could pray according to its own liturgy or tradition. Next a general assembly took place in the *piazza* of the basilica, where representatives of each of the twelve groups took turns reciting a prayer. A pause for silent prayer followed each recitation in order to avoid any appearance of syncretism.

The opening ceremony at St. Mary of the Angels began with the chanting of a Hebrew psalm and closed with a hymn in Japanese. The head of each of the delegations sat in a semi-circle in front of the Portiuncula. The Pope was in the center, flanked by the Dalai Lama on his left and a representative of the Patriarchate of Constantinople on his right. In the middle of the day, the twelve distinct groups met in various locations throughout Assisi for over two hours of prayer. Christians, for example, met in the Cathedral of St. Rufinus; Muslims gathered in a hall at the monastery of St. Anthony; Buddhists met in the Church of St. Peter; and the Jews prayed together in the open air, to avoid praying in a place adorned by Christian symbols.

The general assembly in the cathedral of St. Rufinus was the largest and most significant ever held since the beginning of the ecumenical movement. Wearing a red stole, the Pope opened the service with a few words in English: "What we are doing here today would not be complete if we were to proceed without a stronger resolve to pledge ourselves to continue the search for full unity and to overcome the various divisions which still remain."

The Metropolitan of the Russian Orthodox Church read a passage in Russian from Paul's Letter to the Romans; the President of the World Council of Churches read a selection in English from the Letter to the Ephesians; the Secretary General read from the Letter to the Colossians in Spanish; the representative of the Patriarchate in Antioch read in French from the Letter of James; and finally, the Metropolitan of the Romanian Orthodox Church read from the First Letter of John in Arabic.

The Pope concluded the service with a passage from the Gospel according to John.

The day's principal activities were prayer, pilgrimage, and fasting. To convey a sense of pilgrimage, each of the twelve assemblies walked from their particular assembly points to the general assembly in the *piazza* of the Basilica of St. Francis. Again, the assembly was held in the open air to avoid confronting non-Christians with Christian symbols. Fasting that day consisted in skipping the midday meal.

The three-hour general assembly was televised throughout the world. For the first time ever all the world religions had come together to pray for peace in all the languages of the world. And the symbolism was striking: the distribution of olive branches, the lighting of a flame of peace, rituals of purification, the release of doves into the air, lighted torches, arms raised in prayer, joined hands, inclinations of various kinds, and the fraternal embrace. It was also a day of brilliant colors: the yellow robes of the Shintoists, the orange and red of the Buddhists and Hindus, the bright feathers of the North American Indians, the variegated colors of the Africans, the violet of the Anglicans, the black of the Orthodox and Lutherans, the red of cardinals, and of course, the Pope's white cassock.

John Paul closed the ceremony with a discourse in which he stated: "I humbly repeat here my own conviction: Peace bears the name of Jesus Christ. But, at the same time and in the same breath, I am ready to acknowledge that Catholics have not always been faithful to this affirmation of faith. We have not always been peacemakers. For ourselves, therefore, but also perhaps in a sense for all, this encounter at Assisi is an act of penance."

On October 28, the Italian newspaper *Corriere della Sera* reported that "the truce of God was observed in practically the whole world," but on the very next day the French newspaper *Le Monde* carried the following article under the headline *Une trêve profanée* (a desecrated truce):

> Except for Central America, the Pope's appeal has had practically no effect on the principal theaters of combat. In Lebanon the rival militia of Beirut had promised to silence their guns, but combat between the Shiite militia and the Palestinians resulted in one dead and two wounded, despite a cease-fire that had been agreed upon the previous day. The war between Iran and Iraq goes on, since Teheran has ignored John Paul's appeal. In Afghanistan the radio has not even mentioned the statement from the Vatican, and the news agency *Tass* has likewise neglected to mention it, although it did praise the authorities of the Catholic Church in Rome for the ecumenical initiative. The Afghan re-

sistance did not subscribe to a truce because there was no response from the opposing side. In Sri Lanka, where the two sides had agreed on a truce, the government of Colombo accused the Tamil separatists of breaking the truce by firing on a military plane and killing a soldier. The Punjab Shikh extremists have killed three Hindus and a moderate Shikh politician. In Ireland the day was observed by an attempted act of revenge by the IRA. The army in El Salvador has accused the guerrillas of attacking a military base in the north. There are no reports available regarding the other fronts: Cambodia, the Philippines, Angola, Mozambique or Western Sahara.

It is evident, therefore, that in concrete terms no "universal truce" was observed. A number of governments or factions were willing to observe a day of peace, but the opposition would not agree. The French newspaper *La Croix* stated on October 29, 1986, that "in one way or another the Pope's appeal was known, and it had repercussions in many countries." Although the truce was not universally observed, the day at Assisi did have a great impact on the political world. It brought to everyone's attention the resolve of the Pope and other religious leaders to promote peace in the world and to work toward that end by any means religion can provide. When he had announced the day of prayer for peace at Lyons, France, on October 4, John Paul had stated: "I launch this appeal with great confidence, because I believe in the spiritual value and efficacy of symbols."

A second convocation, also a day of prayer and fasting, took place at Assisi on January 10 and 11, 1993. It focused on peace in Europe, and once again the membership comprised Christians, Jews, and Muslims. Years later, in October 1999, another general assembly took place that involved all the principal world religions.

Ever since the first gathering at Assisi, the Pope always meets with religious leaders when he travels to a religiously diverse country. We saw in Chapter 21 that Muslim leaders in Nigeria had absented themselves from a scheduled meeting with John Paul in 1982. The same thing happened in Nairobi on September 19, 1995; and just two years before, Buddhists of Sri Lanka refused to meet with the Pope because of his comments on Buddhism in the book, *Crossing the Threshold of Hope*. John Paul has suffered greatly because of these rebuffs. In Sri Lanka on January 21, 1995, he said: "This meeting signifies togetherness. We are together; it is necessary to be together; not to be together is dangerous."

Perhaps it is not so difficult to identify the origin of John Paul's eagerness to reach out to other religions. It might be in response to a suggestion that the Swiss theologian, Hans Urs von Balthasar, had offered early on in John Paul's pontificate, published in an interview with the Italian magazine *Trenta Giorni*: "Perhaps the Pope should intensify his dialogue with other religions. He always goes to Catholics. I don't want to criticize him; he has done enough, God knows. But he always surrounds himself with Catholics; any discussion beyond the confines of the Church is lacking."

Some persons in the Curia have not been fully supportive of John Paul's contacts with non-Christian religions. One cardinal, for example, has been quoted as saying that the Pope places too much emphasis on the value of improving dialogue with non-Christian religions. And when John Paul convoked the interreligious assembly at Assisi, he had to defend himself from his critics from the summer of 1986 until the spring of 1987.

NOTES

1. John Paul II, *Dominum et Vivificantem* (Pauline Books & Media, 1986), n. 53.

❈ CHAPTER TWENTY-FOUR ❈

Against War and Violence

N o century in history has seen as many wars as has the twenti-
eth; no century has heard as many popes cry out the words:
"Peace! Peace!" Benedict XV passed into history branding the
First World War as "useless slaughter." Pius XII warned: "Nothing is lost
with peace, but everything can be lost by war." Pope John XXIII is the
author of the encyclical letter, *Pacem in Terris* (Peace on Earth). And
Paul VI issued the call at the United Nations assembly: "No more war!"
He spoke against war many times and instituted the World Day of Peace.

John Paul has received and perfected this heritage. Perhaps no other
pope has preached about peace as vigorously or "confessed" the sin of
war committed by Christians and asked for forgiveness with as much insistence. In addition, John Paul has incorporated four unique dimensions
into his preaching activity on behalf of peace:

❖ support for the condemnation of war as expressed in *Gaudium et
   Spes* (Pastoral Constitution on the Church in the Modern World);

❖ the message he has carried to nations that are at war and his visits
   to regions that are subject to guerrilla attacks and terrorism;

❖ admonitions against particular wars and his encouragement of
   collateral efforts for peace by the episcopate and other religions;

❖ a development of the doctrine on "humanitarian intervention";
   that is, the obligation of the international community to stop wars
   by disarming the aggressor.

John Paul made his most radical statement against war of every type
when he visited the city of Coventry, England—which had been totally

destroyed by Nazi bombardment in the Second World War. He remarked: "Today the scale and the horror of modern warfare—whether nuclear or not—makes it totally unacceptable as a means of settling differences between nations. War should belong to the tragic past, to history; it should find no place on humanity's agenda for the future."

Here the Pope applied the phrase, "totally unacceptable," to *any* war, whether nuclear or conventional, while the document *Gaudium et Spes* had qualified the term "total war" by the use of nuclear weapons. John Paul's courageous statement at Coventry thus stood out among those other popes had made in modern times.

Preparing for the journey to England, John Paul's collaborators continued to advise him against going; but he was determined to carry through with the visit. Members of the Curia were utterly dismayed. When they told him that to visit a country at war could be taken as an offense by the other country, the Pope replied that he would visit them both! And he did, adding onto his visit to Great Britain (May 28 to June 2) a visit to Argentina (June 10 to 13). He explained his decision to the Curia by saying that those two pastoral visits were "atypical"; they had a pastoral character quite distinct from all his others. The Pope had to face the risk involved, because his worldwide pastoral concerns impelled him to do so. He could not abandon two countries at war with one another, and he must show the world at large that the universality of his mission did not conflict with a people's patriotism.

Asking God's Pardon for Violence

Regarding the "confession of sin in waging war," we have already seen the Pope make such an official declaration at Assisi (Chapter 23). There are other occasions as well, and several are cited here. The first was formulated during the second Day of Prayer for Peace at Assisi as a response to the questions: how can there still be enmity in the world if Christ has destroyed enmity, and how can there be war and killing in the heart of Europe at the threshold of the third millennium? The Pope responded: "The only reply to such questions is the humble request for forgiveness for ourselves and for all. Precisely for this reason, our vigil of prayer is also a vigil of repentance, of conversion" (Assisi, Jan. 9, 1993).

The Pope's most fervent plea for forgiveness referred to the Second World War, asserting that Christians were responsible for wars initiated by others either because they did not prevent them or because they actually cooperated in such wars.

We have just recalled one of the bloodiest wars in history, a war which broke out on a continent with a Christian tradition. Acknowledgment of this fact compels us to make an examination of conscience about the quality of Europe's evangelization. The collapse of Christian values that led to yesterday's moral failures must make us vigilant as to the way the Gospel is proclaimed and lived out today.[1]

In marking the fiftieth anniversary of the end of the Second World War, John Paul said:

> In the face of every war, we are all called to ponder our responsibilities, to forgive and to ask forgiveness. We feel bitter regret, as Christians, when we consider that the horrors of that war took place on a continent which could claim a remarkable flowering of culture and civilization—the continent which had remained so long in the light of the Gospel and of the Church. For this the Christians of Europe need to ask forgiveness, even while recognizing that there were varying degrees of responsibility in the events which led to the war.[2]

*T*he "confession of sin" belongs to the later years of John Paul's pontificate, but even in the early years he asserted that it is necessary to ask God's pardon for war and violence. This is what he said after the massacre in the Palestinian refugee camps on September 19, 1982: "I ask the merciful Lord to have pity on our humanity, which has fallen into such excesses of cruelty!"

Among those responsible for the massacre were Lebanese Falangists who called themselves Catholics and who claimed they were acting in defense of their country. The Pope's appeal, therefore, was especially significant. And twelve years later, speaking of the genocide in Rwanda, John Paul explicitly addressed the responsibility Catholics have for that tragic event (see Chapter 39).

Remember that Pope Wojtyła was born in one time of war and lived through another in early adulthood. He has good reason to preach about peace, and he addressed one of his most impressive appeals to Catholics in Ireland:

> I proclaim, with the conviction of my faith in Christ and with an awareness of my mission, that violence is evil, that violence is unacceptable as a solution to problems, that violence is unworthy of man. Violence is a lie, for it goes against the truth of our faith, the truth of our humanity.... Now I wish to speak to all men and women engaged in violence. I appeal to you, in the language of passionate pleading. On my knees I beg you to turn away from the paths of violence and to return to the ways of peace.[3]

Three years later, speaking to the Basques at Loyola, Spain, on November 6, 1982, John Paul spoke to young people "who let themselves be tempted by materialistic and violent ideologies. I would say to them with affection and firmness—and my voice is that of one who has personally suffered from violence—that they should reflect on the path they have taken.... Violence is no way to build up. It offends God, those who suffer it and those who practice it."[4]

The Pope used the same argument in Peru in 1995: "I ask you in God's name: change your course!" Although none of the terrorist or guerrilla groups dropped their tactics because of his appeals, John Paul is convinced that we must continue to hope for results to the Gospel call for the rejection of violence in the Holy Spirit's good time and not according to our own calendar. That is the way he spoke to reporters on the flight from Lima to Rome:

"Wasn't your appeal to the terrorists in Peru a cry in the desert?"

"A voice crying in the desert was necessary. It is often necessary."

"Do you think it will be heard?"

"Ultimately this voice is heard more and more. It has been crying out in the desert for two thousand years" (Feb. 6, 1985).

I consider it a great personal privilege that I was able to be in the airport at Ayacucho, Peru. I witnessed the Pope turn toward the mountains and cry out as he did to the Sandinistas. I was also present on another occasion eight years later at Agrigento, Italy, when he challenged the Sicilian Mafia:

God has said: Thou shalt not kill. No man, no human association, no Mafia can change or trample on this most holy law of God. The Sicilian people are a people that love life, that give life. It cannot live always under a contrary culture, a culture of death. Here you want a culture of life. In the name of Christ, crucified and risen from the dead, of Christ who is the way, the truth and the life, I address those responsible: convert! One day you will see the justice of God!

Written words cannot fully portray the Pope's vehemence in admonishing these people. To feel the full weight of his words, you would have to add the commanding sound of his voice, his stern countenance, his right arm raised and his index finger pointing in accusation. John Paul is capable of strong emotion and of exhibiting legitimate anger. Such scenes conjure images of money tables being overturned in the Temple!

But it may well be not only the Mafia in Sicily and the guerrillas in Peru who threaten peace. Someday soon it may be acknowledged that the powerful nations of the world also pose a threat to peace with their nuclear weapons and guided missiles. Sometimes these very nations send representatives who visit the Pope with great ceremony! Read what he said to them when he departed from his prepared text at St. Peter's Basilica and spoke from the heart: "Why this threat of war? Why these principles of combat? We should reexamine the fundamental principles by which humanity lives, and see if they are not false, if they should not be changed, in order to preserve true justice, to save peace in the world, and in the end to save humanity!" (March 18, 1984)

A few months later John Paul spoke again in the same vein when he visited Ottawa, Canada: "It is necessary to protect people from death—millions of people—from nuclear death and death from starvation. It is necessary to protect from death all that is human!" (Sept. 20, 1984) Finally, on the second Day of Prayer for Peace at Assisi, his speech took on an apocalyptic tone when he prayed that the fire that Christ has brought to the earth should destroy all hatred and all instruments of death (Jan. 9, 1993).

NOTES

1. *L'Osservatore Romano*, English Edition, September 1989.

2. Ibid., June 1995.

3. Ibid., October 1979.

4. Ibid., November 1982.

❧ CHAPTER TWENTY-FIVE ❧

World Youth Days

*J*ohn Paul's pontificate has often focused on young people. In the book *Crossing the Threshold of Hope,* he explains how the World Youth Days began: "No one invented the World Youth Days. It was the young people themselves who created them. Those Days, those encounters, then became something desired by young people throughout the world. Most of the time these days were something of a surprise for priests, and even bishops, in that they surpassed all their expectations."[1]

John Paul minimizes his role in establishing the World Youth Days, but it is true that young people have always responded enthusiastically to him. And it was the Pope who first issued the invitation to the young. So, in spite of his self-effacing words, I want to devote this chapter to one of the Pope's most beautiful initiatives.

The World Youth Days began in the mid-80s, and they have successfully continued because of the support and involvement of young people themselves. In a way, John Paul's invitation to youth can be traced to his call in St. Peter's Square on October 22, 1978: "Open the doors to Christ!" When the Pope appeared at the window of the Vatican that Sunday after a lengthy liturgy, it was already 1:30 P.M. After an improvised prayer, young people in the Square started to chant, *"Viva il Papa!"* "Long live the Pope!" John Paul spontaneously responded, "You are the hope of the world! You are my hope!"

In December of that same year the Pope began his visits to the parishes of Rome, and with each visit he asked for a meeting with young people. The same procedure was followed for his visits outside of Rome and outside of Italy. And one of those meetings with youth that proved decisive was the one in Paris on June 1, 1980. It lasted three hours—a festive event with young people asking questions and the Pope responding. There were prepared questions on topics of which the Pope had been informed in advance, as is the custom. But among the questioners was a young man who ascended the platform with a paper in his hand and who asked the Pope a series of questions: "I am an atheist," he began. "I reject all beliefs and all dogma. I want to say also that I do not object to anyone's faith, but I do not understand faith. Holy Father, in whom do *you* believe? Why do you believe? What is it that is worth the gift of our life and what manner of being is this God you adore?" With that, the young man turned and disappeared into the crowd.

John Paul later wrote to André Frossard about the incident: "How did it come about that I did not reply to that young man's question, or rather series of questions?... Yet that is what happened.... It was only after my return to Rome that I remembered the question that had been left unanswered. I immediately wrote to Cardinal Marty, asking him to find the young man and to present my apologies to him. Shortly afterward the cardinal replied that the necessary had been done and that 'all was well'.... Today there is simply no longer any way of talking about faith without taking into account unbelief and atheism."[2]

The great success of the meeting with young people in Paris surprised everyone. It is true that crowds of young people had gathered for papal events in Mexico, Poland, Ireland, the United States, Africa, and Italy. But people had discounted the success of these encounters by saying that, for one reason or another, it could be expected in those countries. For such an event to succeed in Paris, however, was another matter! When plans for the first World Youth Days were announced, cynics predicted that perhaps twenty young people would be willing to profess their faith in public by attending. Seventeen years later, the surprise exploded to gigantic proportions as over one million young people came out to greet the Holy Father!

The massive crowds of young people attracted to Pope Wojtyła, and the constant growth in their numbers through the years, testify to their unanimous appreciation for this pontificate. Other programs, such as the pro-life movement and the *mea culpas*, have not won unanimous support among Catholics. Those countries that remain close allies of the Soviet system have not appreciated the fall of Communism. Neither the right nor the left has much to say to today's youth, but the fact that young people are flocking to the Pope surprises everyone. Of all the attempts to explain this phenomenon, perhaps one of the best is a statement of

Eugene Ionesco, a Romanian academic in France: "For a long time no one spoke any more of God or of love. Everyone thought that it would make people laugh in derision. But now the crowds have come to listen, and they do not laugh" (*Le Matin,* June 4, 1980). This is true, says Ionesco, of all the French crowds, but it is especially true of young people. An Italian intellectual, Giuseppe Prezzolini, made the same observation: "The reason is that they hear in his words something that transcends everything else."[3]

Among many reasons why John Paul is so well accepted by young people are, undoubtedly, his frankness and sincerity. He does not modify his message so it will be well received; rather, he speaks the truth plainly and candidly, and young people seem to like that. The Pope himself states it this way: "The one being sought out is Christ, who knows that which is in every man (cf. Jn 2:25)...and who can give true answers to his questions! And even if they are demanding answers, the young are not afraid of them; more to the point, they even await them."[4] Moreover, the radical nature of the Gospel message is what motivates young people, as the Pope indicated in Paris: "Permissiveness does not make people happy. Consumer society does not make people happy. It has never done so!" (June 1, 1980) In 1992 at Bergamo, Italy, John Paul spoke ardently to young people in defense of life: "Dear young people, do not be afraid to defend life, all life—life in the womb and life in one's declining years" (June 20, 1992). Finally, during his visit to Holland in 1985, he addressed these strong words to young people when he was asked about new norms of sexual morality:

> Dearest young people, let me speak to you frankly. I know that you are wholly loyal to what is good. But are you really so sure that the idea which you form of Christ is completely in conformity with reality? For the Gospel lets us see a very demanding Christ.... In the area of sexuality we above all find forceful statements concerning the indissolubility of marriage (Mt 19:3–9) and his condemnation of adultery, even when this is committed only in the heart (Mt 5:27ff.). Does it seem realistic to you when people form an idea of a Christ as permissive in the area of married love, regarding abortion, sexual relations before or outside of marriage and homosexual relationships? (Utrecht, May 13, 1985)

Another factor in the Pope's popularity with young people is that he really believes in them, has confidence in them, and loves them. He delights in their company and willingly listens to what they have to say. The young people sense this; they know John Paul is not exaggerating when he tells them that he always learns something from them. Consequently, when André Frossard told him in Paris: "Your Holiness, I think you could lead the young people wherever you want," the Pope replied: "On the contrary; it is they who lead me!"

John Paul believes that beneath one's apparent indifference, there is within every person a strong religious yearning, and young people best exemplify this. "Today's culture sometimes contradicts Christ in a blasphemous way; at other times it smiles at him ironically, but in the depths of one's heart that person is waiting for Christ. The whole person awaits the whole Christ" (Nov. 3, 1984).

Therefore, it is necessary to rid people of the prejudice that smothers their natural longing for God. "Dear friends, let yourselves be captivated by Christ; heed his invitation and follow him!"[5]

"...New generations clearly seem to be accepting with enthusiasm what their elders seem to have rejected. What does this mean? It means that *Christ is forever young.*"[6]

Once individuals allow themselves to be led by Christ, they can convince others to do the same. "Go forth to preach the Good News which redeems; do it with joyful hearts and become communicators of hope in a world not seldom tempted to despair" (Dec. 21, 1993).

But even apart from mission, the Church needs young people: "We need the enthusiasm of the young. We need their *joie de vivre.* In it is reflected something of the original joy God had in creating man."[7] These words are among John Paul's most striking. Perhaps the poems Karol Wojtyła composed in his youth were not particularly noteworthy in themselves, but, providentially, writing poetry has given Pope Wojtyła a feeling for the right word to use.

John Paul's admiration for the *joie de vivre* of the young seems to increase with his advancing years. He confessed at Catania, Sicily, in 1994: "Young people always rejuvenate me"; and the following day at Siracusa, Sicily, he said: "I am always happy to meet with young people; I don't know why, but I am." And the Pope does not cut back on his meetings with young people, despite his age. In fact, in 1996 he said at one of the parishes in Rome: "With all the years that I am carrying, I feel young!" At another Roman parish in 1997 he playfully remarked: "Do you have money in your pockets to return home? I am also among those who would like to return—to my youth!" The Pope frequently speaks to the young in this light-hearted manner, like a father speaking to his children. At Catania in 1994 he spoke to them matter-of-factly about his use of a cane: "Some say that this cane has made me old; others say that this cane has made me young again!"

During his visit to Manila in 1995, the young people began chanting: "John Paul II! We kiss you!" And he replied: "And I kiss you too, all of you! No jealousy!" Sometimes the Pope departs from his prepared text to say, for example: "Rather than speak to you, I want to just look at you as you are: young, spontaneous, authentic, and capable of loving" (at the Vatican, Easter, 1980).

In a discourse to the clergy of Rome John Paul spoke of the importance of young people: "It is necessary to concentrate on young people. I have always thought so. The third millennium belongs to them, and it is our duty to prepare them for it. They are ready" (March 2, 1995).

*A*t the beginning of his pontificate, the new Pope expressed his desire to meet with young people in Roman parishes and elsewhere. At first, bishops and parish priests were surprised by his request, but they soon saw for themselves that the meetings were filled to overflowing. Six years into John Paul's pontificate, the World Youth Days began. The first announcement for such a gathering took place on May 22, 1983. Young people were invited to come to Rome for "an encounter of prayer, of sharing, of conversation, and of joy." The second announcement, made on November 25, 1984, set the gathering for the following Palm Sunday, during the year dedicated to youth by the United Nations. Both events were highly successful, and the World Youth Day was formally inaugurated with an apostolic letter issued on March 31, 1985.

The celebration of World Youth Day follows two patterns. First, each year a day for youth is observed on Palm Sunday in the local churches around the world, and in Rome with the Holy Father. Secondly, every other year the event is held in a different location where young people from all over the world are invited. Thus far, World Youth Day has been celebrated in Buenos Aires (1987), Santiago de Compostela (1989), Czestochowa (1991), Denver (1993), Manila (1995), and Paris (1997). Each celebration attracts an increasing number of participants. In Manila more than two million young people gathered, although the press estimated an exaggerated four or five million. This was said to have been the largest gathering for any of the papal visits up to that time. In Paris, on the other hand, police estimated the crowd on the final evening at 750,000. The number projected for World Youth Day in the year 2000, scheduled to take place in Rome, is two million.

Ecclesial Communities

Through his meetings with young people the Pope has also come into close contact with some of the new movements and ecclesial communities in the Church. He sees them as providential bearers of the Gospel message within our secular society. In fact, John Paul is convinced that the coming of the year 2000 is definitely an opportunity to proclaim the Christian message in all its fullness: "It is time to give witness to the Gospel with renewed, clear vigor, and without commentary" (Jan. 2, 1983).

The Pope has spoken about his hope for the Jubilee to the members of Focolare, a movement he is especially fond of. Speaking at the international center of Focolare, he said: "In the history of the Church there have been so many radical expressions of love, like that of St. Francis of Assisi, St. Ignatius Loyola, Charles de Foucauld, and so many others up to our own day. There is also your radicalism of love, of Chiara, and of the members of Focolare; a radicalism that tries to make love conquer in every circumstance, in every difficulty" (Aug. 19, 1984).

The "Chiara" whom the Pope mentions in this statement is Chiara Lubich, the foundress of the Focolare movement. John Paul honors this woman, who is the same age as the Pope, with special friendship. If she is present at a papal audience, John Paul greets her as his sister, and sometimes he quotes her in a discourse. When he does not see her, he will sometimes ask, "Is Chiara here?"

John Paul has approved the statutes of the Focolare movement, which stipulate that the president must always be a woman. This is how Chiara Lubich explains it: One day she summoned the courage to ask the Holy Father if he would approve the regulation in the statutes that the president of the Focolare movement should always be a woman. His response was: "Why not?" In order to understand the significance of this approval, it suffices to know that the organization exists in more than 100 countries and that its one million-plus members include religious, priests, bishops, and cardinals, as well as laity.

John Paul looks upon the various movements in the Church as signs of the vitality of the Church. Perhaps he sees them as a compensation for the crisis of vocations to the priesthood: "In place of traditional vocations, which lead to the priesthood and monastic orders, another type of vocation has been added to them, the vocation of the lay movements."[8]

In preparation for the Great Jubilee, John Paul called for a reunion of new movements and ecclesial communities to take place in Rome for the feast of Pentecost during the year dedicated to the Holy Spirit (1998). On Saturday, May 30, a truly unusual spectacle unfolded in St. Peter's Square: 180,000 persons, representing fifty-six movements and ecclesial communities from all over the world, listened as Chiara Lubich spoke.

At the end of the event, John Paul explained his reasons for convoking the vast assembly.

In our world, often dominated by a secularized culture which encourages and promotes models of life without God, the faith of many is sorely tested, is frequently stifled and dies. We are urgently reminded, therefore, of the need for a strong proclamation and a deep and solid Christian formation.... And here are the movements and the new ecclesial communities; they are the response, given by the Holy Spirit, to this critical challenge at the end of the millennium.... Their birth and growth have brought to the Church's life an unexpected newness, which is sometimes even disruptive. This has given rise to questions, uneasiness and tensions; at times it has led to presumptions and excesses on the one hand, and on the other, to numerous prejudices and reservations. It was a testing period for their fidelity, an important occasion for verifying the authenticity of their charisms. Today a new stage is unfolding before you: that of ecclesial maturity. This does not mean that all problems have been solved. Rather, it is a challenge, a road to take. The Church expects from you the mature fruits of communion and commitment.[9]

The above discourse is very important because, in it, John Paul gives an historic assignment to his chosen ones.

In moments of difficulty, John Paul has come to the defense of the ecclesial movements, in opposition to the desire of the bishops for the "normalization" of such communities—as religious institutes. With the apostolic exhortation *Christifideles Laici* (Lay Members of Christ's Faithful People), John Paul exhorted the bishops to give the laity their proper place and mission in the life of the Church. John Paul has also approved and recognized several entities whose cases had been pending for years. The Pope has given some ecclesial movements, such as *Comunione e Liberazione* (Communion and Liberation) and *Cammino Neo-Catecumenale* (Journey of the Neo-Catechumenate), permission to establish their own seminaries in Rome when it was not possible to do so elsewhere.

Presiding over a liturgy at an encounter of the Neo-Catechumenate, John Paul encouraged bishops to accept such celebrations in their own churches. He granted recognition to the movement *Rinnovamento nello Spirito* (Renewal in the Spirit), assuring that what had flourished during his pontificate would not be lost.

Ecclesial movements to reach young people, young people to reach all people—this is a practical indication of what John Paul has managed to transmit to the Church. Over the years he has been able to surmount the reluctance of many individuals to these new movements. This may well be another important heritage he will leave to his successor.

NOTES

1. John Paul II with Vittorio Messori, *Crossing the Threshold of Hope* (New York: Alfred A. Knopf, 1994), p. 124.

2. A. Frossard, *"Be Not Afraid"* (New York: St. Martin's Press, 1984), pp. 41–43.

3. E. Cavaterra, *Il Papa dell'uomo nuovo* (Rome: Dino Editori, 1981), p. 111.

4. John Paul II with Vittorio Messori, *Crossing the Threshold of Hope* (New York: Alfred A. Knopf, 1994), pp. 123–124.

5. Message to young people, December 21, 1993.

6. John Paul II with Vittorio Messori, *Crossing the Threshold of Hope* (New York: Alfred A. Knopf, 1994), p. 113.

7. Ibid., p. 125.

8. J. Gawronski, "Il Papa, cresci, uomo europeo" *La Stampa*, April 4, 1989.

9. *L'Osservatore Romano,* English Edition, June 3, 1998.

✺ Chapter Twenty-Six ✺

Conferences of Catholic Bishops

*N*ever, in the preceding thirty-five international pastoral visits John Paul has made, had he spent four consecutive hours in one meeting (which actually turned out to be a work session and dialogue with the members of a national conference of bishops). Yet, that is what he did in Los Angeles on September 16, 1987. Three-hundred-twenty bishops of the United States attended, and they had elected four of their members to speak in their name: Cardinal Joseph Bernardin of Chicago, Archbishop John Quinn of San Francisco, Archbishop Rembert Weakland of Milwaukee, and Archbishop Daniel Pilarczyk of Cincinnati. With full freedom, the speakers discussed four important topics and expressed their concern about advice they had received from Rome. The Pope listened and then replied to each of the four speakers, reemphasizing the boundaries beyond which Rome would not validate the changes and adaptations made in local churches.

At the beginning of the meeting, Archbishop William May of St. Louis, at that time president of the National Conference of Catholic Bishops, greeted the Holy Father, saying: "Very graciously you have acceded to our request for a discussion with us." He then introduced the first speaker, Cardinal Bernardin, who touched on the relations of local churches with Rome. Here is a summation of the cardinal's remarks:

> We live in an open society where everyone prizes the freedom to speak his or her mind. Many tend to question things, especially those matters which are important to them, as religion is. They want to know the reasons why certain decisions are made, and they feel free to criticize it if they do not agree or are not satisfied with the explanations.... Tension

in itself need not be debilitating or destructive.... The practical question that must be addressed today...is how to maintain our unity while affirming the diversity in the local realizations of the Church; how to discern the proper balance between freedom and order.... But at times you are misunderstood; some allege that you do not understand the actual situation in which the Church finds herself in the different parts of the world today. It is also painful for us, the shepherds of our particular churches, when we are cast in an adversarial position with the Holy See or with certain groups within our own dioceses.... We must be able to speak with one another with complete candor, without fear. This applies to our exchanges with the Holy See, as well as among ourselves as bishops.[1]

Responding to Cardinal Bernardin's remarks, the Pope emphasized the importance of the "vertical dimension" of the Church "for understanding the relationship of the particular churches to the universal Church. It is important to avoid a merely sociological view of this relationship.... This universal Church cannot be conceived as the sum of the particular churches or as a federation of particular churches.... The Catholic Church herself subsists in each particular church.... In this perspective too we must see the ministry of the successor of Peter not only as a 'global' service, reaching each particular church from 'outside,' as it were, but as belonging already to the essence of each particular church from 'within.'"[2]

Then Archbishop Quinn, addressed the moral teachings of the Church. After listing some of the critical areas in moral teaching and behavior in the United States, he said:

The recent pastoral letters of the American bishops...employ a moral pedagogy which distinguishes between "universally binding moral principles found in the teaching of the Church" and "specific applications, observations and recommendations" which allow for diversity of opinion on the part of those who assess the factual data of situations differently.... We as pastors are greatly concerned that some particular areas of the Church's teaching on both sexual and social morality are at times subjected to negative criticism in our country and sometimes even by Catholics of good will. This can, in some instances, be ascribed to the permissive, narcissistic and consumer qualities of our society.... Nevertheless, we bishops feel that this problem must be mentioned in any presentation of the current situation of the moral teaching of the Church.... Dialogue and discussion, of course, are never a substitute for the decisions of the Magisterium, but they are, and have been, as Cardinal Newman has so effectively shown, its indispensable prolegomenon.[3]

In his response to Archbishop Quinn's intervention, the Pope said in part:

> It is sometimes reported that a large number of Catholics today do not adhere to the teaching of the Church on a number of questions.... It has also been noticed that there is a tendency on the part of some Catholics to be selective in their adherence to the Church's moral teachings. It is sometimes claimed that dissent from the Magisterium is totally compatible with being a "good Catholic" and poses no obstacle to the reception of the sacraments. This is a grave error that challenges the teaching office of the bishops of the United States and elsewhere.... Within the ecclesial community, theological discussion takes place within the framework of faith. Dissent from Church doctrine remains what it is, dissent; as such it may not be proposed or received on an equal footing with the Church's authentic teaching.... In particular, your dialogue will seek to show the unacceptability of dissent and confrontation as a policy and method in the area of Church teaching.[4]

Archbishop Weakland spoke third, and his topic was the laity—in particular, the role of women in the Church:

> Now the Church in the United States of America can boast of having the largest number of educated faithful in the world.... The faithful are more inclined to look at the intrinsic worth of an argument proposed by the teachers in the Church than to accept it on the basis of the authority itself.... In the area of political issues [they] are jealous of their tradition of freedom and deeply resent being told how to vote on an issue or for which candidate to vote.... The faithful are demanding more help from the teaching authority of the Church on how to bring the Gospel to their professional or work world, their societal and political involvement.... Women, in particular, seek to be equal partners in sharing the mission of the Church.... But no picture would be complete without speaking of other groups which add so much to the vitality and spiritual richness of the Church in the United States of America: the Hispanic, African American, and Asian communities.[5]

In his response to this presentation, the Pope said:

> Primarily through her laity, the Church is in a position to exercise great influence on American culture.... With reference to this question, and in such areas as politics, economics, mass media and international life, the service we bring is primarily a priestly service of preaching and teaching the word of God with fidelity to the truth.... The service of our pastoral leadership, purified in personal prayer and penance, far from bearing an authoritarian style in any way, must listen and encourage, challenge and at times correct.... We serve our laity best when we make every effort to provide for them, and in collaboration with them, a

comprehensive and solid program of catechesis.... Women are not
called to the priesthood. Although the teaching of the Church on this
point is quite clear, it in no way alters the fact that women are indeed
an essential part of the Gospel plan to spread the good news of the
kingdom.[6]

And, finally, Archbishop Pilarczyk discussed the question of lay, religious, and priestly vocations.

Will there be enough priests in the future to do the specifically priestly
work that will need doing? What we are experiencing is a broadening
of the concept of Church vocation and Church ministry, a concept
which formerly included only priests and religious, but which now
includes lay persons in an ever increasing number.... Catholic people
in our country have available to them a depth and variety of ministry
in the Church far greater than ever before.... Most emphatically, the
specific roles and implications of ordained ministry and of vowed religious life have to be carefully maintained, as does the urgency of the
need for Christian witness by lay persons in the world.[7]

In the concluding part of his address to the bishops, the Pope responded to Archbishop Pilarczyk's topic of vocations with some remarks:

My interest in the question of vocations is well known to all of you.... It
is a crucial factor for the future of the Church.... Certainly the more
active participation of the laity in the mission of the Church is an elo-
quent sign of the fruitfulness of the Second Vatican Council.... It is important for our people to see clearly that the ministry of the ordained
priest and the involvement of the laity in the Church's mission are not
at all opposed to one another. On the contrary, the one complements
the other.... In our pastoral mission we must often evaluate a situation
and decide on a course of action. We must do this with prudence and
pastoral realism.... At the same time, your pastoral interest and personal involvement in seminary training are something that can never
end.... The Church of tomorrow passes through the seminaries of today.
With the passing of time, the pastoral responsibility will no longer be
ours. But at the present time the pastoral responsibility is ours, and it is
heavy.[8]

Repeatedly, in his visits around the world, John Paul had faced pro-
tests from Catholics. In Germany and Switzerland, Holland and
Belgium, leaders of ecclesial and social groups had questioned him.
Sometimes, as in Mexico, Chile, Argentina, and Zaire, individual bishops had spoken up boldly to the Pope. Never before the meeting in Los
Angeles, however, had an entire Conference of Bishops expressed its
dissatisfaction with the relations between Rome and the local churches.

Two details from this meeting should be noted: John Paul accepts invitations to dialogue, but he usually adheres to principles grounded in Church law and Tradition. The pontificate of John Paul marks an important step forward in the relations between the Pope and the episcopates, which now meet together, discuss matters, and reach decisions. The Pope is always amenable to discussion, but he is equally intent on making sure the Holy See prevails in matters that are essential or are handed down by Tradition. In substance, the four-hour meeting in Los Angeles enabled the bishops to show the Catholic community that they had transmitted their concerns to the Holy Father; and it gave the Pope an opportunity to let the Catholic community know that their bishops were being asked to put on the brakes.

This notion of restraining certain bishops is one of the characteristics of John Paul's pontificate. Except for countries like Germany, Austria, Switzerland, and Holland, and a few individual cases in France and the United States, "applying the brakes" on episcopates has not caused serious conflicts. But, throughout his pontificate, John Paul has been resolute in following this path, sometimes at the cost of his popularity. His restraint has been felt in the nations that have the largest number of bishops: Brazil, Italy, and the United States. It is another interesting fact that the use of such restraint, which began with the meeting of Latin American bishops at Puebla, reached its peak in the mid-1980s. From that time on, either there has been a gradual lining up of bishops in conformity with the dictates of Rome, or there has been open conflict, as in some German-speaking countries.

John Paul's firmness in dealing with the bishops of the United States was obvious. He acted with similar firmness when dealing with the bishops of Brazil who were too heavily involved in social or political questions. Likewise with the Italian bishops who were concentrating—almost exclusively—on the question of freedom of religious choice (rather than reinforcing the country's "Catholic face" which had been obscured by secularization), the Pope was firm. John Paul is not a man to fear speaking the truth even with bishops and cardinals.

Confronting the Critics

John Paul has also shown great courage when he was publicly criticized or challenged. The first incident occurred in the United States in 1979, when a religious sister assigned to welcome the Pope in Washington, D.C., used the occasion to promote the cause of women's ordination.

In Switzerland, in 1984, a priest and a lay woman objected to compulsory celibacy for priests in the Latin Church and raised the question of the ordination of women. Shortly after, during a 1985 visit to Holland and Belgium, these same questions came up again, more often raised by women than by men. In a particular way, in Holland on May 11, 1985, the Pope received vehement complaints and criticism for naming as bishop a man whom many judged excessively conservative. John Paul told his critics: "Believe me, my dear brothers and sisters, it pains me to know of your sufferings. But be assured that I have truly listened, examined, and prayed. And I have named the one who, before God, I judge to be most suitable. So accept him, in the love of Christ."

More recently, his selection of bishops in Switzerland, Austria, and Germany has been contested. Sometimes the naming of a bishop has served to intensify rather than calm rebellious spirits. In fact, in some cases the Pope has had to hasten "with a stick in hand" to settle things.

This way of acting with bishops is the same John Paul uses with religious institutes. A case in point was the conflict with the Jesuits, which he inherited from Paul VI and resolved authoritatively in 1981 and 1983. Likewise in conflicts with priests or lay associations, the Pope is always disposed to listen, but he is firm in his defense of doctrine and discipline. He is not readily disposed to reforms. In fact, there has been a total lack of reform in the Curia and the government of the Church. In that respect Pope Wojtyła's pontificate, after twenty years, is exactly the same as that of Pope Paul VI. Whatever changes were made, beginning with the so-called reform of the Curia in 1988, have been minimal. The same can be said of the changes in the papal conclave (1987) and in the Vicariate of Rome (1998). Likewise regarding changes in personnel; practically speaking, only Cardinals Ratzinger and Etchegaray were brought into the Curia by John Paul.

As regards the government of the Church, the number of people working in various Curia and Vatican offices, which rose from 89 to 167 during the pontificate of Paul VI, has remained the same. The Synods of Bishops have been held periodically according to the schedule set up by Paul VI. It is true that John Paul has convoked the College of Cardinals five times, something not customary in former times. But there is nothing new regarding its method or content. There has been no change in the number of cardinals (120), though three additional cardinals were named on February 21, 1998. No change has been made in the cut-off age (of 80 years) for entering an elective conclave; neither has the stipulation that bishops should submit their retirement request at 75 been changed, nor the five-year term of office for officials in the Curia.

There have been no reforms of any kind worthy of mention, except for the change in the Secretary of State, just alluded to, and the convoking of an Extraordinary Synod. In addition, there have been two practical changes in administration of the Curia that have not been formalized, but have, in the past twenty years, achieved a remarkable degree of efficiency. These are, namely, the occasional consultations of bishops that have been convoked in Rome to resolve extraordinary questions, and the small working sessions that are held for the discussion and resolution of particular questions. The Pope favors such informal meetings held for the discussion and resolution of problems. Rather than meet with individuals separately, he prefers to discuss matters in the presence of all those concerned. Sometimes these more informal meetings will serve as a follow-up after *ad limina* visits, or when one of the Congregations does not suffice for solving a problem.

In June 1981, the first extraordinary consultation was held in Central America. It lasted four days, and those in attendance were the presidents of the National Conference of Bishops, religious provincial superiors, CELAM (the Council of Latin American Bishops' Conferences), and selected officials from the Vatican Curia. In January 1983, an informal consultation on peace and disarmament was held with members of the National Conference of Bishops from the United States, Belgium, France, Germany, Great Britain, Italy, and Holland, together with some members of the Curia. The episcopate of Peru had a general assembly in Rome in October 1984, to discuss liberation theology. Finally, in 1985, the entire Bishops' Conference of Switzerland met with the Pope and Vatican officials to discuss tensions existing in the diocese of Chur, Switzerland. However, the most compelling assemblies took place in March 1986 and March 1987, and they involved the bishops of Brazil and the United States. The Holy Father has continued to hold similar convocations with other episcopates; for example, in the Persian Gulf, March 4–6, 1991; and in the former Yugoslavia, held at Rome on October 17, 1995.

John Paul leaves the ordinary government of the Church to the various departments of the Curia, but he does not leave everything in the hands of officials. He exercises control in all areas, and when necessary he does not hesitate to convoke extraordinary or special assemblies or to consult with bishops during his international travels. Moreover, the Pope uses particular synods like that in Holland in 1980; extraordinary synods like the one in 1985; special synods, as in Europe (1991), Africa (1994), Pan-America (1997), Asia (1998), and again in Europe (1998). Although Paul VI had planned some of these synods, they never materialized. The journeys, the synods, the extraordinary Holy Year of 1983, the nine years of preparation for the fifth centenary in Latin America (1984–1992), the Marian Year of 1987–1988, the preparations for the Great Jubilee, the beatifications and canonizations, the World Youth Days, and the days for the family—all prove that John Paul does involve others in the government of the Church. He looks ahead and plans in anticipation; he takes the initiative and sets the goals; he is not afraid to give a succinct answer to a complex question.

With regard to governing the Church, the entire pontificate—beyond the particular initiatives—may be interpreted as an effort to seek solutions in advance for every tension that manifests itself. And, when possible, the Pope tries to find solutions that are unifying and directed toward a renewal of the missionary spirit, perhaps experimenting with new forms of episcopal consultations, but without formulating any structural innovations. Apparently John Paul does not have a sensibility for structures, or maybe he has been convinced—through the years—that there is no need to reform in order for him to act outside curial confines. Substantially, John Paul has succeeded in his undertakings. But his successor will need to act promptly and will have to introduce reforms that will render permanent the redimensioning of the Curia and the new papal freedom achieved through the efforts of John Paul II.

NOTES

1. *Origins,* October 1, 1987.
2. Ibid.
3. Ibid.
4. Ibid.
5 Ibid.
6. Ibid.
7. Ibid.
8. Ibid.

❈ CHAPTER TWENTY-SEVEN ❈

Lefebvre's Break with Rome

*W*hat has been the greatest suffering in John Paul's life? The attempt on his life? The death of pilgrims in various incidents during his journeys around the world, for example, at Kinshasa in Zaire (May 1980); Fortaleza, Brazil (July 1980); Montserrat, Spain (Nov. 1982); Cochin, India (Feb. 1986); Maseru, Lesotho (Sept. 1988); or Tuxtla, Mexico (May 1990)? The state of siege in Poland, proclaimed in December 1981, or Poland's drift into secularism after the fall of Communism? Or, in the case of Cardinal Hans Hermann Groer of Vienna, the proof that he was guilty of pedophilia?

Of course, no one could accurately answer for another. We might not even be able to imagine what John Paul's greatest suffering could be. But, objectively speaking, the greatest harm done to the Church during his pontificate was surely the traditionalist schism under the leadership of the French bishop, Marcel Lefebvre. Without authorization from Rome, Lefebvre consecrated four bishops on June 30, 1988, an act for which he was excommunicated on July 2 of the same year. This is the only case involving a group's complete break from the Church during the pontificate of John Paul. After that schism a flurry of disputes arose by innovators in theology. For example, 163 theologians from Germany, Austria, Switzerland, and Holland signed the *Declaration of Cologne* dated January 26, 1989. It contains a denunciation of "the new Roman centralization," and speaks of an "inadmissible extension of the magisterial power of the Pope." The declaration also urges bishops to take a public stand in opposition to the Pope whenever it is necessary. Such a position was taken by 130 French and Belgian theologians on February 20, and by fifty-two Flemish theologians soon after. On April 19, sixty-two Spaniards were added to the list, and sixty-three Italians followed on May 13.

The Pope was caught between schism on one side and strong objections from the other. At the same time, Communism was crumbling and the Pope was very much aware of the approaching end of a millennium. So, while he was enjoying great success in the world at large, he was experiencing his greatest difficulties within the Church. The Lefebvre schism attracted media attention which blew it far out of proportion. The very rarity of such a thing as a schism in the Catholic Church—there had been no event like it since 1870—helped make it a newsworthy event. And it was kept in the news by the slowness with which the situation reached the point of authentic schism and automatic excommunication.

The spectacle attracted and still attracts far more attention than it deserves. Lefebvre's number of followers has not increased; but, for the moment, neither has it diminished. It will take several generations for those who belong to Lefebvre's following to be re-absorbed into the Church. According to a Vatican estimate, some 60,000 to 80,000 members existed at the time of the schism, although the Lefebvrites claimed figures of 120,000 to 200,000. When Lefebvre died on March 25, 1991, these estimates remained stable. Today leaders claim they are present in fifty-six countries and have 300 priests.

Trying to Save Lefebvre

Marcel Lefebvre was the most intransigent adversary of the renewal in the Church desired by the Second Vatican Council. He was the only member of the 2,500 Fathers of the Council who carried his opposition to the point of organizing a community that follows pre-Conciliar norms, especially in the liturgy and formation of the clergy. In so doing, he stood in direct opposition to the popes—Montini, Luciani, Wojtyła—and defied the threat of excommunication. In 1970 he founded the Fraternity of St. Pius X at Econe, Switzerland.

What is interesting in the case of Lefebvre is the action of Pope Wojtyła, who was disposed to grant the French bishop concessions because, at that time, Lefebvre had not yet attacked any doctrine or the authority of the Second Vatican Council. This was a very significant fact, because a stream of objections arose from opponents who accused Pope Wojtyła of "selling out" on Vatican Council II and promoting traditionalist doctrines under the guise of fidelity to the Council. That type of criticism would be repudiated, however, by the Pope's final decision on Lefebvre.

It is true that John Paul tried to save Lefebvre. The Pope received him in an audience on November 1979, thanks in great part to the intervention of Cardinal Siri, who said later: "I was the one who took him to the Pope. They embraced. *L'Osservatore Romano* could have printed the headline: 'Peace has been made.' But instead, the Pope read the dossier from the Congregation for the Doctrine of the Faith."[1] To make unconditional peace with Lefebvre would have been to legitimize his rejection of the doctrinal and normative value of Vatican Council II and the canonical validity of the pontificate of Paul VI. And this would not have been possible for Pope Wojtyła.

Having read the dossier on Lefebvre's case, John Paul advised his representatives, Cardinals Gagnon and Ratzinger, to use every possible means aimed at reconciliation that were not contrary to Vatican II. They drafted a protocol which Lefebvre signed on May 5, 1988, but then immediately retracted—probably due to pressure from collaborators who felt he was being too accommodating to the spirit of Vatican II. The document contained a declaration of "fidelity to the Church, to the Pontiff and to the Magisterium, as well as the obligation to respect canonical discipline and to avoid all polemics concerning the Council and its reforms." The Vatican, on its part, offered Lefebvre the canonical reconciliation of all the priests he had ordained illicitly (after his suspension by Paul VI in 1967); the granting of a statute to the Fraternity, giving a certain degree of exemption from the authority of bishops; permission to use the old Missal; the naming of a bishop selected from among the Fraternity's members; and the establishment of a Roman commission—for settling disputes—with two representatives chosen by the Fraternity from among its members. Lefebvre rejected the agreement because of the last two conditions. He was not content with having only one bishop, and he insisted that his own members should make up the majority on the commission.

For weeks John Paul did everything possible to avoid a schism, but, in the end, the Pope refused Lefebvre's clearly provocative demands, stating that the concept of traditionalism Lefebvre invoked was mistaken. Then the Pope declared the excommunication.

John Paul issued the *motu proprio* on July 2, 1988, under the title *Ecclesia Dei*. This declaration stated that excommunication would result for all those who made a formal act of adhesion to the schism. It included, of course, the four bishops illicitly consecrated on June 30, as well as the two co-consecrators (Marcel Lefebvre, the head of the Fraternity, and the retired Brazilian bishop, Antonio de Castro Mayer).

*T*he followers of Lefebvre publicly voiced their opposition to Pope Wojtyła's program for the Great Jubilee. Franz Schmidberger, Lefebvre's successor as head of the Fraternity, told the news agency *Ansa* on April 28, 1994, that the meeting planned on Mount Sinai in the year 2000 is "against the first commandment of God." On May 22, 1995, following John Paul's request, at Olomouc, for pardon for past religious wars (see Chapter 39), the Fraternity issued a statement. It said, in effect, that the Pope's "words are highly offensive to the Catholic Church and to all those who gave their lives for the Church and for Christian Europe." Hence, John Paul is unacceptable to the Fraternity, especially because of his efforts at dialogue with non-Christian religions and for his *mea culpas*.

Disunity in Other Quarters

No formal schism has occurred on the opposite extreme during John Paul's pontificate, but accusations have been directed back and forth between the Pope and the more radical wing in liberal theology and the base Christian communities. In this area also, Pope Wojtyła has shown himself to be very tolerant on a personal and practical level, but strict when it comes to basic principles of the Faith. There has, in fact, been a rupture on the part of dissident theologians, although they have not been severely censured by the Congregation for the Doctrine of the Faith. Any investigation of theologians still follows the norms and pace established by Paul VI. However, some of John Paul's public statements do carry a more denunciatory tone.

The Pope uttered one of his most severe pronouncements at Paderborn, Germany, on June 22, 1996, calling upon the bishops to exercise their authority.

> One cannot expect people to be enthusiastic about the Church and to find in her the joy of faith when questions, which are really of a secondary nature and significance, are made the focus of public interest; and this all the more so when such questions are presented to believers under the pretext of objective and factual argumentation and with exploitative methods.[2]

The Pope made this statement in reference to the document "We Are Church" (1995), which had received millions of signatures in various countries, especially in Austria where it was first made public, and in Germany where the signers were asked to petition for the ordination of women, the rejection of mandatory celibacy for priests, and more democracy in the Church. These signers sympathized with the "Declaration of Cologne" and other theological manifestoes of 1989. John Paul clarified his attitude toward this type of dialogue two years later in Vienna, when he told the bishops of Austria: "Don't give up dialogue!" He also advised the bishops to be prepared to take risks in advancing dialogue. His statement, however, was not interpreted as a positive exhortation to the bishops because he himself had discontinued dialogue with "We Are Church."

With similar intransigence John Paul spoke against moralists who opposed the Magisterium in matters touching upon family ethics and sexuality:

> The media have conditioned society to listen to what it wants to hear.... An even worse situation occurs when theologians, and especially moralists, ally themselves with the media, which obviously pay a great deal of attention to what they have to say when it opposes "sound doctrine." Indeed, when the true doctrine is unpopular, it is not right to seek easy popularity[3]

The Pope used even stronger language when he spoke about liberation theology at Piura, Peru, on February 4, 1985. He referred to the Gospel passage that states that he who does not enter by the gate is a thief and a brigand. Prior to that, at Managua on March 4, 1983, he had applied that passage to priests who collaborated with the Sandinistas.

The early years of his pontificate were marked by a vehement debate on liberation theology, which now is practically *passé*. John Paul authorized the publication of two documents on the subject by the Congregation for the Doctrine of the Faith, one in 1984 and another in 1986. They offered a critical review of the theology of liberation and called for a message of liberation that is acceptable to the Church.[4]

Perhaps those who have insisted they have always preached a moderate theology of liberation are right. During a 1991 papal visit to Brazil, a journalist asked the Pope if he had ever thought of teaching liberation theology. The Pope replied: "But I always teach the theology of liberation. Even more, I will say that I am a theologian of liberation who remains vigilant at his post."[5]

*I*n accordance with his manner of governing, John Paul tries to promote convergence toward unity at the center, rather than concentrate on traditionalists or on those who question everything. He does this by means of his travels and his weekly catechesis in Rome, frequently mentioning the *Catechism of the Catholic Church* (December 1992) as the *magna* *carta* for the expansion of the Christian endeavor throughout the whole Church. He refers to the *Catechism* more often than to any encyclical or even to the *Code of Canon Law* (revised and promulgated in 1983). Judging from the number of times he speaks of it, we could say the *Catechism* is the chief publication of John Paul's pontificate. When he commissioned the publication of the work on October 11, 1992, he said: "I declare it to be a sure norm for teaching the faith, and thus a valid and legitimate instrument for ecclesial communion."[6] Then, when he presented it to the people of God on December 7 of that same year, he said that its publication "ought to be considered one of the major events in the recent history of the Church."

John Paul, the missionary Pope, points to the *Catechism.* He is more interested in preaching to the nations and in the new evangelization than he is in theological debates or questions pertaining to the internal structure of the Church. He feels an urgent need to reach out to all people; he scrupulously endeavors to proclaim sound doctrine everywhere and to everyone. Faithful to tradition, he is, nevertheless, up-to-date with the Second Vatican Council. And he insists that the norm and instrument for updating is contained in the *Catechism of the Catholic Church.*

NOTES

1. L. Di Schiena, Karol Wojtyła (Rome: Editalia, 1991), p. 384; 75b, pp. 283–286.

2. *Origins,* August 1, 1996.

3. John Paul II with Vittorio Messori, *Crossing the Threshold of Hope* (New York: Alfred A. Knopf, 1994), pp. 172–173.

4. J. Offredo, *Jean-Paul II* (Paris: Editions Carrière-Michel Lafon, 1986), p. 360.

5. D. Del Rio, *Wojtyła. Un Pontificato itinerante,* (Bologna: EDB, 1994), p. 65.

6. John Paul II, *Fidei Depositum* in the *Catechism of the Catholic Church,* p. 5.

※ CHAPTER TWENTY-EIGHT ※

The Role of Women

"*T*hanks to you, woman, for the very fact that you are woman!"
This exclamation belongs to John Paul II, and it is found in
the *Letter to Women* which he published in June 1991. A similar statement appears in the 1996 apostolic exhortation, *Vita Consecrata* (Consecrated Life), when the Pope describes woman as "the
symbol of God's tenderness toward the human race." Eight years before,
John Paul had written in his apostolic letter, *Mulieris Dignitatem* (On the
Dignity and Vocation of Women): "Our time in particular awaits the
manifestation of that 'genius' which belongs to women, and which can
ensure sensitivity for human beings in every circumstance: because they
are human!"[1]

This last document, very personal in tone, occupies a central place in
Pope Wojtyła's pontificate. The French newspaper *Le Monde* said the
document contains a summation of "the re-reading of the concept of femininity in the Bible." In *Mulieris Dignitatem*, John Paul corrects two mil-
lennia of interpretation of the Pauline passage which places man as
"head" over woman (cf. Eph 5:22–23). The Pope, so to speak, corrects
Paul—and no pope had ever done that! John Paul maintains that man and
woman are bound by a "mutual subjection out of reverence for Christ."

The Pope displays a special fraternal tenderness toward women and
freely expresses his warmth. Naturally outgoing, his affection comes
from John Paul's deep admiration for women. He obviously has a high
regard for women's role in society, and he has emphatically encouraged
women's fuller participation in the life of the Church:

> Today I appeal to the whole Church community to be willing to foster
> feminine participation in every way in its internal life.... This is the

179

way to be courageously taken. To a large extent it is a question of making full use of the ample room for lay and feminine presence recognized by the Church's law. I am thinking, for example, of theological teaching; the forms of liturgical ministry permitted, including service at the altar; pastoral and administrative councils; diocesan synods and particular councils; various ecclesial institutions; curias and ecclesiastical tribunals; many pastoral activities, including the new forms of participating in the care of parishes when there is a shortage of clergy, except for those tasks that belong properly to the priest. Who can imagine the great advantages to pastoral care and the new beauty that the Church's face will assume when the feminine genius is fully involved in the various areas of her life?[3]

The document *Mulieris Dignitatem* belongs to a productive period for John Paul: the year 1988, a period of great hopes for Eastern Europe and the Russian millennium; a period which produced the encyclical *Sollicitudo Rei Socialis* and which witnessed the definitive break with Lefebvre. Here are some passages from *Mulieris Dignitatem* in which John Paul sketches his interpretation of the biblical teaching on woman:

"Defer to one another out of reverence for Christ" (Eph 5:21). The author of the Letter to the Ephesians sees no contradiction between an exhortation formulated in this way and the words: "Wives, be subject to your husbands, as to the Lord. For the husband is the head of the wife" (Eph 5:22–23). The author knows that this way of speaking, so profoundly rooted in the customs and religious tradition of the time, is to be understood and carried out in a new way: as a "mutual subjection out of reverence for Christ" (Eph 5:21).... In relation to the "old" this is evidently something "new": it is an innovation of the Gospel. We find various passages in which the apostolic writings express this innovation, even though they also communicate what is "old": what is rooted in the religious tradition of Israel.... However, the awareness that in marriage there is mutual "subjection of the spouses out of reverence for Christ" and not just that of the wife to the husband must gradually establish itself in hearts, consciences, behaviors, and customs. This is a call, which from that time onward does not cease to challenge succeeding generations; it is a call which people have to accept ever anew.... All the reasons in favor of the "subjection" of woman to man in marriage must be understood in the sense of a "mutual subjection" of both "out of reverence for Christ."[4]

Women's movements have recognized the Pope's daring behind such a reinterpretation of Paul's teaching, and theologians have looked favorably upon the Pope's interpretation. Twelve years before the publication of *Mulieris Dignitatem*, Hans Küng had made this request in his famous "Sixteen Theses," published in 1976: "The New Testament statements on the subjection of women should be interpreted in light of the socio-cultural situation of the time and critically transposed to the contemporary socio-cultural situation." That is exactly what Pope Wojtyła has accomplished.

Asking Pardon of Women

During 1995, the year dedicated by the United Nations to women, John Paul expressed regret on two occasions for injustices the Church had committed against women. The first instance took place on June 10, 1995, during his Angelus address: "The equality between man and woman is stated in the very first pages of the Bible, in the stupendous account of creation.... Following in the footsteps of her divine Founder, the Church has been a faithful bearer of this message. If at times, in the course of centuries and with the weight of time, some of the Church's sons have not known how to live accordingly, that is a cause for great regret."

The second example occurs in a statement John Paul made in his *Letter to Women*:

> Unfortunately, we are heirs to a history which has conditioned us to a remarkable extent. In every time and place this conditioning has been an obstacle to the progress of women. Women's dignity has often been unacknowledged and their prerogatives misrepresented; they have often been relegated to the margins of society and even reduced to servitude.... And if objective blame, especially in particular historical contexts, has belonged to not just a few members of the Church, for this I am truly sorry. May this regret be transformed, on the part of the whole Church, into a renewed commitment of fidelity to the Gospel vision. When it comes to setting women free from every kind of exploitation and domination, the Gospel contains an ever relevant message which goes back to the attitude of Jesus Christ himself.... Yes, it is time to examine the past with courage, to assign responsibility where it is due in a review of the long history of humanity. Women have contributed to that history as much as men, and more often than not they did so in much more difficult conditions.... To this great, immense feminine "tradition" humanity owes a debt which can never be repaid.[5]

John Paul returned to the subject of women during another Angelus message he gave on Sunday, July 30, in which he stated that it is time to rewrite history with a less unilateral emphasis. Too much attention has been paid to extraordinary, newsworthy events and achievements of men, and not enough to the faithful performance of the tasks of daily life largely achieved by women. And there is much more to be said and written about the enormous debt men owe to women in areas of social and cultural progress: "Desiring to contribute something toward filling up this vacuum, I would like to speak in the name of the Church and pay homage to women for the multiple, immense but silent contributions by women in every phase and aspect of human existence."

*T*he Pope showed his concern for women very early on in his pontificate, when he visited the tomb of St. Catherine of Siena in Rome and spoke of the varied forms of mission possible for women today. On that occasion he encouraged his listeners to "walk hand in hand with the feminine world of today" (Nov. 5, 1978). A few days later he addressed the International Union of Superiors General of Women Religious and told them: "All sisters have, as it were, conveyed to one another a password: 'Let us first be Christian.' A certain number prefer to add the following: 'Let us first be women.' It is evident that the two do not exclude each other" (Nov. 16, 1978).

Nevertheless, certain groups of feminists have demonstrated against the Pope during some of his travels. Although he is never rude, John Paul has not yet found a way to relate to them. During an international flight, a journalist asked: "Your Holiness, how will you respond to the feminists who have announced they will wage demonstrations while you are in Canada?"

"I shall always respond this way: I love all people."

"Even these women?"

"Yes, very much! It is necessary to have this love for people. But on the other hand, one must speak the truth" (Sept. 9, 1984).

Although the issue of women's ordination is closed, John Paul has encouraged women's participation in other important areas in the Church. In the document, *Vita Consecrata*, issued in 1996, the Pope wrote: "It is therefore urgently necessary to take certain concrete steps, beginning by providing room for women to participate in different fields and at all levels, including decision-making processes, above all in matters which concern women themselves."[6]

John Paul is obviously disposed to involve women to a larger extent in Church matters. For example, from the beginning of his international travels, he authorized women to proclaim the Scriptures during papal celebrations of the Eucharist, even at papal Masses held in Rome. In 1995 John Paul sent a woman—Harvard Professor of Law Mary Ann Glendon of the United States—to represent the Holy See at the United Nations Conference on Women that was held in Beijing, China. And, as noted in Chapter 25, the Pope approved a statute of the Focolare movement specifying that the president must always be a woman. In both of these examples, a woman was given priority choice over a bishop, priest or layman. Both illustrate the Pope's attempts to fully involve the "feminine genius" in ever increasing areas of the Church's life.

NOTES

1. John Paul II, *Mulieris Dignitatem* (Boston: Pauline Books & Media, 1988), n. 30.

2. Ibid., n. 24

3. *L'Osservatore Romano*, Discourse of Sunday, September 3, 1995.

4. John Paul II, *Mulieris Dignitatem* (Boston: Pauline Books & Media, 1988), n. 24.

5. John Paul II, *Letter to Women* (Boston: Pauline Books & Media, 1995), n. 3.

6. John Paul II, *Vita Consecrata* (Boston: Pauline Books & Media, 1988), n. 58.

❖ CHAPTER TWENTY-NINE ❖

Ecumenical Setback in Russia

*T*his is the story of an ecumenical dream—a dream which dawned with the dissolution of the Soviet Union but ended too abruptly with Mikhail Gorbachev's *perestroika*. John Paul was not alone in his belief that when the Communist regime ended, ecumenism would make rapid progress in Eastern Europe; ecumenical efforts would no longer be hampered by atheistic governments. In 1988, John Paul gave substance to this hope by sending a delegation of ten cardinals to the millennium celebration of the Russian Orthodox Church, and by commissioning Cardinal Agostino Casaroli to bring his *Ostpolitik* (the "eastern politics" of the Holy See) to a conclusion.

The reality of the situation, however, was one of underlying resistance. A revival of nationalism had caused local churches to become self-absorbed. The crisis became extreme in the Ukraine; neither the Holy See nor the Patriarchate of Moscow could control the behavior of the national church. And in 1991, when the Pope named a few bishops to serve Catholics living in Russia, misunderstanding and miscommunication surrounding that action led to a definitive break with the Patriarchate that continues to this day, in spite of efforts aimed at reconciliation.

Cardinal Casaroli carried out his mission. He attended the celebration in Moscow as head of the most extraordinary delegation a pope has ever sent to a sister church in modern times. The delegation comprised eighteen members, including Cardinals Etchegaray, Willebrands, Martini, Lustiger, Glemp, and O'Connor. Cardinal Casaroli met with Gorbachev at the Kremlin to prepare him for his visit to Rome and audience with the Pope on December 1, 1989. The Cardinal was also authorized to name bishops in Russia and to seek an invitation for the Pope to visit Russia. While the Russian government was willing to permit such a visit, Russian Orthodox prelates were not. As a result, John Paul's pilgrimage to Moscow, so intensely desired by the Polish Pope in order to normalize ecumenical relations, was vetoed by the Kremlin at the instigation of the Russian Orthodox Church.

Of all the setbacks John Paul experienced during his pontificate, this one was among the most unexpected and painful. He had invested a great deal into the work for full communion with the Orthodox churches; in 1979 he had even dreamed of making a visit to the Patriarch of Constantinople. The opportune moment seemed to have arrived with the celebration of the Russian Millennium coinciding with Gorbachev's reforms.

The challenge of Russian nationalism, which caused the cancellation of Gorbachev's invitation, also caused Patriarch Alexis II to oppose the papal visit and to publicly protest against Rome's "invasion" of Russia. Throughout the following decade, Alexis and John Paul tried in vain to hold meetings in Hungary (1996) and in Austria (1997). Ancient animosities, however, sometimes prevail even over the most earnest attempts of courageous men. As a result, these two prelates have not only been prevented from making reciprocal visits, they have been unable even to arrange a meeting on neutral ground.

Gorbachev's successor, Boris Yeltsin, visited with John Paul on February 10, 1998. The meeting proved cordial and fruitful regarding international questions. For example, the two men agreed on their positions concerning Iraq at a time when new tensions were growing between that country and the United States. The stalemate between the Vatican and the Russian Orthodox Church remained, however, and until now no progress has been made on a papal visit to Russia. The Vatican spokesman has stated that the Pope feels he has an open invitation to visit Russia, because of his invitations from Gorbachev in 1989 and Yeltsin in 1991. But during Yeltsin's visit, a papal trip could not even be discussed because the Orthodox Patriarch still adamantly opposed it.

John Paul's outreach to the East has produced two important results: a series of documents which outline an ecumenical strategy, and a lesson on "ecumenical *kenosis*" which profoundly marked the 1990s and may well have prompted the Pope to propose an examination of conscience at the end of the second millennium.

The most original documents John Paul produced during this projection toward the East have been the encyclical *Slavorum Apostoli* (The Apostles of the Slavs) and the apostolic letter *Euntes in Mundum* (Go

Out to the Whole World). A third and even more important text is the apostolic letter *Orientale Lumen* (Light of the East). During his homily for the feast of Saints Cyril and Methodius on February 14, 1985, John Paul cried out at St. Peter's: "Do away with whatever divides the Church...!" This cry inspired the documents just mentioned.

In his zeal for approaching the Orthodox, Pope Wojtyła has blended biblical and mythical images. A few months before his meeting with Gorbachev, during the flight from Rome to Seoul on October 6, 1989, the Pope said to journalists: "*Lux ex Oriente.* The faith...in Europe again comes to us from the East." The iron curtain was crumbling, and John Paul was anxiously waiting for religious Europe to finally breathe freely with "both lungs."

In Czechoslovakia during April 1990, John Paul announced the special Synod for Europe to be held at the end of 1991. Some accused him of impatience and of rushing things. But in ecumenical matters, John Paul's sense of timing proved far more acute than his critics could have perceived. And in some ways, the Pope's date may even have been too late.

*B*y the time the December 1991 Synod took place, tensions were so great that the Orthodox refused to send delegates. Only the representative for the Patriarch of Constantinople, Metropolitan Spyridon Papagheorghiou, was present. In the name of those absent, he accused Rome of departing from the spirit of Vatican II and of having an expansionistic attitude toward the East, considering the Orthodox countries merely as "mission lands" for Roman Catholicism.

This was perhaps one of the Pope's most painful days, and after Papagheorghiou finished his remarks, an embarrassed silence settled upon the whole assembly. Without a word, John Paul rose and embraced Papagheorghiou, and the entire gathering applauded. With their applause, the assembly seemed to be encouraging the Pope to make a courageous evangelical acknowledgment of the incorrect procedure, of the errors, and of all the mistakes of history, distant and recent.

Five days later, during a penitential celebration in St. Peter's, John Paul spoke in the name of the entire Catholic world when he said that "the Gospel lays bare our sin, which we humbly acknowledge lies at the root of the crisis suffered by the Church in our time." Moreover, said the Pope, difficulties should not make us forget the urgency of working toward the proclamation of one faith. Then John Paul asked: "In Europe, which is on the way to political unity, can we permit the Church of Christ to be a factor in disunity and discord? Would this not be one of the greatest scandals of our time?"

John Paul's switch from a dream for ecumenical unity to a call for ecumenical repentance was finalized on December 13, 1991, in his discourse at the closing of the Synod for Europe. The "examination of conscience at the end of the millennium" would be proposed three years later (see Chapter 39), but his predisposition for it was already there. "Unlike the first millennium," said the Pope, "Christianity is exiting from the second millennium divided but desirous of a new unity. The absence of some of our fraternal delegates has been a unique kind of *kenosis,* but if it is seen and experienced in the spirit of Christ's prayer for the unity of his disciples, it can serve the cause for which this synod was convened" (namely, the new evangelization of Europe to be carried out by *all* the Christian churches).

Kenosis is a word of tremendous significance. The New Testament uses it in reference to Christ's abasement in the incarnation and passion. John Paul used the word to emphasize that the absence of delegates from the Orthodox Churches of Russia, Bulgaria, Greece, Romania, and Serbia was a wound for the synod. It was an experience of failure that must be accepted in a penitential spirit so that it might stimulate a renewed effort toward mutual understanding. From that day on, the Pope has dedicated himself tirelessly, despite great misunderstanding, to the promotion of that penitential act which he calls "the examen at the end of the millennium."

There would have been no *mea culpas* without the Second Vatican Council, and if John Paul had not traveled so much, the *mea culpas* would not have been so numerous. On the other hand, the examination at the end of the millennium—which has been a unique creation of this Pope and is of much greater value than all the *mea culpas* taken together—would perhaps not exist had it not been for this experience of ecumenical failure.

❧ CHAPTER THIRTY ❧

The Fall of Communism

*A*s soon as the door to the East was opened, the Slav Pope was ready to enter. The Berlin wall fell on November 9, 1989, and the first post-Communist government was sworn in at Prague on December 9. Scarcely four months later, on April 21, 1990, John Paul visited Czechoslovakia and announced a synod for the bishops of Europe to evaluate the "significance of that historic event." On his first visit to Poland he had spoken about the mission assigned to him by Providence for the rediscovery of the spiritual unity of Europe. Now he felt that the time was ripe for that rediscovery to begin. The turn-around in the East had been an epochal sign for him, a unique occasion for the Church in non-Communist countries to quickly join together before the consumer mentality of the West could transmit its "virus" to the people of central Europe. Now was the time for the exodus from the desert of long years of religious persecution. As a man from the East living in the West, John Paul would not wait for things to happen; he would anticipate and per-haps even prompt events.

Throughout the entire year of 1990, from his meeting with the diplo-matic corps on January 19 to Gorbachev's second visit to the Vatican on November 18, John Paul enjoyed a continuous celebration of the reli-gious rebirth of Eastern and Central Europe. Speaking to diplomats, he stated that a "Europe of the spirit is being reborn." He expressed gratitude to those people who, at the cost of great sacrifice, had taken the initiative in the events that had led to such a moment, and he paid homage to the political leaders who had supported it.

But the central event in this yearlong celebration was the Pope's April visit to Czechoslovakia. It was his forty-sixth journey outside Italy and, except for his visit to Poland, it was his first papal trip to a country under the Warsaw Pact. He greeted Czech Catholics with a biblical image on April 21, 1990: "Today we stand before the ruins of one of the many towers of Babel in human history." Now, he told them, it was possible to knock down all the walls that divided men and nations.

Eleven years earlier, at Gniezno, Poland, he had launched his program as a Slav Pope called to "manifest" the unity of Europe. At that time some critics accused him of pursuing a medieval dream, of wanting to return to the dark ages. Now John Paul responded to their charge: "A united Europe is no longer only a dream. It is not a utopian memory from the Middle Ages. The events which we are witnessing show that this goal can actually be reached" (April 21, 1990).

John Paul's lofty tone found an echo in the words President Vaclav Havel spoke at the festival celebrated in Prague, and in the staunch Catholicism of the citizens of Velehrad and Bratislava. As a poet President Havel addressed his remarks to the Pope, who is also a poet:

> I don't know if I know what a miracle is. Nevertheless, I dare to say that this afternoon I shall take part in a miracle. In the same place where, five months ago, on the day on which we rejoiced at the canonization of Agnes of Bohemia, the future of our country was decided, and in that same place today the head of the Catholic Church will celebrate Holy Mass and will thank our Saint for her intercession with him who holds in his hands the mysterious course of all things.

In his address to the crowds in Prague, the Pope could well have imagined he had come to the most agnostic and least Christian city of Europe, alongside Berlin, considering the number of baptized persons. In the three meetings during his visit, he praised the 91-year-old Cardinal Frantisek Tomasek, leader of the resistance against Communism, for his "persevering service to the Church, his courageous defense of the rights of the faithful, and his solidarity with those persecuted for the sake of truth and justice" (April 21, 1990).

John Paul then told the people that for many years the door to their country had seemed closed. "Even less than a year ago it was unthinkable that the Pope, himself a Slav and the son of a sister nation, could come to Czechoslovakia." But now, he said, "it is providential that it falls to me to be the first Pope to enter this land in order to bring it a greeting of peace. The faithful of Bohemia, Moravia, and Slovakia have in Rome a Pastor who understands their language. He also understood their silence, when the Church in this country was the Church of silence, and he considered it part of his mission to be their voice." This same theme was interwoven in all ten discourses John Paul delivered during the two days he spent in Czechoslovakia.

Perhaps the most significant statement the Pope made after the fall of Communism, not only during this visit to Czechoslovakia but throughout his entire pontificate, is the following: "The claim to build a world without God has been shown to be an illusion. The only things which remained mysterious [regarding the collapse of the Communist system] were the when and the how" (Prague, April 21, 1990).

John Paul would return to Prague two more times, in 1995 and 1997, but he would not experience the same "magic" he found there in April 1990! During his second visit in May 1995, journalists spoke with the Pope on the flight from Rome to Prague:

"You are returning to countries that were once Communist...."

"That was an incident that lasted about fifty years. The 1,000 years of Christianity represent a period that weighs a great deal more than some forty years of Communism."

*I*n the five years between the Pope's two visits to Prague, John Paul also made trips to Hungary (1991), Albania, Lithuania, Latvia, Estonia (1993), and Croatia (1994). All of these journeys, including the ones to Slovenia and Berlin (1996), gave him the opportunity to speak again about the Communist "incident" and its providential outcome.

When referring to the forty years in which Albania had tried to banish religion, he said: "Nothing like what happened in Albania has ever been recorded in history."

Speaking in Berlin before the Brandenburg Gate, John Paul visibly moved his listeners with these words: "In this place, so full of history, I am prompted to address an urgent appeal for freedom to all of you here present, to the German people, to Europe—which is also called to unity in freedom—to all people of good will" (June 23, 1996).

Caution Regarding Capitalism

While celebrating the fall of Communism, John Paul never failed to warn people to avoid the dangers of capitalism. The first time he touched upon this subject was when he addressed the bishops of Czechoslovakia in Prague:

> Unfortunately, not everything the West proposes as a theoretical vision or as a concrete lifestyle reflects Gospel values.... Thus, it falls to you, revered brothers...to prepare in the churches entrusted to your care appropriate "immunizing" defenses against certain "viruses" such as

secularism, indifferentism, hedonistic consumerism, practical materialism, and also formal atheism, which today are widespread (Prague,
April 21, 1990).

Two weeks after the visit to Prague, John Paul left for his second
journey to Mexico. He told people there that the collapse of Communism
could not be considered a triumph for capitalism, as if that were the only
alternative political/economic system for our world.

Even before the flight to Prague, while borders were only just opening and governments in Central Europe changing, John Paul made a sixth
trip to Africa (Jan. 25 to Feb. 1, 1990). Addressing the diplomatic corps
at Chad, he said: "The great transformations underway in Eastern Europe
must not divert our attention from the South and from the African continent in particular" (Feb. 1, 1990).

And then, as if his realizing his words had too closely resembled diplomatic language, John Paul had a spokesperson add this statement: "The
Pontiff considers it providential and prophetic to make this visit among
people deprived of their freedom, especially at a time when everyone is
looking at Eastern Europe, which has freed itself."

*E*veryone has been able to appreciate the propriety with which John
Paul has spoken about the fall of Communism and the part he played
in it. Of course, he could not have been displeased with Gorbachev's
evaluation: "What has happened in Eastern Europe in recent years would
not have been possible without the presence of this Pope, without the
great role—even political—that he has played on the world scene."[1]
When Paolo Mieli, the director of the Italian paper that printed this statement, presented Gorbachev's words to the Pope, John Paul remarked:
"Gorbachev's words are sincere, and they confirm what I have always
thought about him: he is an honest man."

John Paul himself tends to downplay the providential aspect of the
collapse of Communism. For example, he once said: "It would be sim-
plistic to say that divine Providence caused the fall of Communism. In a
certain sense Communism as a system fell by itself. It fell as a conse-
quence of its own mistakes and abuses."[2]

A year earlier he had told journalist Jas Gawronski: "I think that if
there were a determining factor [in the fall of Communism], it would be
Christianity as such: its content, its religious and moral message, its defense of the human person and his rights. And I have done nothing more
than remind, repeat, and insist that this is a principle to be followed."[3]

In that same interview the Pope surprised Gawronski with a statement on the "good things" and half-truths contained in Communism:

"The followers of capitalism usually tend to refuse to admit any 'good' resulting from Communism: the struggle against unemployment, a concern for the poor. In Communism there is a preoccupation with social questions, while capitalism, on the contrary, is individualistic."[4]

At the end of 1993, the Pope tried to convince collaborators that the fall of Communism could not be interpreted as a moral justification of capitalism: "As it was necessary in the past to tell the truth about the Berlin Wall to the man in Eastern Europe, so now it is necessary to focus on truth for the man who lives in the West. Man is the same all over" (Dec. 21, 1993).

On his two return visits to Poland in June 1991 and June 1997, John Paul had occasion to say something about the risks to liberty his fellow countrymen faced as they hastened to pass from communism to capitalism. When some people accused him, and the Church, of being afraid of freedom, his reply was spontaneous and accurate: "To say that the Church is an obstacle to freedom is a contradiction of words, especially in Poland. Throughout the centuries the Church in Poland has always been the guardian of liberty, and this has been true especially in the last fifty years" (June 1, 1997).

Finally, regarding the part John Paul played in the collapse of Communism, observers are usually of the same opinion as Gorbachev in the statement previously quoted. As for an "insider's" viewpoint, Archbishop Jean-Louis Tauran, the Vatican representative for relations with States, said: "Pope John Paul II has been the detonator that set off the explosion of the [Communist] lies which threatened the life of that society and kept the Church under oppression."[5] More precisely, the Jesuit, Giacomo Martina, gives this evaluation: "Aspirations for religious freedom and for the defense of the human person carried some weight, together with political and economic factors. But with the help the Pope gave to *Solidarność*, Poland cleared the way. The demands of the Poles fed the aspirations of the Russians, the Ukrainians and others, kept secret until now. I believe history will accept this judgment about the personal influence of John Paul II."

NOTES

1. Quoted in the newspaper *La Stampa*, Turin, Italy, March 3, 1992.

2. John Paul II with Vittorio Messori, *Crossing the Threshold of Hope* (New York: Alfred A. Knopf, 1994), p. 132.

3. J. Gawronski, *Il mondo di Giovanni Paolo II* (Milan: Mondadori, 1994), p. 13.

4. Ibid., p. 15.

5. *La Discussione*, Rome, May 8, 1993.

✺ CHAPTER THIRTY-ONE ✺

The Worker and the Marginalized

"*I* have understood what exploitation is, and I have immediately put myself on the side of the poor, the disinherited, the oppressed, the marginalized and the defenseless. The powerful in this world do not always look favorably on a pope like that." Pope Wojtyła spoke these words in an interview with the Polish journalist, Jas Gawronski.[1]

John Paul is not afraid to pronounce uncomfortable words like "exploitation," "the oppressed," or "the powerful." These are words Communist propagandists have used, but they are words found in the Bible as well, words especially familiar to the poor and to workers. And the Pope wants to speak frankly and openly to these sons and daughters: "It is necessary to call every injustice by its name!" This is what he said on February 21, 1979, after his first visit to Mexico, when he addressed the Indians, the *campesinos* and workers.

It was not the sight of the Third World, however, that prompted John Paul to speak out against injustice. He was already determined to march in their defense when he was elected pope, and this determination sprang from his own experience in Poland. When he said, "I have known what exploitation is," John Paul was referring to his experience as a worker who, in his youth, had witnessed and endured the oppression of the Polish people by their "neighbors."

In his contacts with workers, Karol Wojtyła speaks from his own personal experience of manual work, as he told laborers in Rome in 1979: "I was a laborer for 4 years, and for me those 4 years of work are worth more than two doctorate degrees!" A few months later at Turin, a great industrial and secularized city, he invited everyone to experience the "reality" of work: "I am convinced that on the level of this reality we

195

can meet with every person, with every person! On this level we can meet with all, with all!" (Sept. 14, 1979)

Each year the Pope meets with labor unions on the feast of St. Joseph, March 19. He customarily celebrates the feast in an industrial area of Italy, engaging in a dialogue with laborers and answering their questions. He once said the democracy of the workers' world is older than democracy at the parish level, and therefore "I should thank you for giving us an idea for Church life" (Livorno, March 19, 1982).

Workers have criticized the Church for always being on the side of the wealthy, and the Pope has responded with repentance: "I thank you for all your comments, all your words, even if the truths expressed in these words were hard and painful truths" (March 19, 1983). When it comes to the question of the right to work, the Pope goes so far as to suggest that labor unions make it their objective to press for employment opportunities for everyone. He did this at Prato, Italy, on March 19, 1986. Eight years later, Italian unions were still ineffective in addressing workers' situations, and the rate of unemployment was very high. John Paul urged unions to be more demanding because, "if men do not protest, God will!" He told representatives of labor unions that they should "cry out in a loud voice and demand a change of policy" (Rome, March 19, 1994).

The Pope's tone is the same, whether he is addressing laborers in Italy or speaking of social justice elsewhere. Directing his remarks to Brazilian journalists who had accompanied the president of Brazil on a visit to Rome, John Paul said: "Agrarian reform cannot be halted; it is a question of social justice and democracy, and it is necessary to defend democracy" (July 10, 1986).

When there has been criticism, even in the Curia, that the Pope preaches too much on social justice issues, he has promptly responded: "I have made and I still make my option for the poor. I identify with them" (Dec. 21, 1984). He said the same thing a month later at his Sunday Angelus address in Rome: "As successor of Peter, I feel the weight of responsibility to leave nothing untried in serving the cause of justice and solidarity among the citizens of a country and among nations, for a better tomorrow" (Jan. 21, 1985).

In fact, the Pope would have the whole Church embrace the fundamental option for the poor. During his visit to Peru in 1988, he stated that Christians cannot let the banner of justice and the demands of charity be snatched from their hands by any ideology or system. Prior to that, in his Lenten message, the Pope had included the following vehement statement: "When millions upon millions of people lack sufficient food, when millions of infants are irremediably affected for the rest of their lives, when millions of these infants die, I cannot be silent. We cannot remain silent and do nothing" (Feb. 20, 1985).

John Paul has written three encyclicals on social questions: *Laborem Exercens* (On Human Work, 1981), *Sollicitudo Rei Socialis* (On Social Concern, 1987), and *Centesimus Annus* (On the Hundredth Anniversary of *Rerum Novarum,* 1991). These encyclicals contain a critique of capitalism, and they call for solidarity on the part of the Church with working classes. *Laborem Exercens* (especially its section on the rights of unions and ownership of land) became a battle cry for Catholic union members in Latin America and Poland. The Solidarity Movement praised the encyclical for its "personalist" tone and its comments on the participation of workers in management.

John Paul's two other encyclicals, *Sollicitudo Rei Socialis* and *Centesimus Annus*, should be read consecutively, because they were published within three years of each other in order to deal with the new situation resulting from the fall of Communism. Two adjustments are advocated in these documents: *Sollicitudo* criticizes both capitalism and communism and calls for a "radical correction" of both systems in the name of the Third World and spiritual values; *Centesimus* discusses the positive and negative aspects of the economy of the West and suggests some adjustments to the capitalist system.

In *Laborem Exercens*, John Paul uses the Marxist term "alienation," but in *Centesimus Annus* and in his social preaching, he uses the term, "struggle." He states that one can rightly speak of a struggle against an economic system in which capital is considered an absolute priority regardless of the needs of the people. After describing the conditions of inhuman misery existing in the Third World, John Paul calls upon the Church to denounce such situations, even if its cry will not always be favorably received by all. He says that the fall of Communism has not eliminated injustice and oppression in the world, but to those who are looking for a new theory and practice of liberation, the Church can offer not only its social doctrine but the example of Christians who are combating social evils and injustice.[2]

The Pope speaks favorably of certain economic aspects of capitalism, but denounces some of its practical consequences. There is the danger, for example, that like totalitarian Communism, the capitalist system will give the economic factor exclusive priority and will disregard moral values, human rights, culture, and religion.

John Paul has remained faithful to the basic principles he developed in *Centesimus Annus*. He asserted during his visit to Prague in April, 1990, that it was now possible to knock down all the walls that divide men and nations. Then, seven years later when speaking at Gniezno, Poland, he said:

> Can we not say that after the collapse of one wall—the visible one—another invisible wall was discovered, one that continues to divide our continent—the wall that exists in people's hearts? It is a wall made out of fear and aggressiveness, of lack of understanding for people of different origins, different color, different religious convictions; it is the wall of political and economic selfishness, of the weakening of sensitivity to the value of human life and the dignity of every human being. Even the undeniable achievements of recent years in the economic, political and social fields do not hide the fact that this wall exists. It casts its shadow over all of Europe. The goal of the authentic unity of the European continent is still distant. There will be no European unity until it is based on unity of spirit (Gniezno, June 3, 1997).

Although certain Western intellectuals have praised John Paul's actions against Communism, they have never forgiven him for his criticism of capitalism. Only a small number of experts have conceded that, among the voices raised against communism and capitalism, his is most deserving of credibility.

An example of such difficulty with the Pope's message can be found in an editorial published in the French newspaper, *Le Monde.* At a time when there was widespread appreciation for the work of John Paul, the author of the editorial accused the Pope of blatant contradiction. "One cannot at the same time praise freedom, democracy, and economic development—which are the very things lacking to the people of Eastern Europe—and then turn around and denounce what the Pope has called the 'virus' of Western society" (*Le Monde,* April 24, 1990).

On the other hand, Piero Ostellino, a columnist for the Italian journal, *Corriere della Sera,* expressed his complete agreement with the Pope's statement: "A Church that is exclusively anti-communist would be a Church that limps. But a Church that, in addition to condemning Communism, has the courage to denounce all other forms of oppression, is an extraordinary politico-ethical force which everyone should take into account."[3]

NOTES

1. J. Gawronski, *Il mondo di Giovanni Paolo II* (Milan: Mondadori, 1994), p. 18.

2. Cf. *Centesimus Annus,* nn. 26; 43; 61.

3. In an interview printed in the Italian journal, *Il Sabato,* August 22, 1987.

CHAPTER THIRTY-TWO

Opposition to the Gulf War

*T*he pope who fought against Communism, and would not proclaim capitalism's absolute triumph, is also the pope who opposed the Persian Gulf War—from beginning to end. The conflict in the Gulf involved a military campaign approved by the United Nations and carried out primarily by the United States, to force Iraqi leader Saddam Hussein, who had invaded and annexed Kuwait, to withdraw his troops. While recognizing that a gross violation of international law and rights had taken place with Iraq's invasion of Kuwait, John Paul insistently appealed for a peaceful resolution of the crisis; he even reaffirmed his opposition to war after United Nations' forces declared victory.

When the UN ultimatum to Iraq expired and the bombing was about to begin, John Paul stood alone in his opposition to the war. The fact that his was a solitary opposition is decisive in trying to make an historical evaluation of John Paul II, who up until that time was considered a spokesman for the Western world because of his opposition to Communism. But there could not possibly be any doubt about his opposition to the use of military force against Iraq and his criticism of the United Nations for its use of military force under the leadership of the United States. The Pope was not on the side of the Western forces, nor was he on the side of the majority of bishops in the Catholic countries of the Western world.

The Gulf War revealed a great deal about the geo-political sentiments of John Paul. The critical needs of the Third World were predominant in his concern, and he was anxious to speak to Islam so that he could promote a new world order where there would be no dominating superpowers and all people would enjoy equal dignity. Paul VI had attempted a similar dissociation from the Western world's politics and from the war waged in Vietnam (1964–1975). John Paul, however, could do much more than his predecessor simply because there no longer existed a polarization between Communism and the West—something which made it necessary for Pope Montini to be equally distant from the two sides involved.

The principal reason for John Paul's opposition to the Gulf War stems from his personal conviction that the moment has come for Christians to object strenuously to war, and so help to banish it from the international scene. The Pope was faithful to that conviction when he visited Great Britain and Argentina during the Falkland War from May to June 1982; during the war in Lebanon, especially from 1982 to 1984; and during the war in Bosnia from 1993 to 1995. However, during the Gulf War he made a stronger impression and was better understood by the world at large.

A Conflict Unfolds

Iraq invaded Kuwait on August 2, 1990, and on that same day the Security Council of the United Nations unanimously demanded the immediate and unconditional withdrawal of Iraqi forces from Kuwait. On August 10, Iraq proclaimed the annexation of Kuwait as a province of Iraq. Meanwhile, the first American soldiers were assembling in Saudi Arabia, and the Arab League had also decided to send troops to Kuwait.

On November 29, the United Nations Security Council issued an ultimatum: Iraq must withdraw from Kuwait by January 15, 1991. Under the leadership of the United States, a coalition of thirty-nine countries was formed, of which the following have a Catholic majority: Argentina, Austria, Belgium, France, Hungary, Italy, Poland, Portugal, and Spain. The coalition of nations launched their air offensive on January 17 at 12:40 A.M. under the name "Desert Storm." On February 13, allied forces bombed a refugee center, and 300 civilians were killed.

At 4:00 A.M. on February 24, ground forces entered Iraq and Kuwait. The following day, 20,000 Iraqi soldiers surrendered without a battle. An Iraqi scud missile hit Dhahran in Saudi Arabia and killed twenty-seven American soldiers. By February 27, twenty-one out of forty-two Iraqi divisions were destroyed or immobilized. Some of the international humanitarian organizations estimated that the number of Iraqi soldiers killed reached a total of 300,000. When Iraq finally accepted the terms set down by the United Nations, a cease-fire was announced at 6:00 A.M. on February 28, 1991.

Throughout the forty-three days during which the Gulf War was fought—as well as before and after the crisis—John Paul exerted extraordinary efforts: first to avoid hostilities, then to put an end to them, and finally to repair the damage done. He had tried to intervene in the ultimatum issued against Iraq; he suggested that nations in Europe should act as mediators; he appealed to non-allied nations; he supported the suggestions of French President François Mitterand and Gorbachev; he tried to get the United Nations to function as mediator in the crisis; finally, he intervened personally with Saddam Hussein and President George Bush—on the very day conditions for the ultimatum expired.

Between August 26 and March 6, the Pope referred to the Gulf problem, in writing or in speech, some fifty times. Equally numerous were diplomatic efforts and papal statements the Vatican made to various groups and organizations through the spokesman for the Vatican, Joaquín Navarro-Valls. The Pope had never intervened to such an extent in any international problem, not even during the crisis in Poland. What is extraordinary here is not the number of times he intervened, but the extent to which he did so.

Three particular occasions are notable: first, when John Paul appealed to all humanity on Christmas in 1990; second, when he addressed the diplomatic corps on January 12, 1991; and third, when he appealed to the man who, together with Saddam Hussein, had the greatest responsibility for making the final decision in the crisis: the President of the United States, George Bush.

During his address *Urbi et Orbi*, "to the city and the world," on Christmas Day in 1990, the Pope lamented the participation of so many nations in the massive concentration of soldiers and arms in the Persian Gulf:

> The light of Christ is with the tormented nations of the Middle East. For the area of the Gulf, we wait with trepidation for the threat of conflict to disappear. May leaders be convinced that war is an adventure with no return! (Dec. 25, 1990)

Because of these remarks, which the Pope repeated time and again in the following weeks and months, many people labeled him a "pacifist." John Paul eventually felt it necessary to clarify the matter, and he did so at a Roman parish the following February 17: "A just peace, certainly; but we are not pacifists; we don't want peace at any price."

We can look at two quotations from the Pope's address to the diplomatic corps, on January 12, 1991, as concrete proof that John Paul's statements cannot be reduced to pacifist "slogans."

On the one hand, we have before us an armed invasion of a country, and a brutal violation not only of moral law but of international law as defined by the United Nations. These are unacceptable facts. On the other hand, while the massive concentration of men and arms which has followed it has been aimed at putting an end to what must be clearly defined as aggression, there is no doubt that should it end even in limited military action, the operations would be particularly costly in human life, to say nothing of the ecological, political, economic, and strategic consequences whose full gravity and import we have perhaps not yet completely assessed. Finally, without entering into the profound causes of violence in this part of the world, a peace obtained by arms could only prepare for new acts of violence....

Recourse to force for a just cause would only be admissible if such recourse were proportionate to the result one wished to obtain and with due consideration for the consequences that military actions, today made more destructive by modern technology, would have for the survival of peoples and the planet itself. The needs of humanity today require that we proceed resolutely toward outlawing war completely and come to cultivate peace as a supreme good to which all programs and all strategies must be subordinated (Jan. 12, 1991).

Finally, we quote John Paul's letter to President Bush in its entirety. The Pope sent this letter on the very day the United Nations' ultimatum expired; he also sent a letter containing substantially the same message to Saddam Hussein.

I feel the pressing duty to turn to you as the leader of the nation which is most involved, from the standpoint of personnel and equipment, in the military operation now taking place in the Gulf region. In recent days, voicing the thoughts and concerns of millions of people, I have stressed the tragic consequences which a war in that area could have. I wish now to restate my firm belief that war is not likely to bring an adequate solution to international problems and that, even though an unjust situation might be momentarily met, the consequences that would possibly derive from war would be devastating and tragic. We cannot pretend that the use of arms, and especially of today's highly sophisticated weaponry, would not give rise, in addition to suffering and destruction, to new and perhaps worse injustices. Mr. President, I am certain that, together with your advisers, you too have clearly weighed all these factors and will not spare further efforts to avoid decisions which would be irreversible and bring suffering to thousands of families among your fellow citizens and to so many peoples in the Middle East. In these last hours before the deadline laid down by the United Nations Security Council, I truly hope, and I appeal with lively faith to the Lord, that peace can still be saved. I hope that, through a last-minute effort at dialogue, sovereignty may be restored to the people of Kuwait and that international order which is the basis for a coexistence between peoples truly worthy of humanity may be re-established in the Gulf area and in the entire Middle East.

I invoke upon you God's abundant blessings and, at this moment of grave responsibility before your country and before history, I especially pray that you be granted the wisdom to make decisions which will truly serve the good of your fellow citizens and of the entire international community (Jan. 15, 1991).

L ooking at the ensemble of interventions the Pope made during those weeks preceding the war, we see that John Paul was working for three objectives: to avoid war, to bring assistance to the Catholic and Christian communities in the Middle East, and to inform the Arab world that the Catholic Church and Christian ecumenists did not support armed intervention. The Pope may not have achieved his first goal, but he proposed means for realizing the other two.

From March 4 to 6, the Pope convoked an assembly of Catholic prelates from the Middle East and from countries involved in the conflict. The assembly clearly demonstrated to the Arab world that John Paul's position differed radically from that of the Western world, for whom the Pope had been considered a spokesman. Moreover, the entire situation helped demonstrate that the preaching of the Christian churches no longer coincided with the interests of those traditionally Christian nations.

At the Vatican summit, the presidents of the National Conference of Bishops from England and the United States spoke of their difficulty in presenting to their respective governments and people the serious reservations the Church held about the use of military force. Positions similar to that of the Vatican were being taken by Patriarch Alexis of Moscow and the Ecumenical Council of Churches which convened in Canberra, Australia, from February 7 to 20. But if the world knew about the opposition of the Christian churches to the Gulf War, it was due to the tenacity of John Paul, who was largely motivated by the prospect of the total banishment of war. That seems to have been the hope of the majority of Catholic bishops and of members of non-Catholic churches in the countries that had sent troops to the Persian Gulf.

In asserting the unacceptability of armed conflict in the Gulf, the Pope was inferring that of the five conditions necessary for waging a just war—that there be a just cause and a competent authority involved, that the action be taken as a last resort, that there be proper proportionality and reasonable hope of success—two conditions had not been met (i.e., that it be used as a last resort and with due regard for proper proportionality). It has been noted that the Pope never once used the term "just

war" in speaking of the crisis. Nevertheless, when addressing the diplomatic corps on January 12, he did point out that for the sake of justice
and equity, the use of force for a just cause was only admissible when it
was proportionate to the result one wished to obtain. Secondly, the Pope
said in the same discourse: "Now more than ever is the time for dialogue,
for negotiation and for affirming the primacy of international law. Yes,
peace is still possible."

To make an overall judgment on John Paul's interventions during the
conflict, perhaps this statement from his address at the close of the bishops' summit will suffice:

> The war in the Gulf has brought death, destruction, and considerable
> economic and environmental damage.... What can the Catholic com-
> munities of the East and West do? Christians of the East are often called
> to bear witness to their faith in societies where they are a minority. It is
> their wish to do so courageously, as builders and participants wholly at
> one with the society to which they belong. This implies above all a
> genuine and constant dialogue with their Jewish and Muslim brothers,
> and an authentic religious freedom based on mutual respect and reci-
> procity (March 6, 1991).

This is full confirmation of the moral unacceptability of the use of
military force by allied countries, further supported by the lack of any
recognition for the results obtained.

Pope Wojtyła seems to have had three reasons for his willingness to
risk speaking out so courageously against the use of force in resolving the
crisis in the Persian Gulf: his conviction that this war could have been
avoided now that the tension between the East and the West had sub-
sided; his fear that the conflict could have become the prelude to enmity
between North and South; and the possibility that the Arab world would
have interpreted the situation as a declaration of war between Islam and
Christianity.

During a visit to a parish in Rome on February 14, 1991, the Pope
told the people that his greatest preoccupation was "fear for the future:
that people will become even greater enemies rather than advance on the
road to universal solidarity." In addition, there were other areas of concern raised by the Gulf conflict: mutual understanding among peoples;
interreligious dialogue; the mission of the Church historically established in the north, with missionary ventures reaching out to the south.
"We are worried," said John Paul, "about the continuation of the Vatican
Council's vision of the world."

One could ask whether it was prudent for the Pope to involve himself to such an extent in a highly contested and controversial matter as

the Gulf War. Would it not have been wiser simply to repeat the prohibition against killing rather than to get involved in the practical question of how to enforce violations of international law? No doubt others would have acted differently in his place, but John Paul meets challenges head on. He had said on one occasion: "This is a radical time, and it calls for a radical faith." And at the end of a spiritual retreat on February 23, 1991, he remarked that at a time when the world once again found itself in the middle of radical alternatives, the Church necessarily shared in that radicalism because that is the mission of the Church.

Normally prayers uttered in time of war are pleas for God to take one's side, to give victory to one's army. But the Pope's prayers did not distinguish between one side or the other. He simply prayed for the "soldiers on both fronts," and asked the heavenly Father to "free them from feelings of hatred and revenge, and preserve in their hearts the desire for peace" (Feb. 2, 1991).

※ CHAPTER THIRTY-THREE ※

Confronting the Islamic Regime

J ohn Paul's visit to Khartoum, Sudan, on February 10, 1993, was
perhaps the most hazardous of all his missionary journeys. The
country had been under Islamic law for the past two years, and for
ten years there had been violent civil war between the Muslims of the
north and the Christians and animists in the south. The war in Sudan was
simply a smaller version of the conflict between Christianity and Islam
that had been going on in sub-Sahara Africa for a century.

Sudan is the only African country ruled by the Koran that John Paul
risked visiting. The results of the visit were practically non-existent, but
the Pope had primarily wanted to bring the solidarity of the Catholic
Church to a persecuted Christian community and, secondly, to bring the
Sudan question to the world's attention. A third effect of the visit trig-
gered an open confrontation with Islamic fundamentalism. The Pope
spoke frankly, as usual, but received no response. After the visit to Casablanca (see Chapter 21) this visit to Khartoum was the second time that
John Paul had preached to the followers of Islam.

To have some idea of the atmosphere in which the papal visit took
place, it suffices to recall that at the time, Sudan had been denounced
internationally for its violations of human rights. Both the United Nations
and the European community had condemned Sudan, and the United
States had branded it as a country that supported international terrorism.
To understand how much of a risk John Paul faced (he denounced the
persecution of Christians in the south and repeatedly quoted the document issued by the Conference of Bishops that had been censored by the
Sudanese government) it suffices to say that when the Anglican Archbishop of Canterbury, George Carey, met with the heads of rival factions

a year later, the Sudanese government called the visit "undesirable" and completely broke diplomatic relations with London.

W hen the Pope landed at Khartoum after visiting Benin and Uganda, the last stop on his tenth journey to Africa, he was well aware of the risk he was taking. During the flight he had told reporters: "The duty of the Church, the Holy See, the nuncio, and the bishops is to remind the government and those governed, who are Muslims, that the law of the Koran applies only to believers in Islam; it absolutely cannot be imposed on those of another faith, on Christians."

John Paul was aware that his visit to Khartoum would be misinterpreted, but that did not stop him. During the flight he further acknowledged: "There is always a risk.... There is a risk wherever one goes, but especially now the principal risk is the one I have mentioned, the risk that Jesus took in sending out twelve fishermen.... In that context we can make a calculated risk. We shall see; I don't say it is, but for me it seems to be a providential situation."

What John Paul considers providential another pope might have avoided for fear of being misinterpreted or of having the Catholic community he wanted to help incur some greater risk. Four days before his arrival in Khartoum, while he was still in Uganda, John Paul had met with Paride Taban, a bishop from central Sudan. The area had been conquered by government forces, and the bishop had been living for months in the jungle with the liberation army. If government forces could capture the bishop, it would be tantamount to capturing a rebel leader.

Bishop Taban gave the Pope a list of names of catechists who had been buried alive by government forces. He also delivered an appeal addressed directly to the Pope and signed two days before by six bishops: two Catholics, two Episcopalians, one Anglican, and one Presbyterian. It was a dramatic report, describing the bombing of civilians while the Pope was already in Africa and explaining that a column of seventy military vehicles was moving toward rebel headquarters. "In Khartoum," wrote the bishops, "you will receive the red carpet and hear numerous official discourses, but you should know, Holy Father, that these are the same people who are waging a military offensive against us and are intensifying the war; who are holding 300,000 Sudanese hostages at Juba; who are restricting the preaching of the Gospel and the activity of the Church. They are discriminating on the basis of race, and they are capturing and selling African children into slavery."[1]

Actually, John Paul was well aware of the conditions in Sudan even before he left Rome for the pastoral visit. He had received detailed information from the nuncio and from Sudanese bishops during their *ad limina* visit on October 2, 1992. The bishops had also held a news conference in Rome on October 6, at which they described how the Sudanese regime was denying people's basic human rights. Freedom of speech was not allowed, and it was forbidden to evangelize or to profess their Christian religion. Islamic fundamentalist authorities were terrorizing the people. The non-Muslim population was subjected to forced conversion to Islam, and murder of the innocent was the order of the day. Gradually and systematically all foreign missionaries were being expelled from the country, and native Christians were often subjected to imprisonment and torture.

The official propaganda from Islamic leaders stated that the Christian churches in Sudan were foreign powers that were anti-Islam. It further asserted that the Christian religion was imported from the West and was particularly odious to Muslims not only because Christianity originated in Palestine, but also because it was present in Sudan, as well as in Egypt and Ethiopia, long before Islam had arrived out of Arabia.

Against this gloomy background the papal visit took place, restricted to the capital city. On the eve of the Pope's arrival, the Sudanese government showed its willingness to make some concessions regarding a Mass celebrated in the open, transmission of the visit by radio, and the liberation of certain priests and catechists. The government denied involvement in any Islamic pressure or any religious discrimination. General Omar Hassan Ahmed al Bashir, who greeted the Pope at the airport, told John Paul that he would see with his own eyes that Sudan was a "multireligious, multiracial and multicultural country" where everyone could live peacefully in "harmony, brotherhood and tranquillity."

This blatantly contradicted reports John Paul had already received, and in his reply he emphasized that he could not be silent, because "when a people is poor, weak, and defenseless, I must raise my voice on its behalf.... All that the Church asks is the freedom to perform its religious and humanitarian mission."

At the airport only government officials were present to greet the Pope, but on the streets Catholics lined up on either side, most of them refugees from central Sudan. They waved white-and-gold flags and they held aloft cloth banners marked with a cross, beneath which were the names of the victims of Islamic oppression. One such banner was written in English: "Holy Father, speak in the name of those who cannot speak for themselves."

And speak John Paul did! He delivered his second public address to priests and catechists in the cathedral. He told them that he understood the grave difficulties in which they lived and the sad plight of their country because of the war and because of the "absence of good relations which should exist between Christians and Muslims." But he implored them "not to think that they have been forgotten by the rest of the world," because the Pope and the entire Church were praying for them.

Next he paid a return visit to General Omar Hassan Ahmed al Bashir at the general's palace. In addressing the head of State, John Paul expressed his hope that Sudan would be able to establish a constitutional government that would provide peaceful cohabitation for the various religious communities.

> Your Excellency, this is the hope which I renew here today. It is a hope born of confidence, for peace is always possible. Man is a rational being endowed with intelligence and will; therefore he is capable of finding just solutions to situations of conflict, no matter how long they have been going on and no matter how intricate the motives which caused them. Efforts to restore harmony depend on the parties involved being willing and determined to implement the conditions required for peace. But when constructive action does not follow declarations of principle, violence can become uncontrollable.... The building-blocks of peace were succinctly indicated by the Sudanese bishops themselves when they said: "Without justice and respect for human rights, peace cannot be achieved" (Communiqué, Oct. 6, 1992). In a multiracial and multicultural country, a strategy of confrontation can never bring peace and progress. Only a legally guaranteed respect for human rights in a system of equal justice for all can create the right conditions for peaceful coexistence and cooperation in serving the common good. My hope for your country can therefore be expressed more concretely in a heartfelt desire to see all its citizens—without discrimination based upon ethnic origin, cultural background, social standing or religious conviction—take a responsible part in the life of the nation, with their diversity contributing to the richness of the whole national community (Feb. 10, 1993).

Later the Pope celebrated an outdoor Mass with 200,000 people in attendance. In Green Square, during the liturgy in honor of Blessed Josephine Bakhita, a former Sudanese slave and later a religious who had been beatified by John Paul nine months before, the Pope assured the Sudanese bishops of the entire Church's solidarity: "Today the successor of Peter and the whole Church reaffirm their support for the call of your bishops for respect for your rights as citizens and as believers."

Seven of the nine Sudanese bishops concelebrated with the Pope, along with a retired bishop living in Khartoum. Two other bishops, living in the war zone, could not be present, but they listened by radio. "I hope with all my heart," said John Paul, "that my voice reaches you, brothers and sisters in the south."

The Pope also insisted on the peaceful intention of his visit, which he made in order to "promote a new relationship between Muslims and Christians." At the end of his remarks John Paul warned against fundamentalism—something no one had ever done in Khartoum, before or after his visit: "To use religion as a pretext for injustice and violence is a terrible abuse and ought to be condemned by all who truly believe in God." This is much stronger than his later statements against those who commit violence in the name of religion, such as the one he made during a visit to Tunisia in 1996: "No one may kill in the name of God; no one may cause the death of a brother!" And more recently, in Nigeria, he said: "Every time violence is used in the name of religion, we must explain to all that under those circumstances, we are not looking at a true religion" (March 22, 1998).

The Pope's statement at Khartoum was stronger not because of the words he used, which when addressing justice and human rights are always forceful. Neither was it because the situation in Sudan was more dangerous or violent than in Nigeria or Tunisia. The reason John Paul's appeal in Khartoum was more forceful was because it was the same appeal that he had made a month before at Assisi on behalf of Muslims who were being murdered by Serbs and Croatians. The pope who on February 10 in Sudan condemned violence committed against Christians by Muslims, is the same pope who on January 10 had defended Muslims against violence perpetrated by Christians!

Perhaps his reflection on the violence that Christians have inflicted on others in the past has helped John Paul understand the drama in which Islam is involved today. The Pope prays ardently over the entire situation: "I pray every day for Algeria in order to persuade—through heaven—our Muslim brothers, and especially Islamic [fundamentalists], that they must not do what the others have done" (flight from Rome to Manila, Jan. 11, 1995).

Notes

1. D. Del Rio, *Wojtyła: Un Pontificato Itinerante* (Bologna: EDB, 1994). A volume that presents the pontificate of John Paul II through his travels.

CHAPTER THIRTY-FOUR

The Cross of Suffering

S ince the mid-1990s, the courageous and once physically strong Pope has been obliged to use a cane and to slacken his pace even as the new millennium rushes forward. It is a paradox that by the end of 1994, when John Paul's image resembled that of a man of suffering, *Time* magazine selected him "Man of the Year."

John Paul recovered after the 1981 assassination attempt, but from then on physical pain and suffering became a daily part of his life. According to Dr. Corrado Manni, the anesthesiologist at Gemelli Hospital, "John Paul II has never fully recovered from the psychological trauma resulting from the attempt on his life in 1981. That is why he now seems to be so much weakened. It is not due to senility, but to interior suffering. If you are a person who loves, and someone shoots at you, the effect on your psyche will be profound."[1]

The fourteenth year of his pontificate, 1992, was also the year in which a tumor was discovered in the Pope's colon and he began to experience a tremor in his left hand. Since then, John Paul has carried his cross. On November 11, 1993, he suffered his first public fall in the Hall of Benedictions. On April 28, 1994, he fell again, this time in the bathroom of his private quarters, and fractured his right femur. He has since had to resort to a cane. On Christmas Day of 1995, John Paul interrupted his *Urbi et Orbi* message because of an upset stomach, something which occurred again in March and August of 1996. Finally, on October 8, 1996, doctors performed an appendectomy. It was his sixth medical treatment during his twenty years as Pope, and this time, doctors kept him in Gemelli Hospital for 116 days—a stay of nearly four months!

In 1997 the doctors noted a progression of the tremor in John Paul's left hand. This condition has also affected his ability to walk and his speech, and it gives his face a stiff appearance. The official word was that the Pope suffers from an affliction related to Parkinson's disease. In January 1998, at the beginning of a Mass in the Sistine Chapel, the master of ceremonies moved suddenly to support the Pope when he began to fall forward, perhaps as a result of vertigo or drowsiness.

None of these physical problems has caused any substantial changes in the Pope's scheduled appointments. He still journeyed to Cuba in January of 1998 and kept his tradition of making the Good Friday Way of the Cross at the Colosseum—despite gusty winds and a heavy rain that would have challenged persons much younger!

One thing characteristic about John Paul's hospital sojourns is the way he relates to the public. He greets crowds from the window of his hospital room; he jokes about the way he walks, twirling his cane for effect; he candidly answers questions media people put to him. To a crowd in St. Peter's Square on July 12, 1992, for example, he said: "Now I would like to tell you something confidential: This evening I shall go to Gemelli Hospital for some diagnostic tests."

The tumor found in the Pope's colon was the size of an orange; it was benign, and surgeons were able to remove it completely. A year later, during the flight from Rome to Kingston, Jamaica, John Paul reported to journalists: "Up until now I have been able to walk on my own two feet, even in the mountains. I do everything possible to keep myself in shape, to avoid causing problems" (Aug. 9, 1993).

While John Paul continues to "turn out" great performances, his afflictions sometimes impede him. Occasionally he confesses this openly. In November 1993 he told a crowd: "Last Thursday, as you know, I had a brief stay in the hospital because I fell while descending the steps to greet people after an audience." When he fell again some months later, doctors examined him more closely. Speaking to the crowd from his hospital window, John Paul said: "They are giving me a thorough examination. I never knew there were so many organs and so many possibilities" (May 22, 1994).

The fracture of the Pope's right femur was a greater setback, because it restricted this athletic man who now had to use a cane. Initially there was concern he would never walk again. When John Paul reflected on the experience and later spoke about it at an audience, he compared it to the attempt on his life: "I have known that I am to lead the Church into the third millennium with prayer and various activities, but I have also known that that is not enough. The millennium must also be introduced with suffering: the assassination attempt thirteen years ago and this new sacrifice" (May 29, 1994).

John Paul has become accustomed to his afflictions. True, he walks slowly, but he can laugh at himself and even joke about the conjecture surrounding his pontificate: "It is nice to have so many cardinals at the Vatican when there is no conclave" (June 14, 1994). But the world press is beginning to speculate about who will be the next pope, and John Paul himself has remarked that even the faithful attending the Sunday Angelus want to know how he *really* is. "Every Sunday check up on the Pope to see if he is well or if he is better. I'll do my best!" (June 19, 1994)

This man has changed his fatherland and his life, his name and his language with the greatest ease, but how much it costs him to change his pace! He once remarked to doctors: "I don't like to make a spectacle of myself, walking with a cane" (July 1994). On another occasion, when the people in St. Peter's Square were shouting, *"Viva il Papa! Viva il Papa!"* he murmured: "For the time being he lives!" And when he observed journalists using binoculars to see if his hand trembled or if he would stumble, he indicated the sheaf of papers in his hand and said: "Look, not a single sheet has fallen! All the pages have stayed in my hand!" (Nov. 5, 1994)

His physical weakness has been a heavy blow to the Pope, but when he travels he is rejuvenated. During the flight from Rome to Manila, he confessed to reporters: "I am a little surprised. I did not think I would again find myself on Alitalia [Airlines], with the prospect of going all the way to the Philippines. Ten or eleven hours, while it is only one hour to Zagreb!" (Jan. 11, 1995)

Even when in Rome the Pope does not neglect visitation of the parishes. In March, 1995, he told the Roman clergy: "This year I have had to miss the parish visitations. I missed them because of this leg, which is now famous.... But now, on the first Sunday of Lent, I shall return, by the grace of God, and I hope that [these visits] can continue, as long as Providence permits" (March 2, 1995).

Naturally, when serious illness or affliction overtakes a person, the thought of death inevitably arise. The Pope made one of his earliest references to death in a lighthearted manner. When the crowd at Castel Gandolfo shouted: "Long live the Pope!" he replied: "With this uproar, it would be difficult to die, but the time will come!" (Dec. 26, 1994) He first referred to death in a serious way when he told young people: "All of you belong to the third millennium. Perhaps I do not" (April 30, 1995).

A popular Polish song contains the phrase, *"Sto lat!"* meaning, "May you live a hundred years!" Once, when the Pope was greeted with this expression, he playfully observed: "Then I still have twenty-two or twenty-three years left!"

NOTES

1. F. Margiotta Broglio, "Il papato degli ultimi cinquant'anni," *Revista de studi politici internazionali*, n. 1, 1989, p. 59.

CHAPTER THIRTY-FIVE

In Defense of Life

*D*uring the night of April 28, 1994, John Paul slipped and fell on his bathroom floor. An x-ray revealed he had broken the femur of his right thigh, forcing him to cancel his trip to Sicily the following morning. Instead, he paid a fifth visit to Gemelli Hospital. How did Wojtyła react? He told an aid: "Maybe this was needed for the Year of the Family."

Perhaps the Pope meant that suffering was needed because everything else had been done in his attempts to gain international recognition of the sacredness of human life. In the past month and a half he had intervened a dozen times, sometimes speaking at the top of his voice, to halt the United Nations proposal for a September conference in Cairo on population and development. The Church's concern over the conference centered on the possible harm it might deal to human life and family issues because of family planning programs for poor nations that included contraception and even abortion.

John Paul vigorously opposed the project; his action led to an unprecedented conflict between the United Nations and the Catholic Church. Only at the time of Poland's Solidarity movement and during the Gulf War had the Pope waged such a vehement personal campaign.

Protesting the UN's Plans

John Paul first publicly objected to the Cairo Conference on March 18, 1994. He received in audience Mrs. Nafis Sadik, the secretary general for the conference, and told her: "The proofs for the final documents are a source of great concern to me. Some of the proposals contradict basic ethical principles. And this is a discussion of the future of humanity." The Pope objected that the document did not condemn sterilization and abortion, and it ignored the institution of matrimony, as if marriage were something that belonged to the past. Further, he complained the document stressed a limitation of the family rather than its development.

The Pope knew that behind that document were the powerful interests of developed nations, which worry about the increase of the poor on the planet. He realized his voice was powerless against such interests, but he raised it anyway. The following day, March 19, he spoke to workers, telling them that among the solutions that all-powerful possessors of capital were trying to impose on poorer nations, the principal one was the destruction of the right to life. "Isn't that an obvious absurdity?"

To get the United Nations to listen, however, it is not enough to raise one's voice. Therefore on March 25, by a mandate of the Pope, the Cardinal Secretary of State convoked a meeting with all the ambassadors accredited to the Vatican in order to explain to them the Holy Father's great preoccupation concerning the scheduled Cairo Conference. Yet, not even that was enough for the Pope; he wanted to reach those in power directly. Consequently, on Easter Sunday, April 3, in his *Urbi et Orbi* message, John Paul announced that he had written a letter to all the Heads of State. In that letter he asked them to exert every effort to prevent the value of the human person, the sacred character of life, and the capacity of the human person to give one's self in love, from being diminished: "The family remains the principal source of humanity, and every nation should protect it as a precious treasure."

After the Easter liturgy, John Paul spent a day at Castel Gandolfo and went hiking in the mountains of Abruzzo (his last mountain excursion before fracturing his femur). He returned to Rome for the General Audience on April 6, where he spoke even more passionately: "We are concerned lest this Year for the Family become a year *against* the family. And it could very easily become a year against the family if these plans really become the projects of the World Conference in Cairo. We protest! We cannot advance into the future with such a systematic plan of killing the unborn!"

"We protest!" is an unusual cry for a pope. John Paul used this expression only one other time: in Poland in 1991, and again in defense of life—"As Bishop of Rome I protest against the manner in which they want to establish the unity of Europe. What should the criterion be? Freedom? But what kind of freedom? The freedom to destroy the life of an unborn infant?" Very likely it was easier for the Pope to shout in Polish than in Italian, so he felt he should excuse himself for his vehemence: "Pardon my heated words, but I had to say them!" (Wloclawek, June 7, 1991)

During that same 1991 journey to Poland, John Paul justified his manner of speaking out against abortion: "This land is my country, so I am permitted to speak this way. And all of you who are tempted to take these matters lightly should understand that they hurt me; they also ought to hurt you" (Kielce, June 3, 1991).

On April 17, 1994, John Paul announced the battle in which he was going to engage: "I am returning to the Vatican to fight against a project of the United Nations which wants to destroy the family. I simply say: no! Reconsider. Convert. If you are the United Nations, you should not destroy!"

Later that day, from the window of his study, he again spoke with exceptional passion to the crowd listening to him in the rain: "To what kind of society will this ethical permissiveness lead? Are there not already disturbing symptoms that make us fear for the future of humanity? I don't intend to be an alarmist or to indulge in pessimism, but I claim my absolute duty to raise the voice of the Church regarding a very important cause."

Meanwhile, the preparatory committee for the Cairo Conference was working in Washington, D.C. On April 28, the Vatican diplomat taking part in that work, Diarmuid Martin, sent word that "the Holy See finds itself in the minority" on the question of abortion. However, Martin added, the Holy See had "succeeded in having the texts on the question put in parentheses, to be discussed again at Cairo."

The Pope listened to that meager report. Seemingly everything possible had been done to alter the purpose of the conference, but perhaps the offering of suffering was still needed. John Paul's accident now prevented him from intervening for an entire month. The waiting increased the Pope's vexation, already augmented by his physical suffering. It was for the Church a time of sadness, filled with fear that the Pope might never walk again.

By May 29, the Pope had returned to the Vatican. From his window he shared with the crowd how the past month's hospitalization had been a "gift." He promised to defend the family and to try to make his defense prevail before "the powerful of this world." Four days later he would receive President Clinton, the first of the "powerful" leaders he was to meet. This was the substance of John Paul's discourse at the Angelus:

Today I would like to express through Mary my gratitude for this gift of suffering, once more connected with the Marian month. [The attempt on his life had also occurred in May.] I have understood that it is a necessary gift that the Pope should find himself in Gemelli Hospital; that he should be absent from this window for four weeks, four Sundays; that he must suffer this year as he had to suffer thirteen years ago. I have meditated on all this and thought it through again during my stay in the hospital. Once again I found at my side the great Primate of Poland, Cardinal Stefan Wyszynski, who told me at the beginning of my pontificate: "If the Lord has called you, you must lead the Church into the third millennium." He led the Church in Poland into the second millennium, and that is what he told me. So I have understood that I must lead the Church of Christ into the third millennium with prayer and through various activities, but I have also seen that that is not enough. It is also necessary to lead by suffering, with the [assassination] attempt thirteen years ago and with this new sacrifice.... But why now? Why in this Year of the Family? Precisely because the family is. threatened. The family is being attacked. So the Pope must be attacked. The Pope must suffer, so that the world may see that there is a higher gospel, as it were, the gospel of suffering, with which to prepare the future...of the family, of every family, of all families.

I thank the Virgin Mary for the gift of suffering. I understood that it was important to place this argument before the powerful of the world. Once again I must meet the powerful of the world and I must speak to them. With what arguments? What is left for me is the argument of suffering (May 29, 1994).

The concept that the Pope personifies the Church and suffers in the name of the Church is an ancient one, linked to the Pope's title as "Vicar of Christ." But there is another point worth mentioning here. John Paul was suffering for the sake of the family, but his suffering was of value also for "the powerful of the world."

Documents in Defense of Life

To complete the picture of John Paul's passionate defense of human life, two texts are especially significant. The first is a passage from the *Letter to Families*, dated February 22, 1994, the same year the above passages are quoted. Here the Pope criticizes the culture of the West, which has in recent times "passed laws contrary to the right to life of every human being." Consequently, "we are facing an immense threat to life; not only to the life of individuals but also to that of civilization itself. The statement that civilization has become in some areas a 'civilization of death' is being confirmed in disturbing ways."[1]

The second document is the 1995 encyclical *Evangelium Vitae* (The Gospel of Life), a magisterial synthesis on the defense of life. The document also contains something new by way of a statement on the death penalty. In spite of the uninterrupted tradition in its favor, the encyclical opposes the death penalty in order to be consistent with the fundamental teaching on abortion and euthanasia.

John Paul approves of the teaching that opposes the death penalty, and he has imposed it on the Curia, which has resisted and tried to soften the Church's position on this issue. The proof that he supports such teaching is found in the fact that, as his encyclical (a personal document) was being composed, the *Catechism of the Catholic Church* (an institutional document) had already taken a step forward on the question of capital punishment. And note that the *Catechism* represents seven years of work by an international commission in consultation with the episcopate. This general principle is stated in the *Catechism:*

> If...non-lethal means are sufficient to defend and protect people's safety from the aggressor, authority will limit itself to such means, as these are more in keeping with the concrete conditions of the common good and more in conformity with the dignity of the human person.[2]

The above statement indicates the Church is basically opposed to the death penalty. But questions have been raised about the Church's teaching on the legality of the death penalty and the fact that the Church, as a political entity, practiced capital punishment until the 1800s. Publicly, the Church has frequently been accused of using a double standard. On the one hand it radically prohibits abortion and on the other it allows the qualified possibility of using capital punishment.

John Paul himself, who has consistently intervened against the death penalty in every part of the world, was not satisfied with the wording of the *Catechism*. He recognized an element of truth in such public criticism, and he wanted a clear pronouncement on the issue. John Paul formulated that clear statement in his encyclical, and in 1997 he also had a corrected text inserted into the definitive edition of the *Catechism of the Catholic Church*.

In the encyclical the Pope praised as "a sign of hope" ever-increasing public aversion to the death penalty. It was precisely such an aversion that had led to the dispute over the *Catechism's* wording. It was becoming evident that in the Church also there was a growing tendency to seek the total abolition of the death penalty. In the end, the corrected text was to read: "the cases in which the execution of the offender is an absolute necessity are very rare, if not practically nonexistent."[3]

If he had been able to do so, John Paul would have addressed the death penalty in much the same way he spoke out against war, namely, by urging humanity to move toward its absolute prohibition. The world should be grateful for what the Pope has already said and done in defense of life. Christians at least ought to appreciate his efforts to help their brothers and sisters recapture the fundamental Gospel teaching within our own epoch.

NOTES

1. Pope John Paul II, *Letter to Families* (Boston: Pauline Books & Media, 1994), n. 21.

2. *Catechism of the Catholic Church*, n. 2267.

3. Ibid., n. 2267.

❀ CHAPTER THIRTY-SIX ❀

Visits to Sarajevo and Beirut

*T*he year 1994 was one of intense pain and apostolic projects for John Paul. That year marked some of his greatest sufferings— the fractured femur, clashes with the United Nations in the defense of life, and the cancellation of planned trips to Sarajevo and Beirut—and yet, it was also a time of great fruitfulness for him. While newspapers began to speculate about possible successors, John Paul continued to plan for the Great Jubilee with the energy of a newly elected pope.

Encountering Delays

Everyone knows John Paul suffers when he cannot travel, especially when he is forced by reason of war to cancel trips already announced. One of his greatest disappointments must have been the 1994 cancellation of journeys to Beirut and Sarajevo, due to guerrilla warfare in Lebanon and the outbreak of war in Bosnia.

John Paul had always wanted to visit Lebanon; he had spoken about it since the beginning of his pontificate, but every year he had to forego the trip. Finally, the visit was scheduled for May of 1994, but, once again, a series of attacks on Catholic churches led to the trip's postponement.

Even more frustrating for the Pope was the cancellation of his visit to Sarajevo, then under siege by Serbian-Bosnian forces and weakly defended by United Nations troops. John Paul had waited three years and it was still impossible to schedule a visit, so he simply announced unilaterally that he would visit Sarajevo. His original plan included a visit to Sarajevo (Bosnia), Belgrade (Serbia), and Zagreb (Croatia) in one journey, but he had to omit the Belgrade stop because of the opposition of the

Orthodox Patriarch (another sad event in the ecumenical *kenosis* discussed earlier in Chapter 29). All summer long John Paul repeated his intention to visit Sarajevo on September 8. But just two days before the visit, it had to be cancelled when the head of the United Nations forces announced he could not guarantee the Pope's safety.

Unable to visit Sarajevo, John Paul celebrated a Mass on September 8 in the courtyard of Castel Gandolfo instead, "in union with the Catholic community" in Sarajevo. He delivered the homily he would have given in the stadium of Sarajevo. He called out, "Enough war!" and asked Catholics to forgive and to ask forgiveness. He condemned "ethnic cleansing" and asked that sanctions against Serbia be reviewed. And he sent a kiss of peace to the Serbian Orthodox Patriarch who opposed the Pope's visit to Belgrade.

On September 10 and 11 the Pope did visit Zagreb, and he repeated there the same appeals and warnings. On television he appeared to be in pain and somewhat bewildered, unsteady on his feet and not yet able to get around well with his cane. He did not speak extemporaneously or in his usual light-hearted manner. His physical suffering, never so evident before, indicated the spiritual pain he felt in not being able to embrace together fraternally Croatians, Serbs, and Bosnians. And not even once did the Pope's repeated calls for forgiveness win the people's applause.

From the very beginning of the Bosnian war in 1991, John Paul had intervened repeatedly. To understand just how much the Pope suffered because of the war, we need only recall his words at a service for peace in the Balkans which he conducted in St. Peter's on January 23, 1994: "You should not feel that you are abandoned. You are not abandoned! We are with you, and we shall be with you, and we shall always be more and more with you!" And this is how he spoke at the end of 1994, when he announced the publication of a letter to children: "This letter is addressed also to those who are responsible for wars, near and far. We are thinking of all wars, but perhaps especially of those close to us on the other side of the Adriatic. We say to [those who are responsible] today, the fourth Sunday of Advent, stop! Stop in the name of the infant Jesus!" (Dec. 18, 1994)

Despite his impassioned outcry, the war escalated. On July 16, 1995, the Pope warned: "What is happening before the eyes of the whole world is the destruction of civilization!"

Unable to reconcile Croatians and Serbs, Catholics, Orthodox and Muslims, John Paul called together all the heads of the Catholic communities in the former Yugoslavia and told them: "Our faith tells us that we cannot be happy without each other, and much less, against each other" (Oct. 17, 1995). He sent the same message to the bishops and nuncios at Bosnia and Herzegovina, Croatia, the Yugoslav Federation, the former Yugoslav Republic of Macedonia, and Slovenia.

*T*he Pope had to wait another year and a half before he could set foot in Sarajevo, on April 12 and 13, 1997. During the Mass he celebrated in the stadium, it began to snow even though it was not the season. Cardinal Vinko Puljié showed the Pope his city, now in ruins, and read a list of the wounded. Between 1991 and 1995, the number of dead rose to 270,000; there were one million refugees and more than one million displaced persons.

As at Zagreb, the visit to Sarajevo was an uninterrupted sermon on forgiveness and reconciliation. "We forgive and we ask forgiveness" is the statement the Holy Father repeated in seven of his nine discourses. He spoke to the people and to leaders, to crowds at Mass and to bishops, to Muslims and Jews, to the Orthodox and to volunteer workers of Caritas. He spoke this message to everyone in every place he visited.

Naturally, the most forceful appeal John Paul made was to the four Catholic bishops of Bosnia and Herzegovina. He told them to consider the work of reconciliation as their primary duty, and to carry it out "by healing souls tested by sorrow and perhaps brutalized by feelings of hatred and revenge."

There is no family in Sarajevo that does not mourn a member killed in the war. One must keep this grievous condition in mind to understand the courage the Pope demonstrated in his preaching. This was his message: Sarajevo is "a city that symbolizes the sufferings of this century," but it can become "a city that is a symbol of reconciliation in Europe." This transformation can take place only through an authentic renewal that begins with forgiveness; otherwise the way of revenge will prevail, and it will ultimately destroy what remains of the cohabitation of Muslims, Orthodox Serbians, and Catholic Croatians.

Only the Pope could have brought such a message to the martyred city and be heard, if not followed.

John Paul's intense feelings toward Lebanon are much older than those for Sarajevo. They originated before his election, when the cardinals sent a message during the conclave "for the crisis in Lebanon"; they surfaced again during his discourse in the Sistine Chapel on the day after his election. The Pope prayed for "peace in freedom for the beloved land of Lebanon." He frequently mentioned his desire to visit Lebanon, or at least the city of Beirut.

The Pope's attraction for the city of Beirut is similar to that for the city of Sarajevo. Both places have a long tradition of multicultural and interreligious cohabitation, and both require the awareness of the international community for peaceful intervention, because Islam is the predominant faction and the Catholic community is always in danger of being crushed.

Of all the interventions John Paul has made on behalf of Lebanon, perhaps two best illustrate the intensity of his passion. The first was a spontaneous statement which he made in faulty Italian, but which was perfectly in accord with the Gospel: "We cannot allow an entire people to be destroyed, a whole country. They are our brothers, our Catholic brothers and our Muslim brothers. I again repeat this cry of alarm!" (April 23, 1989)

In the statement above, the Pope had used the word "*confratelli*" (religious friars) rather than the correct "*fratelli*" (brothers) when referring to the Muslims. The word was certainly not the one he had intended to use, and yet, what a beautiful concept of fraternity and even of fellowship John Paul extended to the Muslims!

The second example is from a Pope who confesses that sons of the Church are responsible for the conflict in Lebanon, and he entreats them not to fight among themselves. It involved a very tense moment between the country's regular army under General Samir Geagea and the troops of General Michel Aoun. The world press described it as a "Christian war." In a message to the Maronite Patriarch, Pierre Sfeir, the Pope said: "I ask that this fratricidal combat be suspended at once!" (Feb. 6, 1990)

John Paul was finally able to visit Beirut on May 10 and 11, 1997, a month after his visit to Sarajevo. He managed to enter both countries during a cease-fire, but peace still eluded hearts on both sides of the conflict. In both countries despair especially seemed to grip Catholics who could not even view peace as a solution—not in Sarajevo because Christians were immersed in a Muslim majority, and not in Lebanon because there seemed no hope for ending Syrian occupation.

It was an impossible mission, therefore, first because of war and then because of the difficulties involved in talking about peace and reaching an agreement. Any political ambassador or mediator would have found it difficult to deal with troubled areas like this, where people made promises but nothing came of them. But that's not the way John Paul felt. In both cases he spoke the whole truth, without minimizing the responsibility Catholics had in the situation. At Beirut, and also at Sarajevo, the crowds understood him.

Besides, he who speaks the truth speaks in the name of all. Consequently, when John Paul spoke about the sovereignty of Lebanon, Muslims knew he was speaking in their name. As he was leaving for Lebanon, the Pope had said to journalists: "I am going to Lebanon, to the sovereign nation of Lebanon"; it sounded almost like a challenge. Then, at the end of his two-day visit, he explained that the persons who govern in the world must respect international law so that the Lebanese nation would be guaranteed sovereignty, legitimate autonomy, and security.

John Paul raised another troubling truth pertaining to Israel when he used the word "threatening" in reference to the occupation of Southern Lebanon. And the third truth the Pope spoke about referred to Syria when he mentioned that the presence of non-Lebanese armed forces in their territory was the greatest difficulty for the country.

Last of all, the Pope addressed a very disturbing truth to his own Catholic sons, by commenting on the war they had been waging for many years in favor of the occupation by Israel and the protectorate of Syria. This, he said, "wounds the Church," which must see her sons killed and killing each other.

John Paul's frankness won him the favor of the crowds. People flocked to him during the two days of his visit, even in the Shiite and Sunnite quarters. Young Muslims and Orthodox mingled with Catholics on Saturday night at the shrine of Our Lady of Lebanon. They also made up a good part of the crowd on Sunday morning at the outdoor Mass in the center of Beirut; perhaps as many as 50,000 out of 300,000 Muslims came to see the Catholic Pope.

❖ CHAPTER THIRTY-SEVEN ❖

The Holy Spirit Breathes Upon Cuba

Cuba... The first image that comes to mind is the Pope, bent over and leaning heavily on his cane as he leaves the *Plaza de la Revolución* in Havana on January 25, 1998. The celebration of the Mass, with Fidel Castro and an estimated one million people in attendance, has just ended after three hours. Removing his vestments, John Paul makes his way alone to the Popemobile. The crowd does not notice him as he walks slowly along the grass. It matters little to him that he takes more time than is perhaps necessary; he has completed his mission.

Seeing this tired Pope walking with a cane, it is easy to recall the energetic pontiff who began his mission carrying his crosier high. That is the way people knew him twenty years ago, on October 22, 1978, when they saw him walk, tall and resolute, through St. Peter's Square after he had proclaimed the theme of his pontificate: "Open the doors to Christ!" Now he repeated that same missionary appeal during this Mass. Perhaps it has contributed to the opening of a door here as well.

A second image comes to mind from the Mass in the *Plaza de la Revolución*. In the middle of his homily, the Pope was interrupted by a cry for freedom. He had just quoted from Scripture, "The truth will make you free," and a group of young people immediately started chanting a slogan that organizers of the event had not anticipated: "The free Pope wants us to be free!" A wave of concern passed over the face of Cardinal Ortega, who would have to handle affairs after the papal visit. Anxiety also appeared evident on the faces of Vatican staff members. None of it appeared on the Pope's face, however. He listened serenely as the chant was repeated; when it stopped, as if to show that he had understood completely, he responded: "Yes, free with the freedom Christ brought."

The cry for freedom had burst forth before, for example in Poland in 1979, 1983 and 1987; in Brazil in 1980; in Chile in 1987; in Paraguay in 1988; in East Timor in 1989. On other occasions—such as in the Philippines in 1981, Argentina in 1982, Guatemala, El Salvador and Haiti in 1983, Zaire in 1980 and 1985, and Sudan in 1993—no shouts had come from the crowds, but the crowds had listened, thirstily drinking in the Pope's message. John Paul's serenity and self-confidence during those journeys enabled him to confront every form of governmental absolutism in the name of the Gospel—as he did in Cuba.

It is incredible that so preoccupied a man could be alert enough to handle a potentially difficult situation so well. Moreover, John Paul had to contend with the nervousness of Cuban officials and a crowd that easily could have become uncontrollable. Added to this was the fact that from one hour to the next, no one knew for certain if Fidel Castro would even be present at the Pope's Mass or if the Mass would be televised.

Some individuals tried to provide a psychological explanation for the Pope's exceptional physical endurance during the Cuban trip. He appeared rejuvenated by his confrontation with Communism, and even with the possible opposition of young people. At least that was the impression journalists had during the flight to Cuba. John Paul was prompt and alert in answering a dozen questions for a half-hour. This had not happened since January 1995 during the flight from Rome to Manila, when the Pope was eager for conversation during the lengthy international journey.

The Truth Sets People Free

The visit to Cuba can be synthesized in three distinct phrases of the Pope. The first and most incisive words John Paul uttered during the flight from Rome to Havana were in response to the question: "What would you like to hear from Fidel Castro?" The Pope replied: "I want him to tell me the truth, his truth as a man, as the President, as the Commander in Chief. Then I want him to tell me the truth about his country, the relations between the Church and the State, and everything that is of interest to us."

To tell the truth. In other words, to drop the propaganda and engage in an authentic exchange which could also become a collaboration. It is interesting to look at the relation between John Paul's hope and the young people's cry for freedom, which burst forth when they heard the scriptural quotation: "The truth will make you free."

John Paul improvised the second statement at the end of his homily during the Mass: "The wind today is very meaningful, because the wind symbolizes the Holy Spirit. The Spirit breathes where he will, and today he breathes upon Cuba." There is no need for further comment; this is one of the most beautiful, spontaneous statements the Pope has voiced in all his journeys!

The third statement comes from John Paul's General Audience in Rome on January 28, after the visit to Cuba: "My visit to Cuba reminded me very much of my first return to Poland in 1979. I wish for our brothers and sisters on that beautiful island that the fruits of this pilgrimage will be similar to the fruits of that pilgrimage to Poland."

Still weary from his journey but satisfied, indeed very satisfied with the papal visit to Cuba, and trusting in the good results to come, the Pope continued: "Since my return I have been surrounded by a great number of people who have marveled, as have I, at the great enthusiasm of the Latin American people."

In his evaluation of the papal visit, John Paul emphasized the public testimony of faith the visit had made possible. In particular the Polish Pope exulted in the fact that the figure of Christ had been raised high above the plaza in Havana. Very likely it reminded the Pope of the cross that dominated Victory Square in Warsaw on June 2, 1979. "In the great *Plaza de la Revolución* in Havana I saw an enormous picture of Christ with the words: *Jesus Christ, I trust in you.* I gave thanks to God because in that particular place, named after the revolution, I found him who has brought to the world the true revolution, the revolution of the love of God, which frees man from evil and injustice and gives him peace and fullness of life."

With his responses to questions during flight, and with the twelve discourses he delivered in Cuba, John Paul conveyed three messages. They were addressed to three different entities, and the topics they touched upon were also threefold: the visit to Cuba, Fidel Castro, and the United States.

First, the Pope asked the United States to change its policy regarding the 35-year-old embargo that has impoverished the Cuban people. He repeated the request three times. When he was asked during the flight what he had to say about the U.S. policy, John Paul answered tersely: "It must change! It must change!" Later on at Camaguey he said, "Economic embargoes must always be condemned insofar as they are harmful to those who are most needy." Finally, when saying farewell to Castro at the airport, he remarked: "Economic restrictions imposed on a country from outside are unjust and ethically unacceptable."

Over and above the speeches, however, the visit itself was, objectively speaking, a criticism of the United States government. The official spokesperson for the Clinton administration described the Pope's visit as "premature." On January 26—as the Pope flew back to Rome—Mike McCurry stated at the White House: "We understand and we respect the position of the Pope, but the embargo is a question of law, a law that enjoys strong and widespread support on the part of the [American] people and of both political parties."

Over and above the Pope's comments on the embargo and the objective fact of his visit to Cuba, other aspects of the papal visit are significant for the United States. The Pope met with Castro several times: on his arrival at the airport, on the evening of January 22 at the presidential palace, on the evening of January 23 at the university (where Castro was not expected), and at the Mass on January 25 (the greeting at the foot of the stage was not scheduled on the program, but the Vatican spokesman, Joaquín Navarro-Valls, went to Castro and accompanied him to John Paul). Over and over again, the most respected man in the world extended his hand to the man the U.S. government wished to banish from the world community. During the visit at the presidential palace, Castro presented his brothers, Raúl and Ramón, and his sisters, Agnes and Agostina, to the Pope. "My sister Agostina," Castro explained, "would like to embrace you as they do in Rome." "Let us do it," agreed the Pope. They embraced and she wept.

The Pope had asked Castro for the truth, but he also made three specific requests to give the truth substance:

❖ *A gesture of clemency for political prisoners.* This request was made by Cardinal Sodano, Vatican Secretary of State, to Carlos Lage, the number-two man of the Castro regime. Lage's reply? The request would be attended to.

❖ *Reforms that would join freedom and justice.* Neither freedom nor justice should be placed above the other; for example, no yielding to the blind force of the market and to capitalistic liberalism that enriches a few while increasingly impoverishing the many.

❖ *Full religious liberty.* The Pope discussed this topic in his address to the fourteen bishops of Cuba, specifying in writing to the papal nunciature on January 25 to give the Church space and means to carry on its mission, which is not only liturgical, but also prophetic and charitable.

Finally, the Pope told the Church in Cuba to claim insistently as Catholics the right to sufficient freedom in public life and in education. He urged young people especially not to emigrate, but to take part in political life, working "gradually and peacefully" for change (Santiago de Cuba, January 24).

*I*t would be well to say something about the "public witness to the faith" that took place in Cuba (the Pope used the expression in his message to the Cuban people on December 20). Perhaps this was the greatest gift of the papal visit. In view of his visit, the Pope had already obtained the restoration of Christmas as a civil holiday, authorization for a pilgrimage throughout the whole island in honor of the *Madonna del Cobre,* and Cardinal Ortega's first televised appearance. During the papal visit, the crowds of faithful increased day by day until, on the last day, an estimated one million people assembled. In addition, the national radio and television networks carried all five major events. The government had cooperated by declaring each day a semi-holiday in the areas the Pope's visit touched.

The papal visit to Cuba resulted in establishing a collaborative relationship between Church and State, though on an experimental basis. To assure a more permanent relationship, the Pope gave the bishops specific instructions. He left a strengthened Church, one destined to play an important role in the country's future transition. He also provided a model of confrontation that is firm but flexible and respectful.

The papal visit did have some immediate results. A communiqué published on February 12 stated: "The Secretary of State has been informed that the Cuban government has freed a certain number of prisoners as an act of clemency and good will in recognition of the Pope's visit to Cuba." A month later, the United States, "acknowledging the Pope's request," announced a reduction of its economic embargo against Cuba. So the Pope's visit has already borne the fruit of gestures of good will on the part of both the Cuban and the United States governments. Perhaps these gestures do not amount to a great deal, but they are a sign of increased openness compared to what his predecessors, and John Paul himself, experienced until now.

With the January visit to Cuba, the Pope began a landmark year in which the duration of his pontificate surpassed that of any previous modern pope. And this Pope is certainly unprecedented in attracting increasing numbers of people with the passing of the years.

❊ CHAPTER THIRTY-EIGHT ❊

Preparing for the Third Millennium

Since the middle of the 1990s, the days and activities of John Paul have centered on his dream of celebrating the Great Jubilee and leading the Church into the third millennium. With each passing year he has experienced more of the fatigue of being pope, but with each day he has intensified his effort to realize the dream of that goal. And a dream can carry one very far.

With the project of the Great Jubilee, John Paul has given a renewed impetus to his pontificate, aiming it specifically at the year 2000. The Jubilee has become not only an appointment with the third millennium; a schedule of activities has been announced for specific dates throughout the year. Tentative projects outside of Italy include a visit to the Holy Land, a gathering of monotheistic religious leaders on Mount Sinai, and an assembly of Christians in Jerusalem or Bethlehem. With the publication of the calendar of the Holy Year 2000 on May 26, 1998, the Pope announced some very precise activities for himself and for the Church:

❖ the opening of the holy door at St. Peter's Basilica which took place on Christmas night, 1999, and will be closed again on Epiphany, 2001. The Great Jubilee began with the new millennium and was symbolized by a ceremony in which the Pope led the Church into the third millennium;

❖ the opening of an "ecumenical holy door" at the Basilica of St. Paul outside the Walls on January 18, 2000. The door was opened at an ecumenical celebration that preceded a week of prayer for Christian unity;

❖ a day of pardon and repentance of past errors and instances of infidelity and inconsistency, on the First Sunday of Lent, March 12, 2000, in Rome;

❖ an "ecumenical commemoration" at the Coliseum on May 7, 2000, of all the martyrs from all the Christian churches in this century;

❖ a day of prayer and reflection on the duties of Catholics toward humanity: proclamation of Christ, witness, and dialogue, on Pentecost Sunday, June 11, 2000;

❖ a day for Judaeo-Christian dialogue on October 3, 2000.

With his plans for the Great Jubilee, John Paul is acting like the father in the Gospel who takes out of his sack old things and new. We have just seen some of the new things John Paul wants to accomplish; some of the "old things" include planned days for children, for the elderly, for migrants, for workers, for women, for priests and deacons, for religious, for artists, for men of science, for journalists, for police, for the military, for persons in sports, the theater, movies, etc. The international Eucharistic Congress will be held in Rome at the end of June 2000, and World Youth Day is scheduled to take place in Rome in the middle of August.

And precisely what will John Paul be doing during the Great Jubilee? Every evening he will be at the window of his study, greeting the pilgrims assembled in St. Peter's Square. He also is scheduled to visit the Holy Land from March 21–26, 2000. He mentioned this hope in *Tertio Millennio Adveniente:* "It would be very significant if in the year 2000 it were possible to visit the places on the road taken by the people of God of the Old Covenant, starting from the places associated with Abraham and Moses, through Egypt and Mount Sinai, as far as Damascus, the city which witnessed the conversion of St. Paul."[1]

What can one say about these grand plans for the Great Jubilee? The machinery that has been put into motion does have some excessive elements, but the new and original initiatives listed above cover all the essential points (ecumenical, interreligious, historical and social). It seems nothing has been overlooked; plans for the Great Jubilee have followed a coherent and progressive development up to the present time.

An Historic Celebration

Preparations for the Jubilee began with a memorandum to the cardinals early in 1994 for an extraordinary Consistory to be held June 13–14. On November 14, 1994, the Pope promulgated the apostolic letter, *Tertio*

Millennio Adveniente, followed on March 16, 1995, by the establishment of the central committee for the Jubilee. The first consultative meeting with bishops took place on February 15–16, 1996, and the Jubilee Calendar was published on May 26, 1998.

Cardinal Roger Etchegaray was named director of the central committee for the Great Jubilee. Under his direction, there are eight commissions—the most important are the ecumenical, the historical-theological, the interreligious, and the one dealing with the Christian martyrs of this century. Since the ecumenical commission is especially important, it was decided to add to the ten Catholic members, six representatives of other churches and ecclesial communities as "adjunct" members. This would make possible a more detailed examination of concrete ecumenical possibilities and collaboration. In view of the Pope's desire to place great emphasis on the ecumenical dimension, the ecumenical commission became a top priority.

The purpose of the commission on ecumenism was to find ways of participating in the preparation and celebration of the year 2000. A further goal was to organize the pan-Christian meeting so that the Christian churches could publicly and solemnly profess their common faith. There will also be reflection on certain practices in the past that have caused tensions with other Christians (such as indulgences), taking into account that the celebration of Jubilees is a Catholic practice unknown to the Orthodox and rejected by the followers of the Protestant Reform.

The commission for interreligious dialogue has planned to present the Great Jubilee not as an exclusively Christian event and therefore irrelevant to members of other religions, much less as something opposed to them. Like the ecumenical commission, it has the task of preparing a gathering for prayer with Jews, Muslims and members of other religions. The Jubilee is being presented as an opportunity for a mutual examination of conscience and a period of repentance and forgiveness. This is another daring initiative our Pope has embraced. It suffices to repeat his statement in the apostolic letter, *Tertio Millennio Adveniente*: "In a certain sense Christ belongs to all of humanity."

The commission for new martyrs of the past century does not have the task of working for their beatification, but emphasizing the importance of martyrdom today in an ecumenical context. Its task is to gather testimonials of the as yet unexplored examples of martyrdom in our day. With the assistance of the conferences of bishops and the sister churches, the commission has been asked to prepare a catalog of new martyrs. As of this writing, the commission has already compiled 8,000 file cards. The tentative date for publication of the catalog is May 7, 2000.

John Paul's "Folly"

This program is truly audacious and typical of Pope Wojtyła, but it caused some concern in the Curia. The *mea culpas* alarmed almost everyone; but the project on the "new martyrs" especially jolted the Congregation for the Causes of Saints. Moreover, even progressive organizations working for ecumenical and interreligious dialogue felt they were being pushed in a direction that was still premature. But the Pope is in a hurry, and it is necessary for others in the Church to take risks with him!

In past centuries the sun rose and set without haste over the Roman pontificate, with the expectation that it would remain unchanged. Jubilees simply emphasized papal stability. But during John Paul's pontificate, days and nights rush by rapidly, almost as if they are engaged in a contest with one another.

To invite our "separated brethren" to open a holy door with us at the Basilica of St. Paul, which was the church marked for ecumenical hospitality, seemed rash, to say the least. Some of those churches separated themselves precisely because of such holy doors and indulgences! And to call Jews to a celebration of the 2,000 years since the birth of Christ seemed to be another beautiful gamble! But John Paul has already seen some positive results. The Chief Rabbi of Rome, Elio Toaff, has said that his community will participate in the Jubilee if it will advance the strong desire of this pontificate for a dialogue among the monotheistic religions, including Islam. Furthermore, the rabbi offered to make a visit to Jerusalem together with the Pope.

As for the proposal to compose a "contemporary martyrology," it too is an audacious plan. It demonstrates a great deal of trust in humanity, a certain ecumenical courage and some liberty with canon law. The martyrs are those who died *for* the faith and *because of* their faith. But John Paul already canonized Maximilian Kolbe with the title of martyr, explaining that his witness to charity at Auschwitz was the greatest possible testimony to the Christian faith. He expressed the same idea concerning the Sicilian judge, Rosario Livatino, who was murdered by the Mafia, and others like him: "They are martyrs for justice and indirectly for the faith."

In focusing his attention on the martyrs, John Paul clearly communicates his sentiments about the age in which we are living. He sees it as both a severe test and a great opportunity for the faith. Never before have there been such crimes committed against humanity, and never before has humanity given such testimonies of courage. Yes, even non-Christians and non-Catholic Christians!

*A*nyone who does not understand the dialectic of John Paul's vision of history, but sees it simply as a conflict between good and evil, will be disorientated by the way the Pope alternates between fear and confidence in his discourses. He had stated in the encyclical *Redemptor Hominis* that "our age especially is hungering for the Spirit." And he once told André Frossard: "We have reason to fear this future. We have reason to fear that the countenance it will unveil will be more terrible than all we know of the past."[2]

John Paul once referred to the threat of nuclear destruction and the plague of worldwide hunger as reminiscent of the four horsemen of the Apocalypse (January 1, 1984). But in *Redemptoris Missio* he seems to vie with John XXIII in announcing a new Pentecost: "As the third millennium of the redemption draws near, God is preparing a great springtime for Christianity, and we can already see its first signs."[3] John Paul does not hesitate to speak even to young people in an apocalyptic tone: "In this world one constantly experiences the cosmic and apocalyptic jolts of the first disobedience" (St. Peter's Square, March 31, 1985). Nevertheless, he tells young people: "This is not an old world that is ending; it is a new world which has begun" (Lisbon, May 10, 1991).

As for raw emotion, see how dramatically he poses theological questions to the survivors of the atomic bomb and concentration camps: "Where was God at Auschwitz, at Hiroshima and Nagasaki? Where is God when infants die of starvation, when men and women are tortured, when young people full of hope must die?" (Lichtenstein, September 8, 1985)

But the language most typical and authentic for John Paul is that which describes the future, filled with good and evil, hopes and challenges: "A new dawn seems to be breaking in the sky of history, inviting Christians to be the light and salt for a world which has tremendous need for Christ, the Redeemer of man" (Lisbon, May 10, 1991).

The Pope sees in the passing of the second millennium a summation of an era and of history. At the same time he acknowledges the ordeals and the blessings it holds for the present generation. For that reason he would like to speak to all people, and he would like to purify the Church. He would like to gather all the testimonies of salvation (the martyrs) from this period in time, and he would like to meet all believers on Sinai and all Christians in Jerusalem.

One day, while conversing with journalists, John Paul spoke about his travels and made this observation about a possible trip to Jerusalem: "Up to this time I have traveled around the world, but at the end I must arrive at the holy places, the land of Jesus. It was also the land of Moses.

Some have said of me that I am another Moses, I don't know why, but they have told me so. Here is the author of the book that bears that title."[4]

Actually, there were two authors of the book, *Wojtyła: The New Moses,* Domenico del Rio and myself. We knew the Pope would not like the title, but it did make him think of the comparison. Moses had to lead his people across the Red Sea, and John Paul must lead the Church into the third millennium. Moses did not enter with the chosen people into the Promised Land, but had to be content with seeing it from afar. John Paul, however, was confident he would set his feet in the third millennium. On one occasion he asked the Polish people to help him with their prayers so that he could complete his mission. "On October 16, in the Conclave, Cardinal Wyszynski said to me: 'You must lead the Church into the third millennium!' Since the years are passing and I see that I am getting older, help me with your prayers so that I can fulfill that mission!" (Poland, June 2, 1997)

NOTES

1. John Paul II, *Tertio Millennio Adveniente* (Boston: Pauline Books & Media, 1994), n. 24.

2. A. Frossard, *"Be Not Afraid!"* (New York: St. Martin's Press, 1984), p. 191.

3. John Paul II, *Redemptor Missio* (Boston: Pauline Books & Media, 1990) n. 86.

4. Accattoli was among the journalists speaking with the Pope who referred to him for his work, *Wojtyła: Il nuovo Mosé* (Milan: Mondadori, 1988).

※ CHAPTER THIRTY-NINE ※

"I Ask Forgiveness"

"*T*oday I, the Pope of the Church of Rome, in the name of all Catholics ask forgiveness for the wrongs inflicted on non-Catholics during the turbulent history of these peoples; at the same time I pledge the Catholic Church's forgiveness for whatever harm her sons and daughters suffered."[1] John Paul spoke these words in Olomouc in the Czech Republic on May 21, 1995. If any discourse in John Paul's pontificate might be said to express completely and succinctly the *mea culpa* he envisioned, it is here. His very choice of words shows he intended it to be an exemplary text.

On the day John Paul made this statement, he beatified Jan Sarkander with the title of martyr. Sarkander was a Bohemian priest who was put to death by the Protestant authorities during the religious wars in Europe. The Evangelical Church considered the beatification a deliberate provocation, and some of its representatives refused to take part in the ecumenical meeting scheduled for May 20 in Prague. Instead, they staged demonstrations in memory of the martyrs of the Evangelical Church who were put to death by Catholics.

Against this confrontational background, John Paul pronounced his *mea culpa* in the name of all Catholics. International media interpreted his gesture positively; Evangelical Lutherans confessed that his action simply amazed them. The Pope succeeded in reversing the situation, to the point that on his third visit to Prague in April, 1997, he did not encounter any opposition at all. In fact, everyone who had been invited to the ecumenical service in St. Vitus Cathedral accepted, and were later pleased to see that some of the speakers were Lutherans.

John Paul succeeded in reversing another unfavorable situation similar to the one he experienced in Prague. A little more than a month later, he was in Kosice, Slovakia, for the beatification of three priests who were put to death by Protestant authorities in 1619. As had happened at Olomouc, this event also provoked a negative reaction among the Evangelical Protestants in Slovakia. On the night before the Catholic ceremony was to take place in Kosice, a group of Protestants assembled in the ancient city of Presov, in front of the monument dedicated to twenty-four Protestant martyrs condemned to death by Catholic authorities. In his homily at the beatification ceremony the following morning, the Pope mentioned the "spiritual greatness" of the Protestant martyrs; then, in the afternoon, he decided at the last moment to go to Presov. In silence he walked across the city square in the rain and prayed at the monument.

Of all John Paul's ecumenical gestures, this was one of the most humble and unexpected. Standing before that memorial, the Pope was perhaps asking forgiveness of those poor Christian martyrs who had died for their faith because they had refused to submit to the papacy and had been killed by other Christians defending it. The Lutheran Bishop of Presov, Jan Midriak, came into the square and, after the Pope had finished his silent prayer, thanked John Paul for having come to Presov. Then Catholic pope and Lutheran bishop recited the Our Father together. Speaking later to journalists, the bishop said: "We are truly grateful for this gesture; we never thought that anything like this would ever happen."

A Program to Forgive and Ask Forgiveness

Where did Pope Wojtyła's inspiration for these ecumenical gestures come from? As we have seen, on numerous occasions between 1982 and 1992 the Pope had referred to negative incidents in the history of the Church, and sometimes he had asked forgiveness for them. But in the words at Olomouc and the silent prayer at Presov there was a new energy, tone of voice, and evangelical quality in John Paul. What was new and original about these words and gestures was that they formed a penitential program in view of the Great Jubilee. This program, which we have called "an examination of conscience at the end of the millennium," is meant to lead to a purification of the historical image of the Church and the actions for which "we forgive and we ask forgiveness."[2] The program was announced in the apostolic letter, *Tertio Millennio Adveniente*, one of the key texts of John Paul's pontificate and perhaps the most personal of all his documents. It had already been discussed in the extraordinary consistory in the spring of that same year. The first reference to this program, however, appeared in an interview which John Paul granted to Jas Gawronski and which was published in *La Stampa* on November 2, 1993.

> At the end of this second millennium we must make an examination of conscience: where we are, where Christ has brought us, where we have deviated from the Gospel.[3]

These words are important. The examination of conscience at the end of the millennium, described in the media as *mea culpa*, is not only one of the most original initiatives of John Paul's pontificate; it is also the one most open to the future. For that reason it is of critical importance to understand the significance of his statement. And the first hint is contained in the words "where we have deviated from the Gospel." How could that have happened, and what was our sin? Looking at such questions is the first step the Pope has taken in this area.

The second source for reconstructing the genesis and development of the Pope's initiative is a memorandum sent to the cardinals assembled for an extraordinary consistory and that worked its way into the newspapers through a news leak. The twenty-three-page memorandum is entitled *Reflections on the Great Jubilee of the Year 2000*. Five initiatives are listed for the cardinals' consideration:

- ❖ the convocation of synods for America and Asia;

- ❖ a meeting with all the Christian churches;

- ❖ a meeting with Jews and Muslims;

- ❖ the updating of the Church's *Martyrology*;

- ❖ a detailed examination of the Church's second millennium in order to "acknowledge the errors committed by its members and, in a certain sense, in the name of the Church."

This final initiative, found in paragraph seven of the memorandum, is titled *Reconciliatio et Paenitentia* (Reconciliation and Penance), the same title used for the apostolic exhortation published after the Synod of 1983. In part it reads: "As it approaches the end of the second millennium of Christianity, the Church should be aware with ever greater clarity of how much the faithful have proven to be unfaithful throughout the centuries, sinning against Christ and his Gospel."[4]

Then, after recalling recent efforts in the Galileo case, the memorandum continues:

> A close look at the history of the second millennium can perhaps pro-
> vide evidence of other similar errors, or even faults, as regards respect
> for the autonomy due the sciences. How can we be silent about so
> many kinds of violence perpetrated in the name of the faith? Religious
> wars, courts of the Inquisition, and other violations of the rights of the
> human person.... In the light of what Vatican Council II has said, the
> Church must on its own initiative examine the dark places of its history
> and judge it in the light of Gospel principles.... It could be a grace of
> the coming Great Jubilee. It would not in any way damage the moral
> prestige of the Church; on the contrary, it would be strengthened by the
> manifestation of loyalty and courage in admitting the errors committed
> by its members and, in a certain sense, in the name of the Church.[5]

Although the text was never officially published, the press got hold
of it in the middle of April 1994, and immediately the paragraph on the
examination of conscience provoked a great deal of argument. Some
characterized the entire memorandum as "apocryphal." Others claimed
that an official in the Curia had inserted paragraph seven without the
Pope's authorization. Numerous objections were piling up against the
memoranda both within and outside the Curia.[6] At the opening of the
consistory of June 13, 1994, however, John Paul acknowledged he was
the author, and repeated his proposal concerning the examination of conscience at the end of the millennium:

> With the approach of this Great Jubilee, the Church needs a *metanoia*,
> that is, a discernment of the historical faults and failures of her mem-
> bers in responding to the demands of the Gospel. Only the courageous
> admission of the faults and omissions of which Christians are judged to
> be guilty to some degree, and also the generous intention to make
> amends, with God's help, can provide an efficacious initiative for the
> new evangelization and make the path to unity easier.[7]

The Pope repeated his proposal energetically because it had aroused
among some of the cardinals doubts and objections, which were
expressed even during the work of the consistory. But the majority of
cardinals, who had applauded the Pope's proposals, suggested it would
be better for the examination to have a Christological rather than an
ecclesiological orientation. Moreover, while the examination of conscience at the end of the millennium should not bypass the present, it was
necessary at all costs to avoid embarking on an endless series of self-
examination. Finally, care must be taken not to look at the past through
the eyes of the present.

A significant difference of opinion existed on the basis of geographical origins as well. For example, cardinals from the East feared that an

examination of conscience at the end of the millennium would reactivate anti-Catholic propaganda that had been prevalent under Communist regimes. Cardinals from the Third World, on the other hand, showed a significant lack of interest in the historical quarrels of Europe and expressed their fear that an admission of faults foreign to the culture of their people would have a negative impact and no particular pastoral benefits.

At the opening of the consistory, Cardinal Angelo Sodano, Secretary of State, delivered a report on the previous written consultation. He mentioned hesitancy on the part of some cardinals regarding the examination of conscience: "As regards a global, general examination of the past history of the Church, some of the cardinals have advised extreme caution and prudence, since this is a very difficult and delicate question, especially if it is handled in a summary fashion."

In the end, the Secretary of State suggested that the entire question should be submitted to the judgment of the cardinals:

> A public review of the dark periods in the history of the Church, in the light of the Gospel and the teaching of Vatican Council II, would have a special impact and importance. This could be done through the work of a few, but it should demonstrate in an especially credible and efficacious way the sincerity of adhesion to Christ on our part.

Strong support for the Pope came from Cardinal Cassidy of Australia, who gave his report immediately after Cardinal Sodano's. He emphasized "the importance for the future" that would result from the purging of memories, if it were done with "an objective presentation of history, even when such objectivity would not be to the advantage of the ecclesial community." He asked that the Church admit that "we have not always been at the level that was expected of us in our relations with those who, in the majority of cases and without any fault on their part, did not share the riches we enjoy."[8]

All the cardinals of the Church—including those who were over 80 years of age and would have been excluded from voting in a papal conclave—attended this extraordinary consistory. The discussions were held behind closed doors, but we know from Vatican reports, and comments from other individuals, that the majority of cardinals either directly opposed the examination of conscience or else felt doubtful. The cardinal who seems to have been most decidedly opposed was Giacomo Biffi of Bologna. In his pastoral letter, *Christus Hodie,* published in 1995, Cardinal Biffi criticized the Pope's proposal in detail:

> With great insistence Pope John Paul II exhorts us to prepare for the Great Jubilee of the year 2000 with a profound and sincere spirit of

repentance and self-accusation. It is a topic of great importance and of great delicacy as well. It could become a source of ambiguity and even of spiritual uneasiness, especially among the young and the simple faithful.... Considered in the very truth of its being, the Church has no sins because it is "the total Christ." He is the Head of the Church and the Son of God, to whom nothing morally objectionable can be imputed. But the Church can and ought to make its own the sentiments of sorrow and regret for the personal transgressions of its members.... Her children, not their sins, belong to the Church, although the sins of her children always deserve the tears of an undefiled mother.... Is it right and fitting that we should ask pardon for the errors of the Church in centuries past? Yes, it is right, because these have been proven by objective investigations, especially without any anachronistic estimates (something that doesn't always happen). It can also serve to make us less defensive and improve our relationship with the representatives of the so-called lay culture. They would be pleased with our breadth of spirit, even if they will usually not find there any encouragement to overcome their state of incredulity.[9]

Cardinal Biffi recommends a great deal of prudence in conducting the examination proposed by the Pope; he does not say explicitly whether or not the examination should be made. However, the tone of his critique implies that it would be better not to, because the examination could be "a source of ambiguity and even of spiritual uneasiness."

Cardinal Biffi is a person of some authority. Pope John Paul chose him to preach the spiritual exercises at the Vatican in 1992, and even after the Cardinal's criticism, John Paul treated him with great esteem and warmth during the Eucharistic Congress held at Bologna in 1997. Preparing for the concluding ceremony in Bologna, the Cardinal had an opportunity to visit the Pope at Castel Gandolfo. He personally explained his objections to the examination of conscience at the end of the millennium. Later, in an interview with journalists, Cardinal Biffi told them he had cautioned the Pope that the Church might be the only one to ask pardon for errors of the past, and that the Pope was aware of that risk.

Some months later, during the flight from Rome to Rio de Janeiro, the Pope commented to reporters: "It is interesting that it is always the Pope and the Church who ask for forgiveness, while others remain silent. But maybe that is the way it should be." For John Paul II, reciprocity in this penitential gesture is simply not an issue. He is convinced that this penitential act is a Gospel imperative and must be done come what may. In his apostolic letter, *Tertio Millennio Adveniente*, the Pope answers objections to the proposal:

Hence, it is appropriate that, as the second millennium draws to a close, the Church should become more fully conscious of the sinful-

ness of her children, recalling all those times in history when they departed from the spirit of Christ and his Gospel and, instead of offering
to the world the witness of a life inspired by the values of faith, in-
dulged in ways of thinking and acting which were truly forms of
counter witness and scandal.... The holy door of the Jubilee of the Year
2000 should be symbolically wider than those of previous Jubilees, because humanity, upon reaching this goal, will leave behind not just a
century but a millennium. It is fitting that the Church should make this
passage with a clear awareness of what has happened to her during the
last ten centuries. She cannot cross the threshold of the new millennium without encouraging her children to purify themselves, through
repentance, of past errors and instances of infidelity, inconsistency, and
slowness to act. Acknowledging the weaknesses of the past is an act of
honesty and courage which helps us to strengthen our faith, which
alerts us to face today's temptations and challenges, and prepares us to
meet them.[10]

The examination of conscience at the end of the millennium was
entrusted to the most important and the most numerous of the eight
commissions set up by the organizing committee for the Great Jubilee:
the historical-theological commission, under the direction of the Swiss
Dominican, Georges Cottier, theologian of the papal household. In February, 1986, the secretary of the General Council, Archbishop Sergio
Sebastiani, stated that the historical-theological commission "will bring
to light the dark pages in the history of the Church so that a spirit of
metanoia will lead to the request for forgiveness.... For the moment, the
commission is delaying the study of particular cases...in order to look
again at two historical themes that have ecclesial, historical, and cultural
significance—namely, anti-Semitism and the Inquisition. This reevalua-
tion of history will probably call for two international congresses, to be
held in Rome before the celebration of the Great Jubilee."[11]

Archbishop Sebastiani then continued: "The commission is convinced that these two choices will assure an understanding of the events
that actually took place; will help in the discovery of historical truth,
without being influenced by subjective polemics; and could serve as a
basis for the creation of a new culture that is not founded on any kind of
prejudice. At the same time it will make it possible to fulfill the desire of
the Holy Father to perform concrete acts of forgiveness."[12]

The "concrete acts of forgiveness" have been scheduled for the First
Sunday of Lent, March 12, 2000, as an occasion for John Paul II
to ask pardon of the Jews and of victims of the various Inquisitions. In
preparation for that ceremony, an international dialogue took place at the

Vatican from October 30 to November 1, 1997, on the roots of anti-Semitism.

After the publication of *Tertio Millennio Adveniente* and the establishment of the General Council for the Great Jubilee, the Curia realized John Paul would not be deterred. Various episcopates also began to publish statements. For example, when the document on the *Shoah, We Remember*, was issued on March 16, 1998, seven other bishops' conferences had already published similar statements. A document issued by the Argentine bishops on the local church and the dictatorship (April 27, 1996) makes explicit reference to the Pope's call for an examination of conscience. Public support for the Pope's project also came from various cardinals, some of whom had initially expressed doubts or were completely silent at the beginning.

The gradual increase of affirmative voices, however, did not mean those of doubt or disagreement had fallen silent. In general, various reasons were given for the objections: the examination might concentrate too much on the past and lead to a "reductive" mentality; there was no evident connection between historical problems and the Great Jubilee; the positive aspects of Catholic history seemed to be given little account; and there was fear that the very mention of the Inquisition could feed old Communist propaganda.

Responding to these concerns, Cardinal Etchegaray gave his assurance that "the historical-theological commission was aware of the importance and the delicacy of these questions. The members will present proposals for evaluation and decision by the presidential council. However, in all things they will follow the directives given by the Holy Father in *Tertio Millennio Adveniente*."

There are great expectations for the penitential act for the Jubilee and much progress is being made, thanks to John Paul's courage in carrying on with his program despite criticism and polemics.

Holding Catholics Accountable

Chapter 13 presented an overview of the *mea culpas*, clearly showing the expansion of the material, from year to year, and its increasingly pronounced evangelical aspect. This present chapter has dealt with the concrete formulation of John Paul's examination of conscience, and has given a detailed look at important texts. Now we will pause at a text from 1994, which differs greatly from the Pope's other *mea culpas* and touches on a contemporary event rather than a merely historical fact.

The date is May 15; the Pope is in Gemelli Hospital. The consistory scheduled for this date has had to be postponed. A tribal massacre is raging in Rwanda, and John Paul speaks of it with strongly self-critical language—unheard of words from the mouth of a pope concerning an actual event: "This is a case of true and actual genocide, for which, unfortunately, Catholics are also responsible." Surely the lessons that have been learned from confronting the dark pages of past history have prompted the Pope to face history in the making. Moreover, his comment on the massacre in Rwanda is a very effective reply to those who object to any kind of examination because it "always comes too late."

Numerous texts on ecumenical repentance emerge beginning with the year 1995. The most important is found in the encyclical *Ut Unum Sint*, and it has to do with the history of the papacy. But, before coming to that statement, which is directed to Christians separated from Rome, notice the sadness in the following text with which John Paul addresses the Eastern Orthodox:

> The sin of our separation is very serious. I feel the need to increase our common openness to the Spirit, who calls us to conversion, to accept and recognize others with fraternal respect, to make fresh, courageous gestures able to dispel any temptation to turn back.... We have deprived the world of a joint witness that could perhaps have avoided so many tragedies and even changed the course of history (*Orientale Lumen,* May 2, 1995).

The same tone characterizes the confession of sin signed by both the Patriarch of Constantinople and Pope John Paul II. It serves as a response to those who say nothing will come of the Pope's notion to "forgive and ask forgiveness." "In the course of history and in the more recent past there have been attacks and acts of oppression on both sides. As we prepare, on this occasion, to ask the Lord for his great mercy, we invite all to forgive one another and to express a firm will that a new relationship of brotherhood and active collaboration will be established" (June 29, 1995).

Chapter 13 spoke about the confession of sin on the part of the Mafia of Calabria, which the Pope made in September 1983, in the name of the people in whose midst such organized violence flourished. Twelve years later, the Pope made a similar statement to the Mafia of Sicily, calling them to an examination of conscience at the end of the millennium. This is proof, if any is needed, that in the penitential itinerary of John Paul nothing is done by chance or left to improvisation. Rather, every action or statement has a purpose and is well planned.

Dear Sicilians, the moment has come to make an appeal to every good resolution. On approaching the new millennium, I have frequently invited the entire Church to make a courageous examination of conscience, so that the power and grace of God will be able to open a new page in history. I propose the same to you, dear faithful of Sicily.... The Mafia was born of a society that is spiritually incapable of recognizing the wealth of which the people of Sicily are bearers (St. Peter's, June 22, 1995).

During 1995, the Year of the Woman, John Paul spoke frequently about the condition of women, expressing sorrow for the behavior of some men in the Church (Chapter 28). Here also is a sentence from the Pope's message to the Vatican delegation to the Conference on Women in Beijing: "I appeal to all the men in the Church, that they undergo, where necessary, a change of heart and make their own, as their faith demands, a positive vision of women" (Aug. 29, 1995).

The Church's self-examination also includes a reference to the 1572 massacre in Paris on St. Bartholomew's Night. On the eve of that anniversary, in Paris on August 23, 1997, John Paul said: "On the vigil of the feast of St. Bartholomew, we cannot forget the St. Bartholomew's Massacre. For motives very obscure in the political and religious history of France, Christians performed acts which the Gospel condemns."

With these words, John Paul was extending his hand to French Protestants, who had accused organizers of World Youth Day of intentionally assigning that night for the Pope's meeting with young people. When John Paul spoke the above words, there were 750,000 people in attendance, and on the following day there were one million! Protestants were deeply touched by the Pope's gesture, and they too acknowledged that the sin was not committed by only one side. In this situation John Paul had again handled a delicate situation with superb diplomacy and tact.

*E*ven before the penitential ceremony scheduled for the Great Jubilee, what the Pope has already done in this area will have left a permanent impression on his pontificate. Over the past twenty years there have been hundreds of texts in which John Paul has corrected a statement, admitted a fault, or asked pardon. The whole world has witnessed how he holds the Church responsible, with the same frankness with which he has proclaimed its rights.

NOTES

1. L. Accattoli, *When a Pope Asks Forgiveness* (Boston: Pauline Books & Media, 1998) p. 146.

2. Ibid., p. 51.

3. Ibid., p. 53.

4. Ibid., p. 57.

5. Ibid., pp. 57–58.

6. L. Valente, E. Zanussi, E. Cajati, *Giovanni Paolo II* (Rome: Rai-Eri, 1997), p. 54.

7. L. Accattoli, *When a Pope Asks Forgiveness* (Boston: Pauline Books & Media, 1998), p. 58.

8. Ibid., p. 61.

9. Ibid., pp. 63–64.

10. John Paul II, *Tertio Millennio Adveniente* (Boston: Pauline Books & Media, 1994), n. 33.

11. L. Accattoli, *When a Pope Asks Forgiveness* (Boston: Pauline Books & Media, 1998), pp.74-25.

12. Ibid.

CHAPTER FORTY

That They May All Be One

*P*ope Wojtyła's pontificate has been one of great expectation and uncertain destiny, as is true of all pontificates in which the message predominates over government or reforms. Twenty years after his election, many people have spoken about John Paul's legacy. But, at the moment, the only thing that I would call a "bequest" is his call to all the churches to seek, together with the Catholic Church, new ways of exercising the "Petrine ministry," so that one day it might be acknowledged by all.

This call is found in the 1995 encyclical *Ut Unum Sint* (That They May Be One). Although up until now it has received little response, the document is much more than a simple declaration, and it will bear fruit for a long time to come. With this call the Pope, who has profoundly modified the image of the papacy but has done nothing to change its rules and structure, has posed a problem and laid a foundation for a reform of the papacy in view of the third millennium. His successor—or successors—will be the ones to perform the task. In this respect, therefore, his legacy will be one on which others can build.

John Paul consigns to us an image of a pope linked to this era: freed from the tradition that would have rendered him immobile, committed to the actions and language of common humanity. Everyone has witnessed his enjoyment of good health and his struggle with illness. Even his piety is better understood.

He has transmitted to us his concept of a theology of the body, of sexuality, of woman, which can prove to be decisive for Christianity in the coming centuries. He has transmitted that theology to us by his rereading of Genesis, but also by his expressions of warmth toward people, and even by interpreting favorably Michelangelo's portrayal of the human body. Christian churches are moving toward a better appreciation of human sexuality and, thanks to John Paul, the Roman pontificate will continue to favor this appreciation.

Linked to the theology of the body, another great gift John Paul has given the Church is an appreciation for the *joie de vivre* of young people, a joy similar to that which God had when he created man and woman. It is an appreciation young people view as sincere and willingly reciprocate. Moreover, the Pope's empathy for the feminine charism of women has borne fruit in the apostolate. He has spoken to women and taken their part; he has acknowledged, without resolving, the conflicts they experience within the Church.

John Paul has given us a certain anxiety about the destiny of the human person and the Gospel, which at first seemed irrelevant to our time, but which we soon discovered was capable of being intimately interwoven with the drama of our age. His conscience is attentive to our epoch, and he will leave to his successor the encouragement to trust that he is being listened to. The world may not accept his tenacious defense of life—his unambiguous stand against abortion, against the death penalty, against all war—but it listens. This listening, facilitated by the media and the scheduling of papal visits, has given him a greater degree of independence from the Curia than any other pope in modern times has enjoyed. John Paul has not instituted reforms, but he has prepared a freedom from rules that will help his successor to attempt the unheard of.

Pope Wojtyła's zeal for the Gospel has prompted him to be a world missionary and to devote the best of his energies to remaking the Catholic Church as missionary and expansive. As he wrote in the encyclical, *Dominum et Vivificantem*, John Paul urges the Church to "look further and go further afield,"[1] to relate to every person, however new and difficult that may be. His visits—to Islamic lands, Lutheran churches, the Synagogue in Rome, Orthodox and Protestant churches, to countries at war, to suffering peoples everywhere, to Sarajevo, Beirut, and Cuba— have all inspired and prompted the Catholic Church to rediscover her traditional missionary zeal, updated by the Second Vatican Council.

In his approach to non-Christian religions, John Paul has gone beyond Vatican II's proposals. He calls the Jews our "older brothers," he calls the Muslims our "brothers," and he invites both to the Great Jubilee. He is convinced that the figure of Christ belongs to all humanity, and he is driven by that conviction.

Under the impetus of apostolic zeal, John Paul remains adamant in his opposition to communism, but he refuses to assign victory to capitalism. There is no one in the world today who speaks in the name of the disenfranchised of every type as the Pope continues to do. In choosing the Third World, as did his predecessor who bore the same name, John Paul frees the Roman pontificate from the influence of the North and the West; he thus confers a truly universal dimension on the promotion of peace and the rights of the human person. Likewise from his restless spirit emanate his *mea culpas* for the historical responsibility of the "sons of the Church."

Looking at the Primacy of Peter

After this overview of the gifts John Paul has already given us, we want to speak about his legacy in the field of ecumenism, and in particular, his proposal that all look together for a new way of exercising the papal primacy. In spite of the ecumenical failure at the beginning of the 1990s, which he once called a *kenosis*, John Paul issued a statement that reaffirmed his ecumenical dream: "To achieve the much desired union of all the believers in Christ would constitute, and certainly will constitute, one of the great events in human history" (Estonia, Sept. 10, 1993).

In the face of great difficulties, John Paul resumed the dialogue with the publication of the encyclical *Ut Unum Sint* in May 1995. It was the first time a pope had ever opened for discussion the papal ministry and its historical exercise. In a way, he was actually asking pardon for the exercise of papal authority.

We have become accustomed to his calls for forgiveness for the sins of the members of the Church, but this time John Paul was asking forgiveness for himself and his predecessors. He admitted that the ministry of the Bishop of Rome, as it has been exercised throughout history, has been a "difficulty" for the majority of other Christians, because of painful memories connected with past events:

> The Catholic Church's conviction that in the ministry of the Bishop of Rome she has preserved, in fidelity to the Apostolic Tradition and the faith of the Fathers, the visible sign and guarantor of unity, constitutes a difficulty for most other Christians, whose memory is marked by certain painful recollections. To the extent that we are responsible for these, I join my predecessor Paul VI in asking forgiveness."[2]

At the beginning of his pontificate, Paul VI spoke at the opening of the second session of Vatican Council II. Turning to the non-Catholic observers, he said: "If any fault has been imputed to us for this separation, we humbly ask pardon of God and forgiveness of the brethren who were offended by us. We are ready, so far as it pertains to us, to forgive the offenses of which the Catholic Church has been the object, and to overlook the pain that has been suffered throughout the long years of dissent and separation" (Sept. 29, 1963).

*P*ope Montini's request for forgiveness made a deep impression on Bishop Wojtyła; perhaps it was one of the inspirations for his *mea culpas*. But, it did not produce the ecumenical results Paul VI had expected. In fact, during a visit to the Ecumenical Council of Churches at Geneva on April 28, 1967, Paul VI had to admit that Rome and his primacy were seen as an obstacle rather than an incentive to unity. "We know very well that the Pope is without a doubt the greatest obstacle on the road of ecumenism."

Paul VI's words caused something of a sensation, but John Paul has said a great deal more: If the exercise of the Petrine ministry has been a problem, let us see what we can do to correct it. That is the substance of paragraphs 88–96 of the encyclical *Ut Unum Sint*, and it contains the extraordinary proposal to search together for new ways of exercising that Petrine ministry.

> After centuries of bitter controversy, the other churches and ecclesial communities are more and more taking a fresh look at this ministry of unity.... I am convinced that I have a particular responsibility in this regard, above all in acknowledging the ecumenical aspirations of the majority of the Christian communities and in heeding the request made of me to find a way of exercising the primacy which, while in no way renouncing what is essential to its mission, is nonetheless open to a new situation.... I insistently pray the Holy Spirit to shine his light upon us, enlightening all the pastors and theologians of our churches, that we may seek, together, of course, the forms in which this ministry may accomplish a service of love recognized by all concerned.

> This is an immense task, which we cannot refuse and which I cannot carry out by myself. Could not the real but imperfect communion existing between us persuade church leaders and their theologians to engage with me in a patient and fraternal dialogue on this subject, a dialogue in which, leaving useless controversies behind, we could listen to one another, keeping before us only the will of Christ for his Church and allowing ourselves to be deeply moved by his plea "that they may all be one...so that the world may know that you have sent me" (Jn 17:21)?[3]

*P*erhaps what has affected John Paul most profoundly during the last twenty years has been his failure in the ecumenical endeavor. Perhaps he still has something important to tell humanity, something about how to bring believers together. He continues to prepare for an ecumenical gathering of Christian churches to take place sometime during his pilgrimage to the Holy Land from March 20–26, 2000. Although new initiatives usually occur at the beginning of a pontificate, with John Paul, they could just as easily continue until the end. He might very well be saving the best for last.

NOTES

1. John Paul II, *Dominum et Vivificantem* (Boston: Pauline Books & Media, 1986), n. 53.

2. John Paul II, *Ut Unum Sint* (Boston: Pauline Books & Media, 1995), n. 88.

3. Ibid., nn. 95–96.

Chronology

1920

MAY 18   Karol Jozef Wojtyła is born at Wadowice, Poland, to Karol Wojtyła and Emilia Kaczorowska. He is nicknamed "Lolek."

1929

APRIL 13   Lolek's mother dies.

1932

DECEMBER 5   Lolek's older brother Edmund, a doctor, dies of scarlet fever, age 26.

1938

AUGUST   Eighteen-year-old Karol Wojtyła moves with his father to Kraków and begins undergraduate studies at Jagiellonian University.

1941

FEBRUARY 18   Lolek's father dies.

MARCH   Karol Wojtyła begins work in a stone quarry at Zakrzèwek; with a friend, he founds a theatrical group at Kraków.

1942

OCTOBER   The Archdiocese of Kraków accepts Karol as a clandestine seminarian; he secretly attends classes in theology at Jagiellonian University. Shortly after, he is transferred from the stone quarry to the Solvay factory.

1944

FEBRUARY 29   Wojtyła is hit by a German army truck and spends the next two weeks recovering in the hospital.

AUGUST   Archbishop Sapieha establishes an underground seminary in his own residence; Wojtyła is a student.

1946

NOVEMBER 1   Karol Wojtyła is ordained a priest and sent to Rome to complete graduate studies.

1948

JUNE   Karol completes his first doctorate. He submits his doctoral thesis, *Faith according to St. John of the Cross*, and returns to Poland.

JULY 8   Father Wojtyła is assigned as a curate to the country parish of Niegowic.

1949

AUGUST   Karol returns to Kraków as a curate in the parish of St. Florian.

1953

DECEMBER 1   At Jagiellonian University, Karol Wojtyła qualifies for teaching with a thesis on Max Scheler.

1956

DECEMBER 1   Wojtyła becomes professor of ethics at the Catholic University of Lublin, a post he will hold until his election as Pope.

1958

JULY 4   Father Karol Wojtyła is ordained auxiliary bishop of Kraków.

1960

Love and Responsibility, Karol's first book, is published.

1962

OCTOBER   Pope John XXIII opens the Second Vatican Council; Bishop Wojtyła travels to Rome to attend.

1964

JANUARY 18   Pope Paul VI names Karol Wojtyła Archbishop of Kraków.

1967

JUNE 28   Karol Wojtyła is made a cardinal.

1969

FEBRUARY 28 — Cardinal Wojtyła visits a Synagogue in the Kazimierz quarter of Kraków.

SEPTEMBER–OCTOBER — Wojtyła participates for the first time in the Synod of Bishops in Rome.

1971

OCTOBER 5 — Karol Wojtyła is elected to the Council of the Secretary General of the Synod of Bishops (he will be reelected in 1974 and 1977).

1972

MAY 8 — The Archdiocesan Synod at Kraków opens. Wojtyła publishes *Sources of Renewal*.

1974

SEPTEMBER 27–OCTOBER 26 — Cardinal Wojtyła is appointed as relator at the Synod of Bishops on evangelization.

1976

MARCH — Wojtyła preaches the Lenten spiritual exercises at the Vatican to Pope Paul VI.

1978

SEPTEMBER 19 — Wojtyła visits Germany with a delegation of Polish Bishops.

OCTOBER 16 — Karol Wojtyła is elected pope, taking the name John Paul II.

OCTOBER 22 — Celebration marking the inauguration of John Paul's papal ministry takes place at St. Peter's.

1979

JANUARY 25–FEBRUARY 1 — John Paul begins his papal journeys with trips to the Dominican Republic, Mexico, and the Bahamas; he addresses the third general conference of Latin American bishops at Puebla, Mexico.

MARCH 4 — Publication of John Paul's inaugural encyclical, *Redemptor Hominis*.

APRIL 28 — Agostino Casaroli is named Pro-Secretary of State.

JUNE 2–10 — John Paul's first visit to Poland.

SEPTEMBER 29–OCTOBER 8 — The Pope visits Ireland and the United States. On October 2, he addresses the United Nations.

NOVEMBER 10 — John Paul announces a reexamination of the Galileo case.

NOVEMBER 28–30 — John Paul visits Turkey and meets with Dimitrios I, the Ecumenical Patriarch of Constantinople.

1980

MAY 2–12	The Pope's first African pilgrimage.
MAY 30–JUNE 2	John Paul's first pastoral trip to France.
JUNE 30–JULY 12	The Pope's first pastoral visit to Brazil.
SEPTEMBER 26–OCTOBER 25	The International Synod of Bishops explores the role of the family in the modern world.
NOVEMBER 15–19	John Paul's first papal visit to Germany.
NOVEMBER 30	Publication of the encyclical, *Dives in Misericordia.*

1981

FEBRUARY 16–27	The Pope's first pastoral visit to Asia: Pakistan, the Philippines, Guam, and Japan.
MAY 13	John Paul is shot in St. Peter's Square by Ali Acga.
SEPTEMBER 14	Publication of the encyclical, *Laborem Exercens.*
NOVEMBER 25	Cardinal Ratzinger is named Prefect of the Congregation for the Doctrine of the Faith.

1982

FEBRUARY 12–19	The Pope's second visit to Africa: Nigeria, Benin, Gabon, Equatorial Guinea.
MAY 12–15	John Paul visits Portugal (he makes a pilgrimage to Fatima on the anniversary of the assassination attempt).
MAY 28–JUNE 2	The Pope visits Great Britain (and meets with the Anglican Primate, Archbishop Runcie).
JUNE 10–13	The Pope visits Argentina.
JUNE 15	Papal visit to Geneva.
AUGUST 29	The Pope visits the Republic of San Marino.
OCTOBER 31–NOVEMBER 9	John Paul's first pastoral visit to Spain.

1983

JANUARY 25	The revised *Code of Canon Law* is promulgated.
MARCH 2–10	John Paul visits Central America: Costa Rica, Nicaragua, Panama, El Salvador, Guatemala, Honduras, Belize, Haiti.
MARCH 25	The Holy Year of Redemption opens.
JUNE 16–25	The Pope's second pastoral visit to Poland (which has been under martial law since December, 1981).
AUGUST 14–15	John Paul goes on pilgrimage to Lourdes.
SEPTEMBER 10–13	The Pope's first pastoral visit to Austria.

SEPTEMBER 29– OCTOBER 29	The Synod of Bishops takes place on the theme: reconciliation and penance.
DECEMBER 11	The Pope visits the Lutheran Church in Rome.
DECEMBER 27	John Paul II visits Ali Agca in prison.

1984

FEBRUARY 11	Publication of the Apostolic Letter, *Salvifici Doloris,* on the Christian meaning of suffering.
APRIL 9	John Paul appoints the Secretary of State to represent him in the exercise of power over Vatican City State.
MAY 2–12	Second pastoral visit to Asia and Oceania: Fairbanks, Alaska, South Korea, Papua New Guinea, Solomon Islands, Thailand (in Seoul, John Paul canonizes 103 Korean martyrs).
JUNE 12–17	The Pope visits Switzerland (in Geneva, he addresses the World Council of Churches).
SEPTEMBER 9–21	Pope John Paul's first pastoral visit to Canada.
DECEMBER 11	Publication of the Apostolic Exhortation, *Reconciliatio et Paenitentia* (a basis for the examination of conscience to be proposed in 1994).

1985

JANUARY 26– FEBRUARY 6	Pastoral visit to Latin America: Venezuela, Ecuador, Peru, Trinidad, Tobago.
MARCH 31	John Paul's Apostolic Letter, To the Youth of the World.
MAY 11–21	Papal visit to the Netherlands.
JULY 2	Publication of the encyclical, *Slavorum Apostoli.*
AUGUST 8–19	John Paul's pastoral visit to Africa: Togo, Ivory Coast, Cameroon, Republic of Central Africa, Zaire, Kenya, Morocco (on August 19, he speaks to 50,000 young Muslims in Casablanca).
SEPTEMBER 8	The Pope visits Lichtenstein.

1986

JANUARY 31– FEBRUARY 11	John Paul II visits India (on February 4, he meets with Mother Teresa of Calcutta).
APRIL 13	The Pope meets with the Jewish community in the Synagogue of Rome.
MAY 18	Publication of the encyclical, *Dominum et Vivificantem.*
JULY 1–8	The Pope visits Colombia and Santa Lucia.

OCTOBER 4–7	Third pastoral visit to France.
OCTOBER 27	World Day of Prayer and Fasting for Peace at Assisi, Italy.
NOVEMBER 18–DECEMBER 1	John Paul visits Asia and Oceania: Bangladesh, Singapore, Fiji Islands, New Zealand, Australia, Seychelles.

1987

MARCH 25	Publication of the encyclical, *Redemptoris Mater*.
MARCH 31–APRIL 13	Pastoral visit to Latin America: Uruguay, Chile, Argentina on APRIL 12, John Paul travels to Buenos Aires for World Youth Day).
APRIL 30–MAY 4	John Paul's second visit to Germany.
JUNE 6	In Rome, John Paul opens the Marian Year.
JUNE 8–14	Third pastoral visit to Poland.
SEPTEMBER 10–21	Second pastoral visit to the United States.
OCTOBER 1–30	The Synod of Bishops looks at the vocation and mission of the laity.
NOVEMBER 22	John Paul II beatifies eighty-five English martyrs.
DECEMBER 3–7	Ecumenical Patriarch Dimitrios I visits the Vatican.

1988

FEBRUARY 19	Publication of the encyclical, *Sollicitudo Rei Socialis*.
MAY 7–19	Pastoral visit to Latin America: Uruguay, Bolivia, Peru, Paraguay.
JUNE 19	Pope John Paul canonizes 117 Vietnamese martyrs.
JUNE 23	Second pastoral visit to Austria.
JULY 2	Marcel Lefebvre and his followers incur automatic excommunication.
AUGUST 15	Apostolic Letter *Mulieris Dignitatem*.
SEPTEMBER 10–19	Pastoral visit to Africa: Zimbabwe, Botswana, Lesotho, Swaziland, Mozambique.
OCTOBER 8–11	Fourth pastoral visit to France.
DECEMBER 30	Apostolic Exhortation *Christifideles Laici*.

1989

APRIL 28–MAY 6	Pastoral visit to Africa: Madagascar, La Reunión, Zambia, Malawi.
JUNE 1–10	First papal visit to Norway, Iceland, Finland, Denmark, Sweden.
AUGUST 19–21	Third pastoral visit to Spain (John Paul travels to Compostela, Spain, for World Youth Day).

SEPTEMBER 30– OCTOBER 3	The Pope receives Robert Runcie, Anglican Archbishop of Canterbury.
OCTOBER 6–16	John Paul's fifth visit to Asia: South Korea, Indonesia, Mauritius.
DECEMBER 1	The Pope receives Mikhail Gorbachev at the Vatican and is invited to Russia.

1990

JANUARY 25– FEBRUARY 1	Papal visit to Africa: Capo Verde, Guinea-Bissau, Mali, Burkina Faso, Chad.
APRIL 21–22	Papal visit to Czechoslovakia (John Paul announces the European Bishops' Synod).
MAY 6–14	John Paul's second pastoral visit to Mexico.
MAY 25–27	The Pope visits Malta.
SEPTEMBER 1–10	Pastoral visit to Africa: Tanzania, Burundi, Rwanda, Ivory Coast.
SEPTEMBER 30– OCTOBER 28	The Synod of Bishops gather to consider priestly formation.
DECEMBER 1	Archbishop Angelo Sodano replaces Cardinal Casaroli as Secretary of State.
DECEMBER 7	Publication of the encyclical, *Redemptoris Missio*.

1991

JANUARY 15	John Paul II writes to Saddam Hussein and President George Bush to prevent the Gulf War.
APRIL 13	The Pope appoints bishops for the territory of the former Soviet Union and provokes protest from the Orthodox Patriarch of Moscow.
MAY 1	Publication of the encyclical *Centesimus Annus*.
MAY 10–13	Second papal visit to Portugal (John Paul visits Fatima on the tenth anniversary of the attempted assassination).
JUNE 1–9	John Paul's fourth pastoral visit to Poland (his first after the end of the Communist regime).
AUGUST 13–20	John Paul travels to Czestochowa for World Youth Day and later visits Hungary.
OCTOBER 12–21	Second pastoral visit to Brazil.
NOVEMBER 28– DECEMBER 14	The Special Assembly of the European Synod of Bishops meets in Rome.

1992

FEBRUARY 19–26	Pastoral visit to Africa: Senegal, Gambia, Guinea.

JUNE 4–10	Pastoral visit to Africa: Angola, Sao Tomé, Principe.
JULY 12–28	John Paul is admitted to Gemelli Hospital for the removal of a tumor in his colon.
OCTOBER 9–14	Pastoral visit to the Dominican Republic for the Fifth Centenary of the evangelization of Latin America.
OCTOBER 31	Conclusion of the examination of the Galileo case; John Paul urges new dialogue between science and religion.
DECEMBER 7	Presentation of the *Catechism of the Catholic Church.*

1993

JANUARY 9–10	World Day of Prayer and Fasting for Peace in the Balkans is held at Assisi.
FEBRUARY 3–10	Pastoral visit to Africa: Benin, Uganda, Sudan (at Khartoum, John Paul asks the Islamic government to respect religious freedom).
APRIL 25	John Paul visits Albania.
MAY 8–10	The Pope visits Sicily and makes his most vehement protest against the mafia.
JUNE 12–17	Fourth pastoral visit to Spain.
AUGUST 9–16	Pope John Paul's sixtieth international journey: Jamaica, Mexico, United States (in Denver, John Paul participates in the World Day for Youth).
SEPTEMBER 4–10	Papal visit to the Balkans: Lithuania, Latvia, Estonia.
OCTOBER 5	Publication of the encyclical, *Veritatis Splendor.*
NOVEMBER 11	John Paul falls and breaks his shoulder.

1994

FEBRUARY 22	Publication of the Pope's *Letter to Families* (for the International Year of the Family).
APRIL 10–MAY 8	Special Assembly of Bishops' Synod for Africa.
APRIL 29–MAY 27	John Paul falls and is again hospitalized with a fracture in his right femur.
MAY 22	Publication of the apostolic letter, *On Reserving Priestly Ordination to Men Alone.*
JUNE 13–14	The Pope convenes an extraordinary consistory in preparation for the Great Jubilee.
JUNE 17	For the first time in 23 years: the Prefecture of Economic Affairs announces a favorable balance for the year 1993.
SEPTEMBER 10–11	John Paul visits Zagreb, Croatia.

OCTOBER 19	Publication of Pope John Paul's book, *Crossing the Threshold of Hope.*
NOVEMBER 10	Publication of the Apostolic Letter, *Tertio Millennio Adveniente,* in preparation for the Great Jubilee

1995

JANUARY 11–21	Papal visits to Asia and Oceania: the Philippines, Papua New Guinea, Australia, Sri Lanka. (In Manila, John Paul attends the World Day for Youth.)
MARCH 25	Publication of John Paul's eleventh encyclical, *Evangelium Vitae.*
MAY 20–22	John Paul visits the Czech Republic and Poland.
MAY 25	Publication of the encyclical *Ut Unum Sint.*
JUNE 3–4	The Pope's second visit to Belgium.
JUNE 27–29	Pope John Paul receives at the Vatican Patriarch Bartholomew of Constantinople.
JUNE 29	Publication of the *Letter to Women*, for the International Year of the Woman.
JUNE 30–JULY 3	Papal visit to Slovakia.
SEPTEMBER 14–20	John Paul visits Africa and issues an Apostolic Letter on the Bishops' Synod for Africa: Cameroon, Republic of South Africa, Kenya.
OCTOBER 1	Pope John Paul beatifies 64 martyrs of the French Revolution and 45 martyrs of the Spanish Civil War.
OCTOBER 4–9	Fourth papal visit to the United States.
NOVEMBER 26– DECEMBER 14	Special Assembly for Lebanon of the Synod of Bishops meets in Rome.

1996

FEBRUARY 5–12	John Paul visits Latin America: Guatemala, Nicaragua, El Salvador, Venezuela.
APRIL 14	John Paul visits Tunisia.
MAY 17–18	Papal visit to Slovenia.
JUNE 21–23	Third pastoral visit to Germany.
SEPTEMBER 6–7	Second pastoral visit to Hungary.
SEPTEMBER 19–22	Fifth pastoral visit to France.
OCTOBER 6–15	John Paul is hospitalized a sixth time for an appendectomy.
NOVEMBER 15	Publication of *Gift and Mystery* for the fiftieth anniversary of John Paul's priestly ordination.
DECEMBER 3–6	The Pope receives at the Vatican Anglican Primate Archbishop George Carey.

1997

APRIL 12–13	Papal visit to Bosnia-Herzegovina.
APRIL 25–27	John Paul visits the Czech Republic.
MAY 10–11	Papal pilgrimage to Lebanon.
MAY 31–JUNE 10	Seventh papal visit to Poland.
AUGUST 21–24	Sixth visit to France (World Day of Youth at Paris).
OCTOBER 2–6	Third papal visit to Brazil.
NOVEMBER 16– DECEMBER 12	Special Assembly for America of the Synod of Bishops meets in Rome.

1998

JANUARY 21–26	First papal visit to Cuba.
MARCH 16	Publication of the Holy See's document: *We Remember: A Reflection on the Shoah.*
MARCH 21–23	Second papal visit to Nigeria.
APRIL 19–MAY 14	Special Assembly for Asia of the Synod of Bishops meets in Rome.
MAY 25	John Paul becomes the longest-reigning pontiff of the twentieth century.
MAY 31	Publication of the Apostolic Letter, *Dies Domini.*
JUNE 19–21	Third papal visit to Austria.
JUNE 25	The Vatican releases the text of a joint Lutheran/ Roman Catholic statement on the doctrine of justification.
OCTOBER 15	Publication of John Paul's thirteenth encyclical, *Fides et Ratio.*

1999

JANUARY 22-28	John Paul II visits Mexico and, on his return trip to Rome, St. Louis, Missouri.
JANUARY 22	Publication of the Apostolic Exhortation, *Ecclesia in America.*
APRIL 4	Publication of John Paul II's *Letter to Artists.*
MAY 7-9	Papal visit to Romania.
JUNE 5-17	Eighth papal visit to Poland.
SEPTEMBER 19	John Paul's pastoral trip to Slovenia.
OCTOBER 1	Publication of John Paul II's *Letter to the Elderly.*
NOVEMBER 5-9	Pilgrimage of the Holy Father to India and Georgia
NOVEMBER 6	Publication of the Apostolic Exhortation, *Ecclesia in Asia.*

Documents of John Paul II

ENCYCLICALS

The Redeemer of Man *(Redemptor Hominis)*
MARCH 4, 1979
In his first encyclical, John Paul outlines the program for his pontificate. The document centers on Christ the Redeemer, the human person and the Church's mission today.

On the Mercy of God *(Dives in Misericordia)*
NOVEMBER 30, 1980
This encyclical focuses on God the Father, recalling his mercy and love for sinful humanity. It treats of people's need for mercy today, and mercy in relation to the Church's mission.

On Human Work *(Laborem Exercens)*
SEPTEMBER 14, 1981
John Paul's first social encyclical discusses the dignity of the human person in relation to work. The Pope draws on his experience as a worker and develops a spirituality of human work, relating it to the redemption.

Eleventh Centenary of Saints Cyril and Methodius *(Slavorum Apostoli)*
JUNE 2, 1985
This encyclical epistle presents the relevance of these two saints as model evangelizers. It covers evangelization, inculturation, ecumenism and Europe's role in spreading Christianity.

On the Holy Spirit in the Life of the Church and the World
(Dominum et Vivificantem)
MAY 18, 1986
This extensive presentation of the Holy Spirit's role in the Church and the world draws heavily from Scripture and from the teaching of the Second Vatican Council.

Mother of the Redeemer *(Redemptoris Mater)*
MARCH 25, 1987
This major document on Mary situates her in relation to Christ the Redeemer and to the Church. The Pope presents Mary as a figure of the Church and explains her role of maternal mediation.

On Social Concern *(Sollicitudo Rei Socialis)*
DECEMBER 30, 1987
Written for the twentieth anniversary of Paul VI's *Populorum Progressio,* this encyclical comments on the world's social and economic development in light of new situations.

Mission of the Redeemer *(Redemptoris Missio)*
DECEMBER 7, 1990
Based on a theology of mission, this encyclical sounds the Pope's call for a new evangelization.

On the Hundredth Anniversary of *Rerum Novarum (Centesimus Annus)*
MAY 1, 1991
Commemorating Leo XIII's important social encyclical, this document addresses social issues in view of the collapse of communism in Eastern Europe.

The Splendor of Truth *(Veritatis Splendor)*
AUGUST 6, 1993
An important papal statement on the Church's moral teaching.

The Gospel of Life *(Evangelium Vitae)*
MARCH 25, 1995
This major encyclical on life issues stresses the dignity of the human person and presents Church teaching on the sanctity of human life.

On Commitment to Ecumenism *(Ut Unum Sint)*
MAY 25, 1995
Based on an ecclesiology of communion, this document discusses the Church's role in ecumenical dialogue.

On the Relationship Between Faith and Reason *(Fides et Ratio)*
SEPTEMBER 14, 1998
The Pope, a professional philosopher himself, reflects on the role of Christian philosophy.

POST-SYNODAL APOSTOLIC EXHORTATIONS

On Catechesis in Our Time *(Catechesi Tradendae)*
OCTOBER 16, 1979
On the role and importance of catechetics in the Church.

The Role of the Christian Family in the Modern World
(Familiaris Consortio)
NOVEMBER 22, 1981
On the nature of the Christian family and its role in society.

Reconciliation and Penance *(Reconciliatio et Paenitentia)*
DECEMBER 2, 1984
On the call to conversion and living in reconciliation.

I Will Give You Shepherds *(Pastores Dabo Vobis)*
MARCH 25, 1992
On priestly formation and ministry in the Church.

Lay Members of Christ's Faithful People *(Christifideles Laici)*
DECEMBER 11, 1994
On the role of the laity in the Church and the world.

The Church in Africa *(Ecclesia in Africa)*
SEPTEMBER 14, 1995
On the Church's mission in Africa today.

Consecrated Life *(Vita Consecrata)*
MARCH 25, 1996
On the nature of consecrated life and its renewal.

The Church in America *(Ecclesia in America)*
JANUARY 22,1999
On the Church's mission in the Americas.

The Church in Asia *(Ecclesia in Asia)*
NOVEMBER 6, 1999
On the Church's mission in Asia.

APOSTOLIC LETTERS

Rutilans Agmen
MAY 8, 1979
For the ninth centenary of the martyrdom of St. Stanislaus.

Patres Ecclesiae
JANUARY 2, 1980
Commemorates the sixteenth centenary of the death of St. Basil.

On the Mystery and Worship of the Eucharist (*Dominicae Cenae)*
FEBRUARY 24, 1980
On the Eucharist and the priesthood.

Amantissima Providentia
April 29, 1980
For the sixth centenary of the death of St. Catherine of Siena.

Sanctorum Altrix
July 11, 1980
For the fifteenth centenary of the death of St. Benedict, patron of Europe.

The Freedom of Conscience and of Religion
September 1, 1980
To the heads of States which signed the Helsinki Final Act on freedom of religion.

Egregiae Virtutis
December 31, 1980
Commemorates Leo XIII's encyclical *Grande Munus* on Saints Cyril and Methodius.

For the Sixteen-Hundredth Anniversary of the First Council of Constantinople and the Fifteen-Hundredth Anniversary of the Council of Ephesus
March 25, 1981
On the Christological and Marian teachings of these Church Councils.

Essential Elements in the Church's Teaching on Religious Life
April 3, 1983
A letter to the bishops of the United States on the renewal of religious life as called for by Vatican II.

On the Christian Meaning of Human Suffering *(Salvifici Doloris)*
February 11, 1984
Suffering in light of the Paschal Mystery.

To Men and Women Religious on Their Consecration in the Light of the Mystery of the Redemption *(Redemptionis Donum)*
March 25, 1984
Issued for the Jubilee Year of the Redemption.

Redemptionis Anno
April 20, 1984
An appeal for peace in Jerusalem and the Middle East.

Les Grands Mystères
May 1, 1984
On the situation in Lebanon.

Establishing the Pontifical Commission for the Apostolate of Health Care Workers *(Dolentium Hominum)*
February 11, 1985

Augustine of Hippo *(Augustinum Hipponensem)*
AUGUST 28, 1986
On the significance of the great Doctor of the Church, St. Augustine.

Sescentesima Anniversaria
JUNE 5, 1987
For the sixth centenary of the Christianization of Lithuania.

Spiritus Domini
AUGUST 1, 1987
For the bicentennial of the death of St. Alphonsus.

On the Twelve-Hundredth Anniversary of the Second Council of Nicaea
(Duodecimum Saeculum)
DECEMBER 4, 1987
To commemorate the Second Council of Nicaea, which dealt with the controversy surrounding icons.

Euntes in Mundum
JANUARY 25, 1988
Commemorates the millennial celebration of the baptism of St. Vladimir and the conversion of Russia to Christianity.

To All Consecrated Persons on the Occasion of the Marian Year
(Litterae Encyclicae)
MAY 22, 1988
On the consecrated life.

On the Dignity and Vocation of Women *(Mulieris Dignitatem)*
AUGUST 15, 1988
On the vocation of women in light of the Pope's "theology of the body."

Ecclesia Dei
JULY 2, 1988
On the situation regarding Archbishop Lefebvre and the Tridentine Mass.

On the Twenty-fifth Anniversary of *Sacrosanctum Concilium*
(Vicesimus Quintus Annus)
DECEMBER 4, 1988
Commemorates Vatican II's *Constitution on the Sacred Liturgy* and gives guidelines for liturgical renewal.

Guardian of the Redeemer *(Redemptoris Custos)*
AUGUST 15, 1989
On the person and mission of St. Joseph in the life of Christ and of the Church.

Fiftieth Anniversary of the Beginning of World War II
AUGUST 27, 1989
On the need for world peace.

On the Situation in Lebanon
SEPTEMBER 7, 1989
An appeal for peace.

For the Centenary of the "Work of St. Peter the Apostle"
OCTOBER 1, 1989
On the work of this association to promote vocations to the priesthood and religious life.

Fifth Centenary of Evangelization of the New World
JUNE 29, 1990
Commemorates the Christianization of the Americas.

On Reserving Priestly Ordination to Men Alone *(Ordinatio Sacerdotalis)*
MAY 22, 1994
Discusses the question of the ordination of women.

On Preparation for the Jubilee of the Year 2000
(Tertio Millennio Adveniente)
NOVEMBER 10, 1994
Outlines the proximate preparations for the great Jubilee year.

Light of the East *(Orientale Lumen)*
MAY 2, 1995
On the significance of Christian traditions from the East.

Fourth Centenary of the Union of Brest
NOVEMBER 12, 1995
Commemorates the union of the Greek Ukrainian Church with Rome.

Three-Hundred-Fifty Years of the Union of Uzhorod
APRIL 18, 1996
On the union of the Ukrainian eparchy of Mukacheve with Rome as a result of the Council of Florence.

Operosam Diem
DECEMBER 1, 1996
Commemorates the sixteenth centenary of the death of St. Ambrose.

Stella Maris
JANUARY 31, 1997
On the maritime apostolate.

Laetamur Magnopere
AUGUST 15, 1997
Promulgates the Latin typical edition of the *Catechism of the Catholic Church.*

Divini Amoris Scientia
OCTOBER 19, 1997
Proclaims St. Thérèse of Lisieux a Doctor of the Church.

On the Theological and Juridical Nature of Episcopal Conferences
(Apostolos Suos)
MAY 21, 1998
On the relation of national bishops' conferences and the Holy See.

By Which Certain Norms Are Inserted into the *Code of Canon Law* and
into the *Code of Canons of the Eastern Churches (Ad Tuendam Fidem)*
MAY 28, 1998
Norms for teaching the Catholic faith in fidelity to the Church's tradition.

On Keeping the Lord's Day Holy *(Dies Domini)*
MAY 31, 1998
On Sunday as the heart of Christian life.

Inter Munera Academiarum
JANUARY 28, 1999
On the Pontifical Academy of St. Thomas Aquinas.

Proclaiming St. Bridget of Sweden, St. Catherine of Siena and St. Teresa
Benedicta of the Cross Co-Patronesses of Europe
OCTOBER 1, 1999

APOSTOLIC CONSTITUTIONS

On Ecclesiastical Universities and Faculties *(Sapientia Christiana)*
APRIL 29, 1979
Norms on ecclesiastical universities and faculties regarding the teaching of
theology.

Magnum Matrimonii Sacramentum
OCTOBER 7, 1982
On the Pontifical Institute for Studies of Marriage and Family.

Apostolic Constitution for the Promulgation of
the New *Code of Canon Law (Sacrae Disciplinae Leges)*
JANUARY 25, 1983
The official text promulgating the *Code of Canon Law.*

Divinus Perfectionis Magister
JANUARY 25, 1983
On new legislation regulating the causes of the saints.

Pastor Bonus
JUNE 28, 1988
On the Roman Curia.

Fidei Depositum
OCTOBER 11, 1992
On the publication of the *Catechism of the Catholic Church.*

On Catholic Universities *(Ex Corde Ecclesiae)*
AUGUST 15, 1990
On the mission of Catholic universities and their role in teaching the faith.

Universi Dominici Gregis
FEBRUARY 22, 1996
New legislation governing the election of a pope.

Ecclesia in Urbe
JANUARY 1, 1998
On the vicariate of Rome.

LETTERS TO SPECIAL GROUPS

To the Youth of the World *(Dilecti Amici)*
MARCH 31, 1985
On the occasion of the International Youth Year.

Letter to Families
FEBRUARY 2, 1994
On the occasion of the Year of the Family.

Letter to Children
DECEMBER 13, 1994
On the occasion of the Year of the Family.

Letter to Women
JUNE 29, 1995
On the occasion of the Fourth World Conference on Women held in Beijing.

Letter to Artists
APRIL 4, 1999

Letter to the Elderly
OCTOBER 1, 1999